MEN'S FASHION

JOHN PEACOCK

MEN'S FASHION

THE COMPLETE SOURCEBOOK

WITH OVER 1000 COLOR ILLUSTRATIONS

THAMES AND HUDSON

For Rowland Warne

© 1996 Thames and Hudson Ltd, London

First published in the United States of America in 1996 by
Thames and Hudson Inc., 500 Fifth Avenue,
New York, New York 10110

Library of Congress Catalog Card Number 96-60141
ISBN 0-500-01725-5

Printed and bound in Great Britain

Contents

Introduction

This book illustrates the evolution of men's fashion from the late eighteenth century to the present day, focusing in the main on clothes worn by the well-dressed gentleman.

One of the main factors determining exactly which clothes the fashionable man keeps in his wardrobe is of course social convention. In the nineteenth century this called for a different set of clothes for every occasion. Garments could be divided into a bewildering number of categories: morning wear, afternoon wear, informal and formal evening wear (the latter in at least two sub-categories of discomfort) as well as country clothes and a developing sub-section of leisure wear and sports wear. It would have been unthinkable for a gentleman to appear in inappropriate clothing – country wear in town, for example, or morning wear in the evening.

Today dress is altogether less structured. Only in certain sections of society do the old rigid codes to some extent still prevail. For most men the more casual, egalitarian High Street style has made getting dressed less painstaking and far less time-consuming. Less frequent, too, since the well-off man may now do what in earlier centuries only the poor could get away with: wear the same outfit from first thing in the morning until last thing at night.

I have chosen the 1790s as my starting point because it was a period of immense social and political upheaval which had a direct influence on dress, particularly in France. Rich fabrics, lavish embroidery and gorgeous plumage gave way to the ideal of the English gentleman, with his well-cut, simple costume. It was a style based on riding wear and there was no place in it for silks and satins, and even less for vulgar colour. A fine-tailored jacket of dark and sober hue, a spotless white starched shirt and cravat, and a pair of close-fitting trousers were reckoned to speak volumes about the taste and style of the wearer. It was an outfit which would in time metamorphose into that most masculine of garments, the suit, which is beyond 'fashion' but by no means merely clothing.

Usually of course there is a difference between 'clothes' and 'fashion'. The beginning of our period – the time of the French Revolution – saw the development of some working-class clothes into bourgeois fashion. Trousers, for example, which began as a practical garment worn by French agricultural workers, evolved effortlessly into the 'trowsers' and 'inexpressibles' of the Regency buck. The same process can be seen more recently in the metamorphosis of the blue denim trousers of American rural workers into the ubiquitous 'jeans' – an indispensable item of the fashionable (and not so fashionable) wardrobe.

Though this book is mainly concerned with man à la mode, I have also included exaggerated outfits worn by what we today might regard as 'fashion victims'. Some 'street styles' make an appearance too. And I have taken into account the fact that in the past decade or so 'labels' have sometimes served in place of style.

The book is divided into sections which cover about ten to twelve years. Within these sections clothes are grouped into headings appropriate to the period under examination. The early headings include 'Day Wear', 'Riding Wear', 'Court and Evening Wear', 'Negligee and Underwear' and 'Accessories and Hairstyles'. As these categories become more fluid, the groupings change to take in 'Sports Wear', 'Leisure Wear', 'Footwear', 'Beachwear', 'Knitwear' and so on. Captions at the end of each section explain details of colour and cut and itemize collars, pockets, belts, buttons, hems, stitching, and other features. It should be noted here that since it is difficult to show detail on black garments, I have for the sake of clarity tended to colour these grey, though their actual colour is clearly stated in the captions.

With men's fashion, as with women's, the silhouette is an instant guide to style. Towards the end of the book, I have included a 7-page chart which illustrates the silhouettes as they change throughout the period and which reveals the chief developments in cut. This chart can serve as a synopsis or summary of the main illustrations and may be useful as easy reference.

The fashion designer has come later to male fashion than to female and has by no means replaced the tailor as the primary source of excellence in men's clothes designs. Where an illustration shows clothing by a particular designer, I have noted this fact in the captions. Concise biographies of designers, tailors and outfitters appear at the end of the book.

For the student who wishes to research further into the period, a bibliography is also included.

Men's fashion moves more slowly than women's and is often concerned with nuances of style rather than with enormous changes, but the developments shown in the two centuries covered by this volume can certainly have an impact on fashion design of today, influenced as it is by elements of historicism. It is permitted to plunder the past in order to enrich the present and it is my hope that the collection of drawings contained here will enable today's fashion student and enthusiast to do just that.

1789

1790

1789

1790

1791

1791

1792

Day Wear 1792–1795

1792

1792

1793

1794

1793

1794

1795

1795

1795

1796

1798

1798

1799

1799

Day Wear 1799–1802

1799

1799

1799

1800

1801

1802

1802

1789

1792

1793

1794

1798

1802

Court and Evening Wear 1789–1802

1789

1789

1800

1795

1800

1802

Accessories and Hairstyles 1789–1802

1803

1804

1806

1807

1807

1807

Day Wear 1807–1809

1807

1807

1807

1809

1808

1809

1810

1810

1810

1811

1812

1811

1812

1812

1812

1812

1813

1813

1813

1814

1815

1803

1806

1807

1811

1808

1815

Evening and Court Wear 1803–1815

1803 1806 1807 1812 1815

1803 1810 1812 1815

1803

1804

1813

1803

1812

1815

1805

1803

1804

1805

1805

1805

1807

1808

1809

1809

1809

1810

1811

1813

1815

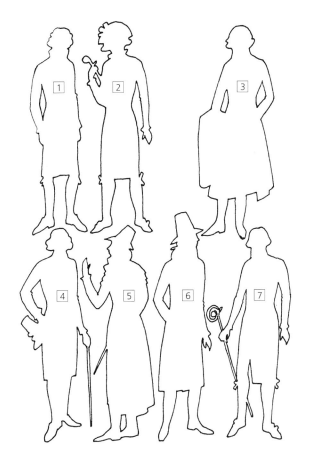

Day Wear 1789–1792

1 1789. British. Red silk single-breasted coat, self-fabric buttons, high collar, tight sleeves, cuffs decorated with buttons. Long waistcoat with flap pockets. Black silk breeches. White neckcloth and lace jabot. Wig tied at back with large bow. White stockings. Black buckled shoes. 2 1790. French. Single-breasted orange silk coat, self-fabric buttons. Yellow silk waistcoat. White neckcloth, jabot and wrist frills. Wig. Cocked hat with ribbon rosette. Leather breeches. White stockings. Black shoes trimmed with large bows. 3 1789. Italian. Knee-length striped silk coat, high collar, tight sleeves. Blue silk waistcoat trimmed with embroidered braid. Black silk breeches. Striped silk stockings. Black leather shoes, large round buckles. Outsized fur muff. 4 1790. French. Double-breasted green silk coat, high waistline, tight sleeves. Lace-edged white neckcloth tied into large bow with matching wrist frills. Checked silk waistcoat. Fine leather breeches. Wig with side-curls. Tall-crowned hat with ribbon rosette. Yellow leather gloves. Walking cane. Buckled shoes. 5 1791. French. Mid-calf-length brown wool coat, three-tier cape with blue velvet collar. Tall-crowned hat trimmed with ribbon. Fine leather breeches. Stockings with embroidered clocks. Shoes trimmed with large bows. Yellow leather gloves. 6 1791. British. Single-breasted blue striped silk coat lined in red. Yellow and blue striped waistcoat. Yellow leather breeches. Blue and white striped stockings. Knee-high brown leather boots. Tall-crowned hat. Leather gloves. 7 1792. Italian. Red silk double-breasted coat with high waistline, lined with blue silk matching the collar, worn open. Striped neckcloth tied into large bow. Red and yellow striped waistcoat, two welt pockets, wide revers. Black silk breeches, red ribbon ties at knee. White stockings with embroidered clocks. Black leather shoes trimmed with silk rosettes. Long cane with twisted handle.

Day Wear 1792–1795

1 1792. French. Ankle-length topcoat, wide striped silk revers and matching high collar. Double-breasted red silk coat, wide revers, high collar. Double-breasted waistcoat. Striped neckcloth tied into large bow. Breeches. Stockings with embroidered clocks. Shoes with flat bows. Leather gloves. Tall-crowned hat trimmed with rosette. 2 1792. French. Double-breasted striped silk coat, high waistline, high collar, wide revers, embroidered self-fabric buttons. White neckcloth. White wrist frills. Mid-calf-length tight knitted-silk pantaloons, side-button fastenings. Striped stockings. Buckled shoes. Cocked hat. Long crooked walking cane. 3 1793. British. Wool coat, wide revers, high collar. Striped silk breeches. Stockings with embroidered clocks. Leather shoes with flat bows. Tall-crowned hat. Outsized fur muff lined with red wool. 4 1793. British. Double-breasted green wool coat, high waistline, gold buttons. White waistcoat embroidered in blue. Yellow breeches. Patterned stockings. Leather shoes trimmed with rosettes. Tall-crowned hat. Walking stick with bird's-head handle. 5 1794. British. Single-breasted lilac silk striped coat, wide revers, high collar. Double-breasted embroidered waistcoat. Long knitted pantaloons. Leather shoes. Leather gloves. Straw hat, tall crown. Walking cane. 6 1794. French. Incroyable. Mid-thigh-length single-breasted wool coat, outsized revers, low-set flap pockets, high blue-velvet collar and matching turned-back sleeve cuffs. Double-breasted striped silk waistcoat, roll collar. Striped neckcloth. Leather breeches. Patterned stockings. Short green leather boots, long pointed toes. Dishevelled hair. Large hoop earring. 7 1795. French. Incroyable. Double-breasted green cloth coat, wide outsized revers, high collar, long tight sleeves, low-placed flap pockets, full skirts. Blue waistcoat. Red under-waistcoat. Spotted neckcloth. Yellow pantaloons. Knee-high leather boots, pointed toes. Long dishevelled hair. Cocked hat with red, white and blue rosette. Leather gloves. Knotted walking stick.

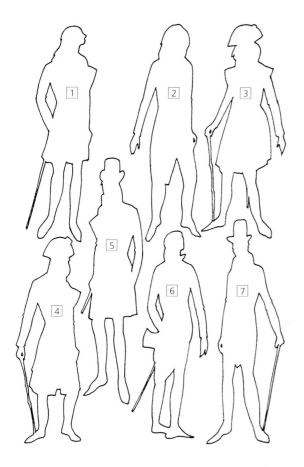

Day Wear 1795–1799

1 1795. French. Incroyable. Double-breasted green cloth coat, wide revers, narrow cuffless sleeves with buttoned wrist openings, low-set flap pockets. Double-breasted yellow silk waistcoat, shawl collar. Yellow cloth under-waistcoat. White shirt and neckcloth. Grey silk scarf. Cream pantaloons. Striped stockings. Long leather boots, pointed toes. Dishevelled hair. Walking cane. 2 1795. Spanish. Single-breasted pink velvet coat, high stand collar, tight cuffless sleeves. Double-breasted embroidered silk waistcoat. Pantaloons. Stockings. Long boots, pointed toes. Dishevelled hair. 3 1796. French. Incroyable. Mid-thigh-length coat, full skirts, long cuffless sleeves flared out over hands. Double-breasted yellow striped waistcoat worn over single-breasted blue waistcoat. Pantaloons. Long boots, deep cuffs, pointed toes. White shirt and neckcloth. Cocked hat with rosette. Dishevelled hair. Walking stick. 4 1798. French. Incroyable. Knee-length orange cloth coat, tight cuffless sleeves flared out over hands, high collar, wide revers, low-set flap pockets in flared skirts. Yellow silk embroidered waistcoat, wide revers. Striped under-waistcoat. Striped neckscarf. Tight breeches. Stockings. Flat pumps. Cocked hat. Long dishevelled hair. Walking stick. 5 1798. French. Incroyable. Double-breasted knee-length coat, velvet collar, cuffs and covered buttons; wide revers; low-set flap pockets in flared skirt. Pantaloons. Striped stockings. Long boots, pointed toes. Leather gloves. Tall-crowned hat. Long dishevelled hair. Walking stick. 6 1798. British. Green wool swallow-tail coat, waist-level flap pockets. Tight pantaloons. Long leather boots. Leather gloves. Tall-crowned hat. Walking cane. 7 1799. British. Double-breasted cloth coat, high waistline, cuffless inset sleeves with slightly gathered head, self-fabric buttons, high collar, wide revers. Single-breasted red silk waistcoat. Knitted pantaloons. Long leather boots. White shirt and neckcloth. Tall-crowned hat. Short hair and side-whiskers.

Day Wear 1799–1802

1 1799. British. Double-breasted knee-length green wool topcoat, three-tier shoulder cape, wide revers, self-fabric buttons. White neckcloth. Striped knitted-silk pantaloons. Stockings. Buckled shoes. Yellow leather gloves. Hat with wide brim. Walking cane. 2 1799. British. Striped cloth coat, cuffless sleeves gathered at head, button opening on wrist. Double-breasted red silk waistcoat, shawl collar. White shirt and neckcloth. Knitted pantaloons. Short leather boots. Short-cropped hair. 3 1799. British. Mid-calf-length single-breasted brown wool topcoat, velvet collar and cuffs, tiered shoulder cape. Leather gloves. Long leather boots, deep cuffs. Tall-crowned hat. Short-cropped hair. Side-whiskers. 4 1800. German. Double-breasted red coat, high waistline, wide revers, stand collar, tight cuffless sleeves, self-fabric buttons. Double-breasted waistcoat. Watch fob. White neckcloth and shirt. Knitted pantaloons. Long leather boots. Walking cane. Short-cropped hair. 5 1801. British. Double-breasted cloth coat, tight sleeves gathered at head, velvet cuffs and matching high collar. Single-breasted pink silk waistcoat. White neckcloth and shirt. Knitted pantaloons. Striped stockings. Buckled shoes. Tall-crowned hat, wide brim. Walking stick. 6 1802. British. Green striped cloth coat, two buttoned-down pockets inset into side/back seams of skirts, tight cuffless sleeves gathered at head. Knitted pantaloons. Cuffed leather boots. Yellow leather gloves. Tall-crowned hat. Walking cane. 7 1802. American. Mid-calf-length cloth topcoat, wide revers and notched collar, cuffed sleeves. Double-breasted blue coat, wide revers, self-fabric buttons. Double-breasted yellow waistcoat. Single-breasted striped under-waistcoat. White shirt and neckcloth. Knitted pantaloons. Long cuffed leather boots. Leather gloves. Walking stick. Tall-crowned hat, curled brim.

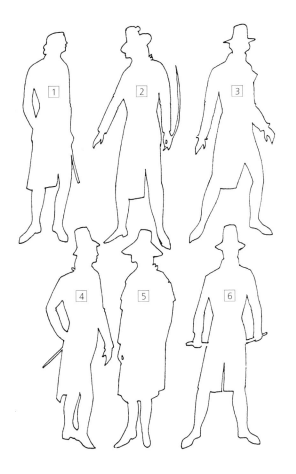

Riding Wear 1789–1802

1 1789. British. Single-breasted blue cloth coat trimmed with red, high stand collar, tight sleeves with stitched cuffs, hip-level flap pockets. White neckcloth, lace-edged jabot. Buttoned leather leggings and long boots worn with spurs. Yellow leather gloves. Wig with side-curls. 2 1792. French. Dark blue coat worn open, brass buttons, high collar, narrow revers, tight sleeves with button trim on wrist. Embroidered silk waistcoat. Striped scarf. White neckcloth. Tight leather breeches. Knee-high cuffed leather boots. Tall-crowned hat trimmed with rosette. Wig with side-curls and tied back with ribbon bow. 3 1793. Red wool coat, high waistline, self-fabric buttons, high collar, wide blue-silk-lined revers. Double-breasted waistcoat. Leather breeches. White stockings. Leather boots worn with spurs. Leather gloves. Tall-crowned hat. Short hair. 4 1794. British. Double-breasted purple cloth coat, high stand velvet collar; white neckcloth with matching wrist frills. Double-breasted waistcoat. Two watch fobs. Leather breeches. Knee-high leather boots worn with spurs. Leather gloves. Tall-crowned hat. Hair dressed into side-curls and tied back with a ribbon bow. 5 1798. American. Double-breasted knee-length blue cloth topcoat, high collar, triple-tier shoulder cape, cuffed sleeves, button trim. Knee-high leather boots with wide cuffs, worn with spurs. Leather gloves. Tall-crowned hat with wide brim. Hair dressed into side-curls. 6 1802. British. Edge-to-edge green wool coat, button-and-strap fastening, high collar and wide revers, tight sleeves with sewn cuffs. White neckcloth tied into large bow. Single-breasted pink waistcoat. Yellow leather breeches. Long boots worn with spurs. Leather gloves. Tall-crowned hat. Short hair.

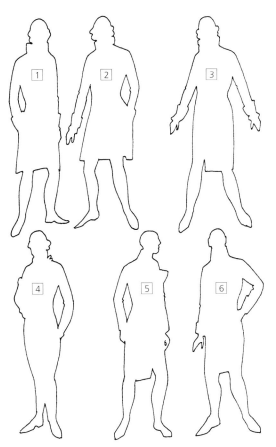

Court and Evening Wear 1789–1802

1 1789. English. Court. Green silk coat embroidered with insects and flowers, high stand collar, tight sleeves with wide cuffs, embroidered buttons. Waistcoat embroidered with gold thread. Lace-edged white neckcloth, matching wrist frills. Green silk breeches. White stockings. Buckled shoes. Powdered wig. Side-curls tied back with large bow. 2 1789. German. Court. Cream and gold striped silk coat with embroidered front panels, stand collar, flap pockets, sleeve cuffs and self-fabric buttons. Single-breasted waistcoat, flap pockets. Knee breeches in matching fabric with embroidered bands and button fastenings. White neckcloth, matching wrist frills. White stockings. Buckled shoes. 3 1789. English. Court. Single-breasted red velvet coat worn open, edges piped with gold-coloured silk, matching stand collar, sleeve cuffs and single-breasted waistcoat. Velvet knee breeches. White neckcloth, matching wrist frills. White stockings. Buckled shoes. Powdered wig. 4 1790. German. Court. Silk coat fastening with single button; embroidered front panels, sleeve cuffs and collar. Single-breasted embroidered waistcoat. White lace-trimmed neckcloth, matching frills. Knee breeches. Silk stockings. Buckled shoes. Powdered wig with side-curls, tied back with ribbon bow. 5 1798. British. Evening. Single-breasted black cloth coat worn open, high collar and wide revers, tight sleeves with stitched cuffs, self-fabric buttons. Double-breasted blue silk waistcoat, shawl collar. Single-breasted white silk under-waistcoat. White shirt. Grey silk neckcloth. Pantaloons. White stockings. Flat pumps. Short-cropped hair. 6 1802. French. Court. Double-breasted velvet coat embroidered with gold thread, high collar, deep cuffs. Double-breasted waistcoat. Knee breeches. White stockings. Buckled shoes. Short-cropped hair.

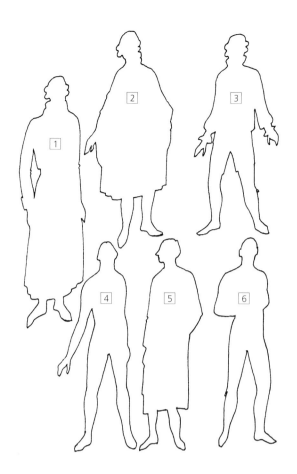

Negligee and Underwear 1789–1802

1 1789. Ankle-length embroidered velvet dressing gown/housecoat, long shawl collar of green silk piped in red, matching deep wrist cuffs and tie-belt. Red leather slippers, pointed toes. Brown wig with side-curls, tied back with ribbon bow. 2 1789. Voluminous knee-length white cotton powdering mantle, single-button fastening under collar, dropped shoulderline, full flared sleeves long enough to cover hands. Black leather mules. Powdered wig with side-curls, tied back with ribbon. 3 1800. Hip-length white cotton shirt, single-button fastening under high stiffened stand collar, chest panel with decorative pintucks at each side, pleated inset sleeves, narrow cuffs, wrist frills, shirt fullness achieved from gathers under narrow shoulder yoke. Short unfitted white cotton drawers. Long knitted-silk stockings. Red silk garters. 4 1795. Knitted cream stockinette foot drawers; legs separate, joined only to the front-buttoned waistband; back lacing. Short-cropped hair. 5 1800. White cotton nightshirt, single-button fastening under collar, front opening edged with waterfall frill, matching wrist frills on full sleeves; knee-length front body gathered onto narrow shoulder yoke, back body cut longer to mid-calf-length. Black leather mules. Short-cropped hair. 6 1802. Knee-length cream stockinette drawers joined through crotch, waistband with back lacing and front-button fastening, drawstring fastening on knee. Knitted white ribbed-cotton stockings.

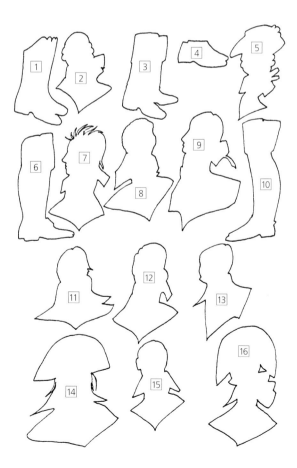

Accessories and Hairstyles 1789–1802

1 1789. Knee-length green leather boots, low heels, square toes, gold braid trim. 2 1790. British. Brown wig, dressed away from face, side-curls, back hair tied with ribbon. White neckcloth, lace-trimmed jabot. 3 1790. Brown leather boots, low heels, square toes, deep cuffs. 4 1791. Laced leather shoes, lined and trimmed with red leather, low heels, rounded toes. 5 1791. French. Black cocked hat trimmed with red, white and blue rosette. Brown wig with side-curls, back hair tied with ribbon. 6 1795. Knee-high brown leather boots, upturned cuffs lined and trimmed with red leather, decorative pull straps, low heels worn with spurs. 7 1795. French. Incroyable. Long hair dressed in dishevelled style. White neckcloth. Striped silk waistcoat. 8 1796. Short-cropped hair worn with side-whiskers. White neckcloth, shirt and waistcoat. 9 1796. French. Incroyable. Long hair dressed in dishevelled style, back hair tied with a ribbon bow. 10 1798. Knee-length leggings, buttoned upturned cuffs, strap-and-buckle side fastening, strapped under foot of black leather boot. 11 1796. Short hair dressed onto forehead and over ears. White neckcloth and shirt. Striped silk waistcoat. 12 1796. American. Natural hair dressed in waves away from face. White neckcloth tied into a large bow. Lace-trimmed jabot. 13 1799. Short hair dressed over forehead, worn with side-whiskers. White neckcloth and shirt with jaw-high collar. 14 1799. French. Black cocked hat trimmed with black silk rosette. Long hair. White neckcloth worn with narrow bow-tie. White shirt. 15 1802. British. Short-cropped hair dressed onto forehead, worn with side-whiskers. White neckcloth tied into large bow. Jaw-high shirt collar. 16 1800. Spanish. Black cocked hat. Long hair tied back with ribbon bow. White neckcloth with narrow tied bow. Shirt with jaw-high collar.

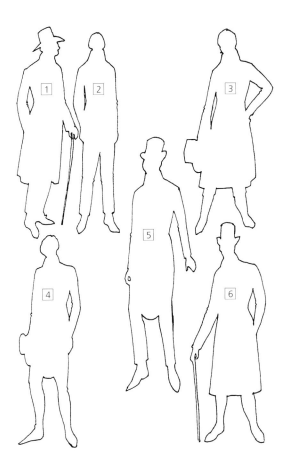

Day Wear 1803–1807

1 1803. British. Single-breasted knee-length blue cloth coat, velvet collar, matching buttons, flap pockets and turned-down flared sleeve cuffs. Red cloth waistcoat, self-fabric buttons, shallow stand collar. Ankle-length striped wool trousers. White shirt, high pointed collar. White neckcloth tied into large bow. Tall-crowned hat, wide curled brim. Short-cropped hair. Leather shoes, silk bow trim. 2 1804. British. Single-breasted green cloth tailcoat, narrow inset sleeves, self-fabric buttons, M-notch collar, wide revers. Grey cloth waistcoat, small self-fabric buttons. Beige ankle-length fitted trousers, side slits. White shirt and neckcloth. Short-cropped hair. White stockings. Black shoes. 3 1806. Spanish. Double-breasted knee-length green wool coat, wide revers, velvet collar and matching covered buttons. Blue and white striped waistcoat. Red and white striped scarf. Light brown pantaloons. Black leather knee boots, yellow cuffs. Black top hat lined in red. Yellow leather gloves. Short hair. 4 1807. British. Single-breasted yellow cloth tailcoat, M-notch collar and wide revers, tight inset sleeves with deep stitched cuffs. Fitted pale yellow trousers flared over foot and held with stirrup under black leather shoe. Blue and white striped waistcoat. White frilled shirt, high pointed collar. White neckcloth. Black top hat lined in red. Short curled hair. Spyglass on ribbon worn round neck. 5 1807. British. Double-breasted wool coat, M-notch collar and wide revers, flap pockets set into waist seam. Ankle-length striped trouser. Spats, side-button fastening, worn over black shoes. Blue waistcoat. White frilled shirt, high pointed collar. White neckcloth. Black top hat. 6 1807. British. Knee-length double-breasted blue cloth topcoat, M-notch collar and wide revers, hip-level flap pockets. Red scarf. Striped waistcoat. White shirt and neckcloth. Black top hat. Yellow gloves. Black leather boots, brown cuffs. Walking stick.

Day Wear 1807–1809

1 1807. Danish. Single-breasted tailcoat worn open, M-notch collar, wide revers, self-fabric buttons matching tiny buttons on sewn cuffs of tight inset sleeves. Single-breasted waistcoat, shawl collar, self-fabric buttons. Watch ribbon and fob. Pantaloons with braided decoration on front waist. Long leather boots, deep cuffs, long decorative straps. White shirt, high pointed collar. White neckcloth. Bicorn hat, ribbon trim. Short curled hair and sideburns. 2 1807. British. Double-breasted ankle-length topcoat, full skirts, M-notch collar, wide revers. White shirt and neckcloth. Tall-crowned wide-brimmed hat. Short hair and sideburns. Leather boots. 3 1807. British. Double-breasted coat, M-notch collar, inset sleeves with turned-back cuffs. Breeches fastened on the knee with laces and buttons; side hip-level pockets. Silk stockings. Long hessian boots. Single-breasted waistcoat, stand collar. White shirt and neckcloth. Tall-crowned hat, curled brim. Walking stick. 4 1808. British. Single-breasted blue wool tailcoat, brass buttons, M-notch collar, inset sleeves with gathered head and deep turned-back cuffs. Single-breasted yellow cloth waistcoat. Frilled and tucked white shirt, high pointed collar. White neckcloth. Beige trousers with stirrups. White stockings. Black leather pumps. Black top hat. Short hair worn with sideburns. Yellow gloves. 5 1809. British. Double-breasted brown wool coat; tight inset sleeves without cuffs, gathered at head; M-notch collar. Single-breasted blue silk waistcoat. White shirt and neckcloth. Beige pantaloons. Long black leather boots. Black top hat. Yellow gloves. Walking stick. 6 1809. American. Dark green single-breasted coat with black velvet M-notch collar, matching coat buttons and buttons at wrist-level on tight inset sleeves. Single-breasted striped silk waistcoat. Frilled white shirt, high pointed collar. White neckcloth. Ankle-length trousers. Black shoes worn with spats. Black top hat. Yellow gloves. Walking stick.

Day Wear 1810–1812

1 1810. British. Tight double-breasted red cloth coat, M-notch collar, wide revers, self-fabric buttons, tight inset sleeves flared over hands, button detail. Waistcoat, high stand collar. Watch fob. Ankle-length cloth trousers. White stockings. Black pumps, ribbon bow trim. White shirt and stock. Short hair. Black top hat. 2 1810. British. Double-breasted cloth coat worn buttoned to high collar, tight sleeves flared over hands. Cream pantaloons. High black leather hessians. White shirt and neckcloth. Black top hat. Yellow gloves. Cane. 3 1810. British. Ankle-length brown cloth topcoat, wrist-length cape, high collar, wide revers. White shirt and stock. Black top hat. Yellow gloves. Black boots. 4 1812. American. Green double-breasted coat, satin-covered M-notch collar and wide revers, matching covered buttons, tight inset sleeves gathered at head and flaring over hands. Blue waistcoat. Ankle-length striped trousers with hip-level pockets. White stockings. Black pumps, bow decoration. White shirt and neckcloth. Black top hat. Cane. 5 1811. German. Long double-breasted topcoat, velvet collar, flap pockets, covered buttons. Long boots. White shirt, high pointed collar. Top hat. 6 1811. British. Single-breasted ankle-length brown topcoat lined in red, triple-tiered wrist-length capes, M-notch collar, wide revers, inset sleeves with deep turned-back cuffs. Brown double-breasted coat. Green waistcoat. White shirt and neckcloth. Pantaloons. High black leather hessians. Black top hat. Yellow gloves. 7 1812. French. Mid-calf-length wool coat lined in red, M-notch collar, wide revers, inset sleeves with gathered head and narrow turned-back cuff. Embroidered waistcoat. Trousers with gathers from waist, narrow legs, centre slit. Black shoes, bow trim. White shirt and neckcloth. Short hair. Black top hat. Yellow gloves.

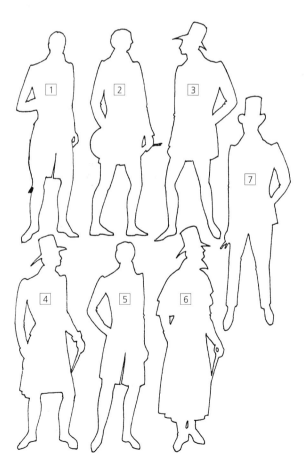

Day Wear 1812–1815

1 1812. German. Double-breasted blue cloth coat worn buttoned to velvet collar, matching flap pockets and covered buttons, tight inset sleeves gathered at head and flared over hands. Yellow waistcoat. Beige breeches. Striped stockings. Grey spats. Black leather shoes. White shirt and neckcloth. Short-cropped hair. 2 1812. British. Hip-length brown wool coat with box and inverted pleats, tight inset sleeves gathered at head with narrow turned-back cuffs, flap pockets. Tight trousers flared over foot, button detail on outside leg from ankle to mid-calf. Stirrups. Black shoes. Short hair. Black top hat. 3 1813. British. Tight double-breasted black cloth coat, velvet M-notch collar and revers, matching covered buttons. Red waistcoat, stand collar. White frilled shirt, high pointed collar. White stock. Grey trousers, hip-level pockets. Stirrups. White stockings. Black pumps. Black top hat. 4 1813. American. Double-breasted pale green cloth coat, black velvet M-notch collar, flap pockets, sleeve cuffs and covered buttons; full knee-length skirts. Yellow waistcoat. White frilled shirt, high pointed collar. White neckcloth. Beige trousers with stirrups. Black leather shoes. Short hair. Black top hat. Yellow gloves. Cane. 5 1813. French. Double-breasted coat, stand collar. White shirt and neckcloth. Fitted pantaloons. High hessian boots. Short-cropped hair. 6 1814. British. Mid-calf-length coat with two-tier elbow-length cape, large collar and wide revers, sleeves with deep turned-back cuffs, strap-and-button fastening, vertical welt pockets with button trim. Long boots. Top hat. Gloves. Cane. 7 1815. American. Single-breasted checked cloth coat, satin M-notch collar and revers, inset sleeves gathered at head and flared over hands, short tails. Double-breasted waistcoat. White shirt and neckcloth. Ankle-length trousers, hip-level pockets. Buckled shoes. Top hat. Gloves.

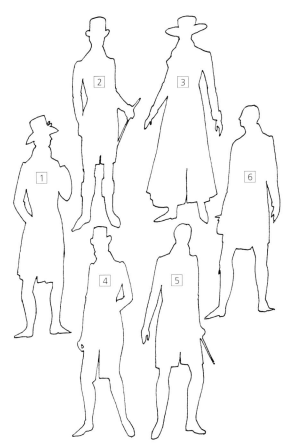

Riding Wear 1803–1815

1 1803. British. Fitted striped wool tailcoat, vertical pockets inserted into back pleats, button decoration, sleeves with gathered head and turned-back cuffs. Leather knee breeches. Long boots, deep turned-down cuffs, decorative tabs. Leather gloves. Top hat, braid trim. 2 1806. British. Single-breasted green and blue striped cloth tailcoat, inset sleeves with gathered head, narrow turned-back cuffs. Pink waistcoat, stand collar. Watch chain and fobs. Long beige leather breeches. Black leather boots, brown turned-down cuffs. White frilled shirt and neckcloth. Black top hat. Yellow leather gloves. 3 1807. British. Ankle-length green cloth topcoat, large M-notch collar and wide revers, sleeves with turned-back cuffs, hip-level flap pockets. Single-breasted brown cloth coat. Waistcoat. White shirt and neckcloth. Red scarf. Beige cloth breeches. Black leather boots, brown turned-down cuffs. Yellow leather gloves. 4 1808. French. Double-breasted green wool spencer jacket, black velvet collar and revers, matching covered buttons. Blue cloth tailcoat. Yellow waistcoat. White shirt and stock. Yellow gloves. Beige breeches. Black boots. Black top hat. 5 1815. British. Double-breasted green cloth coat, M-notch collar and narrow revers, sleeves with gathered head and turned-back cuffs. Single-breasted red cloth waistcoat, stand collar. Beige cloth breeches. Long black leather boots. White shirt and stock. Yellow leather gloves. Short-cropped hair. 6 1811. British. Fitted brown striped wool tailcoat, sleeves with gathered head and turned-back cuffs, hip-level flap pockets, box pleats, centre-back vent. Beige cloth breeches. Black leather hessian boots. Black top hat lined in red. Yellow gloves. Short-cropped hair.

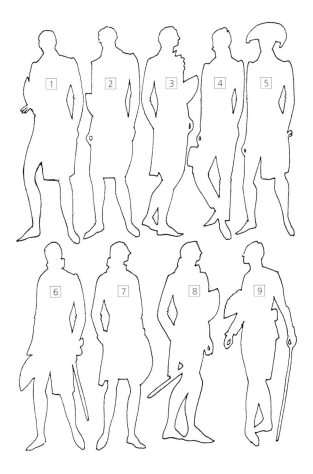

Evening and Court Wear 1803–1815

1 1803. British. Double-breasted blue cloth formal evening tailcoat, M-notch collar and wide revers, tight sleeves with gathered head and cuffs flared over hands. White single-breasted waistcoat, stand collar. White frilled and pleated shirt, pointed collar. White neckcloth. Flesh-coloured breeches. Striped white stockings. Black pumps. Black bicorn hat. Yellow gloves. 2 1806. British. Double-breasted green cloth formal evening tailcoat, black velvet collar and matching covered buttons. White waistcoat, pleated shirt, stock. White knee breeches. Buckled shoes. Bicorn hat. 3 1807. French. Double-breasted blue cloth formal evening tailcoat, M-notch collar. White frilled shirt. White neckcloth. White waistcoat. Beige breeches. Striped white stockings. Black pumps. Bicorn hat. Yellow gloves. 4 1812. British. Black ribbed-silk semi-formal evening tailcoat worn open. Single-breasted white silk waistcoat. White pleated shirt. White neckcloth. Ankle-length trousers. White stockings. Black pumps. Top hat. Yellow gloves. 5 1815. French. Double-breasted blue velvet formal evening tailcoat, gilt buttons, tight sleeves cut without cuffs, M-notch collar and wide revers. White waistcoat. White pleated and frilled shirt. White neckcloth. Flesh-coloured breeches. Buckled shoes. Bicorn hat trimmed with feathers. Yellow gloves. 6 1803. English. Court. Velvet tailcoat embroidered with gold thread. Embroidered waistcoat. White neckcloth, lace jabot and wrist frills. Cream breeches. Red silk sash. White stockings. Buckled pumps. Bicorn hat. 7 1810. German. Court. Blue striped silk coat trimmed with gold braid. White waistcoat. White neckcloth. White lace jabot and wrist frills. White breeches and stockings. Buckled pumps. Bicorn hat trimmed with feathers. 8 1812. German. Court. Green velvet coat. Lace jabot and wrist frills. White stockings. Black pumps. Bicorn hat trimmed with feathers. 9 1815. Spanish. Court. Red velvet tailcoat trimmed with gold braid. Embroidered waistcoat. Blue silk waist sash. Black silk breeches. White stockings. Buckled shoes. Bicorn hat trimmed with feathers.

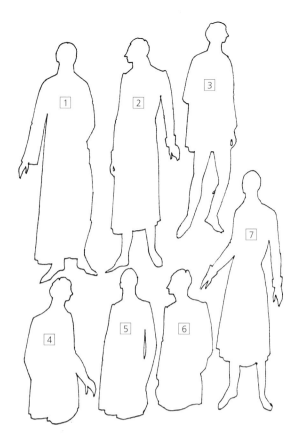

Negligee and Underwear 1803–1815

[1] 1803. Collarless ankle-length wrap-around green corded velvet dressing gown, wide wrist-length flared sleeves, all edges bound with embroidered braid. White shirt and stock. White stockings. Red slippers. [2] 1804. Mid-calf-length striped pink silk dressing gown, plain silk shawl collar, turned-back split cuffs and covered buttons, double-breasted fastening emphasized by decorative twisted cords. White shirt and stock. White stockings. Black leather mules. [3] 1813. White muslin shirt, high stiffened pointed collar, single-button-and-loop fastening, bound slit opening, inset pleated sleeves with deep buttoned cuffs. Knee-length flesh-coloured stockinette drawers. Striped stockings. Black pumps. [4] 1803. White muslin shirt, high stiffened collar with long points, single-button-and-loop fastening, bound slit opening decorated either side with fine pintucks, long cuffless sleeves. [5] 1812. White muslin shirt, high stiffened pointed collar, bound slit opening edged either side with white embroidery, single-button-and-loop fastening, cuffless inset sleeves with gathered head. [6] 1815. White muslin shirt, high stiffened pointed collar, bound slit opening edged with frills, deep buttoned cuffs. [7] 1805. Knee-length edge-to-edge blue velvet dressing gown, front fastening with buttoned-down straps, matching stand collar, fitted bodice, full skirts, long tight sleeves with gathered head and turned-back cuffs. White stockings. Black leather mules.

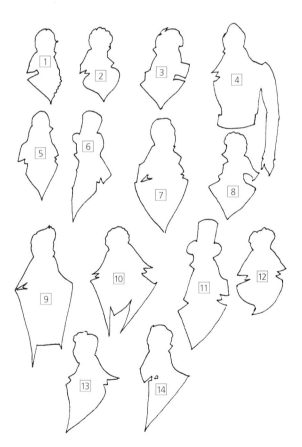

Accessories and Hairstyles 1803–1815

[1] 1803. Blue coat. Green waistcoat. White muslin shirt, high stiffened pointed stand collar, three-tier pleated frill. White muslin neckcloth. Short swept-back hair with long curled fringe and sideburns. [2] 1804. Black coat, M-notch collar and wide rounded revers. Blue waistcoat. White muslin neckcloth. Curled hair with spiked fringe. Sideburns. [3] 1805. Green cloth coat, black velvet collar. Yellow waistcoat. White muslin shirt and neckcloth tied into formal bow. Hair combed back with spiked fringe. [4] 1805. Blue striped spencer jacket, pearl buttons. Yellow waistcoat. White muslin shirt, high stiffened pointed stand collar, frilled front. White stock tied into bow. Hair swept up and dressed into large stylized curl on forehead. [5] 1805. Black coat. Blue waistcoat. White shirt, ruffled front, high stand collar. Neckcloth tied into large one-sided bow. Hair curled and dressed forward. [6] 1807. Blue coat. Blue waistcoat. White shirt, pointed collar. Red silk stock. Yellow beaver hat, tall crown, curled brim, cord trim. [7] 1808. Black coat. Black waistcoat. White shirt, high pointed collar, pleated front. Red silk stock, large bow knot. Short hair and side-whiskers. [8] 1809. Green coat. Grey waistcoat. White shirt, soft pointed collar. White neckcloth tied into large bow. Short curled hair. [9] 1809. Green coat. Double-breasted embroidered waistcoat. White shirt and stock. Short spiked hair. Side-whiskers. [10] 1809. Blue coat. Red waistcoat, shawl collar. White shirt, soft turned-down collar points. White muslin stock tied into large bow. Short hair dressed forward. [11] 1810. Black coat. White waistcoat. White shirt and stock. Grey beaver hat, high crown, curled brim. [12] 1811. Black coat. White waistcoat. White shirt, high stiffened pointed collar. Blue silk stock. Short curled hair with side parting. [13] 1813. Blue coat. Striped waistcoat. White shirt, stiffened collar, pleated front. White neckcloth. Short hair. Side-whiskers. [14] 1815. Green coat, M-notch collar, worn closed. White shirt, soft collar. White muslin stock. Curled hair with spiked fringe.

1816

1816

1816

1818

1818

1818

1819

1819

1820

1821

1822

1823

1823

1824

1825

1825

1827

1827

1829

1829

1829

1829

1829

1829

1829

1829

1829

1829

1829 1829 1829 1829

1829 1829 1829 1829

Evening Wear 1816–1829

1816

1824

1824

1825

1826

1829

1828

1816

1820

1824

1829

1828

1816
1818
1819
1820
1821
1823
1823
1823
1825
1825
1825
1826
1825
1828
1828
1829
1829

1830

1830

1830

1830

1831

1831

1831

1832

1833

1833

1834

1834

1834

1836

1836

1836

1836

1837

1837

1840

1840

Day Wear 1840–1842

1840

1840

1841

1841

1842

1842

1842

1830

1834

1839

1839

1840

1842

1830

1834

1836

1837

1838

1842

1830

1830

1832

1835

1840

1830
1831
1831
1834
1834
1834
1835
1840
1842
1830
1839
1841
1830
1830
1830
1835
1842
1840

Day Wear 1816–1819

1 1816. British. Single-breasted blue tailcoat, M-notch collar and wide revers, tight inset sleeves with gathered head, turned-down flared cuffs. Single-breasted striped silk waistcoat, two welt pockets. Watch fobs. White muslin shirt, stiff high pointed collar, pleated front. White silk stock with red spots. Ankle-length white cloth trousers. White stockings. Black pumps. Yellow beaver hat, tall waisted crown, curled brim. 2 1816. British. Dandy. Single-breasted mid-calf-length coat, shawl collar, tight sleeves, full skirts. Red waistcoat. White shirt, rounded collar. White stock. Trousers gathered into band at ankle level. Black boots. Black top hat, shallow crown, curled brim. 3 1816. French. Fitted blue tailcoat, tight sleeves, large gilt buttons at waistline and hem of back inverted box pleats. White shirt and stock. Grey ankle-length knitted pantaloons, button detail on outside ankle. Ribbed stockings. Black pumps. Yellow gloves. Black top hat. 4 1818. British. Single-breasted ankle-length checked wool topcoat, self-covered buttons, M-notch collar, tight sleeves with gathered head, hip-level flap pockets. White trousers. Grey spats. Black shoes. Yellow gloves. Walking cane. Black top hat. 5 1818. British. Double-breasted cloth coat worn open, M-notch collar and wide revers, tight sleeves with gathered head. Embroidered waistcoat. White muslin shirt, collar points turned down, pleated front. White stock. Ankle-length white cloth trousers. White stockings. Black slippers. Yellow gloves. Walking cane. Black top hat. Short hair. 6 1818. British. Double-breasted brown cloth tailcoat, self-fabric buttons, M-notch collar and wide revers, tight sleeves. Brown waistcoat. White shirt and stock. Ankle-length beige cloth trousers. Black boots. Yellow gloves. Walking cane. Yellow beaver top hat, high waisted crown, deep curled brim. 7 1819. British. Single-breasted blue cloth coat worn open, M-notch collar, tight sleeves. Pink striped silk waistcoat, shawl collar. White muslin shirt. Yellow and white striped silk stock. Ankle-length white cloth trousers, hip-level pockets. Black boots. Yellow gloves. Cane. Top hat. Short curled hair.

Day Wear 1819–1824

1 1819. British. Double-breasted wool tailcoat, high collar and wide revers, tight sleeves gathered at head, stitched cuffs. Red and white striped waistcoat. Watch fobs. White shirt. Blue spotted cravat. White trousers with stirrups. Black boots worn with spurs. Yellow gloves. Cane. Top hat, tall crown, curled brim. 2 1820. American. Knee-length beige wool topcoat, three sets of buttons, wide shawl collar, tight sleeves, hip-level flap pockets. Tight green wool trousers with stirrups. Black boots. Yellow gloves. Black beaver hat. 3 1821. French. Knee-length single-breasted fitted blue wool coat lined in red, tight sleeves, wide shawl collar, self-fabric buttons, flap pockets. White shirt. Blue stock. Brown cloth trousers with stirrups. Black shoes. Black hat. Yellow gloves. Short hair. 4 1822. British. Dandy. Double-breasted grey wool coat, M-notch collar and wide revers, tight sleeves gathered at head, flared turned-down cuffs. Red and yellow broad striped silk waistcoat with shawl collar. White shirt. Black silk stock. Striped trousers gathered at waist and ankle. Black boots, high heels. Yellow gloves. Cane. Dark blue beaver top hat, tall crown, narrow curled brim. 5 1823. British. Knee-length single-breasted fitted ribbed velvet coat, M-notch collar, tight sleeves gathered at head, narrow wrist cuffs. Yellow waistcoat. White under-waistcoat. White shirt. Red and white striped stock. Striped trousers with stirrups. Black boots. Yellow gloves. Walking cane, gilt handle. Black beaver hat. 6 1823. British. Double-breasted black cloth coat worn open, M-notch collar and wide revers, tight sleeves gathered at head. Red waistcoat, shawl collar. White muslin shirt, turned-down pointed collar. Black silk cravat. White trousers with stirrups. White spats. Black shoes. Yellow gloves. Cane. 7 1824. British. Mid-calf-length fitted wool coat, double elbow-length cape, wide collar, tight sleeves. White shirt. Red stock. Blue pantaloons. White spats. Black shoes. Yellow gloves. Cane. Black beaver hat.

Day Wear 1825–1829

1 1825. British. Double-breasted knee-length green cloth coat, high collar and wide revers, tight inset gathered sleeves with stitched cuffs decorated with buttons, waist-level flap pockets. Black waistcoat. White shirt. Red and white cravat. Brown striped trousers. Black shoes. White gloves. Black beaver hat. Cane with gilt handle. 2 1825. German. Double-breasted knee-length coat decorated with cord frogging; black velvet collar, cuffs and covered buttons. White shirt and stock. White trousers. Black shoes. Yellow gloves. 3 1827. British. Dandy. Double-breasted blue cloth coat, gilt buttons, large collar and wide revers, tight cuffed sleeves, waist-level flap pockets. Decorative silk handkerchief. Yellow waistcoat. Watch chains. Black silk stock lined with red and tied into large bow. Black and white striped silk shirt. White trousers with wide hems. Black shoes. Black top hat, high waisted crown. Curled hair. 4 1827. British. Single-breasted knee-length coat, short shoulder cape, tight sleeves with turned-down cuffs. Red waistcoat. White shirt and stock with pleated bow. Checked trousers. Black shoes. Black beaver hat. Curled hair. 5 1829. British. Blue cloth coat worn open, M-notch collar and wide revers, tight inset gathered sleeves, buttoned turned-down cuffs. Green striped waistcoat with shawl collar. White shirt and stock. Grey and white striped trousers with stirrups. Black shoes. Black beaver hat. Yellow gloves. Cane. 6 1829. British. Knee-length blue cloth coat, gilt buttons decorating back waist and below inset pockets, panel seams end in pleats, tight sleeves. White shirt and stock. Grey trousers. Black shoes. Black beaver hat. White gloves. Cane with gilt handle. 7 1829. British. Knee-length double-breasted green cloth coat worn open, gilt buttons, M-notch collar and wide revers, tight inset gathered sleeves. Double-breasted brown cloth waistcoat. Red under-waistcoat. White shirt. Black stock. White trousers. Black shoes. Black beaver hat. Yellow gloves. Cane.

Day Wear 1829

1 1829. British. Ankle-length green wool greatcoat lined in red, triple cape, large fur collar. Double-breasted black cloth coat. Grey and white striped trousers. White shirt. Blue and white checked stock. Black shoes. Black beaver hat. Yellow gloves. 2 1829. British. Double-breasted mid-calf-length brown wool greatcoat worn open, large collar with wide revers, outsized covered buttons, waist-level flap pockets, tight cuffed sleeves. Knee-length double-breasted black wool coat. Blue waistcoat. White shirt. Black stock. Grey trousers with stirrups. Black shoes. Black beaver hat. White gloves. Cane. 3 1829. British. Knee-length double-breasted grey wool frock-coat, high collar, top-stitched edges, tight inset gathered sleeves with button detail on wrist. Grey trousers. White shirt. Yellow striped stock. Black shoes. Black beaver hat. White leather gloves. 4 1829. German. Double-breasted ankle-length brown wool coat worn open, large fur collar with matching lining and sleeve cuffs, outsized covered buttons, hip-level piped pockets. Knee-length double-breasted cloth frock-coat. White waistcoat and shirt. Blue stock. Grey trousers. Black shoes. Black top hat. Yellow gloves. Curled hair with side parting and whiskers. 5 1829. German. Double-breasted knee-length wool coat, edges piped with dark wool matching covered buttons and pockets, tight sleeves with sewn cuffs. Tight ankle-length green wool trousers. Striped stockings. Black shoes. Black beaver hat. White shirt. Yellow waistcoat. Blue stock. White gloves. Cane with gilt handle. 6 1829. German. Double-breasted mid-calf-length green wool tweed greatcoat, elbow-length cape, covered buttons, high collar. White trousers. Black shoes. Black beaver hat. White shirt. White stock. White gloves. Cane with gilt handle. 7 1829. British. Double-breasted knee-length blue cloth frock-coat worn open, large collar with wide revers, tight cuffed inset gathered sleeves, hip-level flap pockets. Grey trousers. Red waistcoat, flat collar. White shirt and stock. Black shoes. Black beaver hat. Yellow leather gloves.

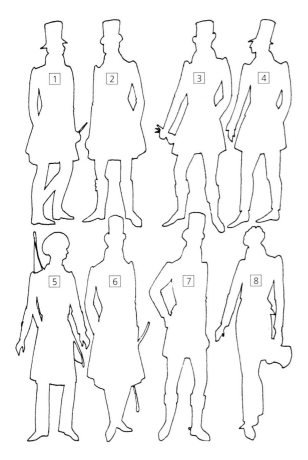

Sports Wear 1829

1 1829. British. Shooting. Single-breasted knee-length blue cloth coat, gilt buttons, velvet collar and matching flap pockets, gathered inset sleeves with turned-down cuffs. Beige trousers. White shirt. Spotted stock. Black shoes. Brown beaver hat. Yellow leather gloves. 2 1829. British. Riding. Edge-to-edge knee-length frock-coat, fastening down the front with hooks and eyes, black velvet collar and matching bound edges. Red waistcoat. White shirt. Blue stock. Beige pantaloons. Black hessian boots trimmed with gold tassels. Black beaver hat. Yellow leather gloves. 3 1829. British. Hunting. Single-breasted knee-length red cloth coat, gilt buttons, bound pockets with matching detail, narrow collar. Double-breasted cloth waistcoat. White shirt. Blue stock. White breeches. Black boots with brown cuffs. Black top hat. Yellow gloves. 4 1829. British. Riding. Short brown cloth coat, velvet collar, fitted waist, inverted box pleats in back skirt, flap pockets, gathered inset sleeves with turned-down cuffs. Tight ankle-length white trousers, laced at ankle. Striped stockings. Black pumps. Black beaver hat. Yellow gloves. 5 1829. British. Archery. Single-breasted knee-length green linen coat buttoning from waist to soft shirt-collar, gathered inset sleeves. Broad brown leather belt. Single leather gauntlet and wrist protector. Flared white linen trousers. Black shoes. Green beret. 6 1829. British. Riding. Single-breasted knee-length coat, full skirts, gilt buttons, shawl collar, flap pockets set into waist seam. Yellow waistcoat. Striped stock. Brown beaver hat. Yellow gloves. 7 1829. British. Riding. Short single-breasted green cloth coat, M-notch collar, gathered inset sleeves with stitched cuffs, hip-level flap pockets, gilt buttons. Striped waistcoat. Black stock. White shirt. White breeches. Brown boots worn with spurs. Black top hat. 8 1829. British. Light riding. Double-breasted brown cloth coat, velvet M-notch collar and covered buttons, gathered inset sleeves with buttoned hem. Embroidered waistcoat. White shirt. White stock. White ankle-length trousers. Short boots. Top hat. Leather gloves.

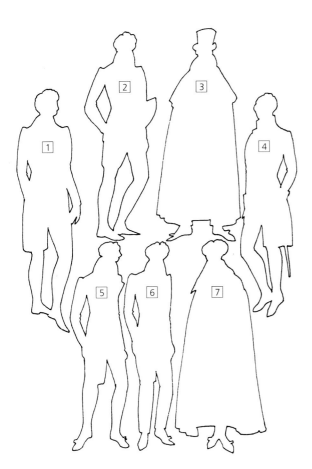

Evening Wear 1816–1829

1 1816. British. Blue cloth tailcoat, inverted pleats in the back skirt, covered buttons, flap pockets set into waist seam, gathered inset sleeves with flared cuffs. Flesh-coloured breeches. White silk stockings. Black buckled pumps. White gloves. 2 1824. British. Single-breasted black cloth tailcoat worn open, M-notch collar and wide revers, gathered inset sleeves with flared cuffs. Black under-waistcoat. Embroidered waistcoat. Gold watchchain and fob. Black breeches. White stockings with embroidered clocks. Black buckled pumps. White frilled shirt. Black stock. Black bicorn hat. White gloves. 3 1824. British. Opera wear. Ankle-length brown silk cape lined with red and white striped silk, elbow-length overcape with fur collar. Black tailcoat. Yellow waistcoat. White shirt and stock. Striped trousers. Silk stockings. Black leather pumps, bow trim. Black top hat. White gloves. 4 1825. English. Court. Pink silk tailcoat, gilt buttons, high stand collar, inset sleeves with deep cuffs. Yellow patterned waistcoat. White frilled shirt. Black silk breeches. White silk stockings. Black buckled pumps. Sword. 5 1826. British. Double-breasted tailcoat worn open, large velvet collar, gathered inset sleeves with flared turned-down cuffs. Under-waistcoat. Waistcoat with shawl collar. Frilled shirt. Stock tied into large bow. Knee breeches. Stockings with clocks. Pumps trimmed with ribbon bows. 6 1829. British. Opera wear. Black double-breasted coat worn open, velvet collar and outsized covered buttons. White striped waistcoat. White striped ankle-length trousers. Black pumps with bow trim. White gloves. 7 1828. British. Opera wear. Ankle-length blue velvet cape lined with red silk, large black velvet collar. Black tailcoat. Waistcoat with shawl collar. White shirt. Black stock. Ankle-length flesh-coloured trousers, buttoned at ankle-level. White stockings. Black pumps with bow trim. Yellow gloves. Black top hat.

Negligee and Underwear 1816–1829

1 1816. British. Edge-to-edge ankle-length wool damask dressing-gown, wide shawl collar from neck to hem, gathered inset sleeves with deep turned-back cuffs. Red leather mules with pointed upturned toes.
2 1820. British. Thigh-length white muslin shirt, high stiffened stand collar, three-button fastening, front opening edged with wide frill, dropped shoulderline, gathered inset sleeves with narrow buttoned cuffs, side vent open from hem to hip. 3 1824. British. Thigh-length white muslin shirt with high stiffened collar, three-button fastening, tucked front panel, opening edged with pleated frill, dropped shoulderline, inset sleeves gathered into buttoned cuffs, side vent open from hem to hip. 4 1828. British. Thigh-length white muslin shirt with high stiffened pointed collar, button fastening to hem of tucked front panel, dropped shoulderline, gathered inset sleeves with buttoned cuffs, side vent open from hem to hip. 5 1829. British. Double-breasted mid-calf-length green wool dressing-gown, large collar and wide revers, gathered inset sleeves with flared turned-down cuffs, velvet-covered buttons. Black silk stock. Black leather slippers with pointed upturned toes.

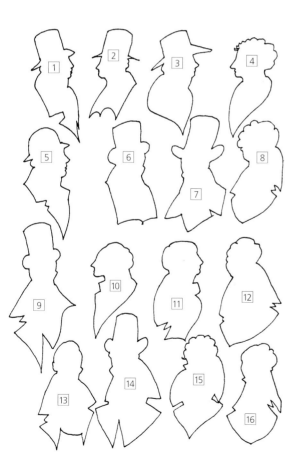

Accessories and Hairstyles 1816–1829

1 1816. Black silk top hat, high straight crown, narrow curled brim. Shirt with curved collar points. Spotted silk stock. Curled hair. 2 1818. Grey beaver hat, straight-sided crown, narrow curled brim. Boned black silk stock. Curled hair. 3 1819. Brown beaver hat, shallow crown, wide curled brim. Striped silk stock. Embroidered waistcoat. Curled hair. Long side-whiskers. 4 1820. Muslin shirt, turned-down collar, single-button fastening. Long curled hair with side parting. 5 1821. Brown bowler hat, rounded crown, narrow curled brim. High collar points. Curled hair. Long side-whiskers. 6 1823. Grey beaver hat, high waisted crown, curled brim. High collar points. Patterned silk stock. Long side-whiskers. 7 1823. Black beaver hat, waisted crown, curled brim. Rounded collar points. Striped silk scarf. 8 1823. White muslin shirt with pleated waterfall frill. White muslin stock. Asymmetrical hairstyle. 9 1825. Yellow beaver hat, tall crown, wide curled brim, central rosette decoration. Boned stock. Long side-whiskers. 10 1825. Curled hair dressed away from face. Boned black silk stock. 11 1825. White silk stock tied into large bow. High collar points. Hair dressed forward with side parting. Long side-whiskers. 12 1826. Boned striped silk stock. Double-breasted striped silk waistcoat. Curled hair. Long side-whiskers. 13 1828. White piqué evening shirt. White stock. White double-breasted waistcoat. Hair dressed away from face. Long side-whiskers meeting to form beard. Moustache. 14 1828. Tall brown beaver hat, curled brim. White stock tied into large bow. Muslin shirt, high collar points, double-pleated waterfall frill. 15 1829. Shirt with high collar points. White muslin stock. Yellow waistcoat. Black coat. Curled hair. 16 1829. Cream silk stock. White shirt with high collar points. Waved hair with side parting. Long side-whiskers.

Day Wear 1830–1831

1 1830. British. Single-breasted wool tailcoat, two extra rows of decorative covered buttons either side main opening, gathered inset sleeves with sewn cuffs, M-notch collar and narrow revers. Yellow waistcoat. White shirt and stock. Striped trousers. White stockings. Black leather pumps. Black top hat. Yellow gloves. Spy-glass on long ribbon worn around neck. 2 1830. British. Single-breasted knee-length green wool tweed coat, black velvet collar, gathered inset sleeves. Single-breasted embroidered collarless waistcoat. White shirt. Blue cravat. Grey trousers, inset stripe on outside leg. Black leather ankle-boots. Black top hat. Yellow gloves. Walking cane. 3 1830. British. Single-breasted knee-length green checked wool overcoat, black velvet collar. Red waistcoat. White shirt. Black stock. Striped trousers. Ankle-boots. Black top hat. White gloves. Umbrella. 4 1830. British. Double-breasted knee-length black wool overcoat, tight inset sleeves. Red waistcoat. White shirt and stock. Blue and white checked trousers. Ankle-boots. Black top hat. Yellow gloves. 5 1831. German. Single-breasted black wool tailcoat, inset sleeves with gathered head and flared cuffs, M-notch collar and wide revers. White shirt, high points. Black silk stock. Wool trousers, central seam. Stirrups. Black leather ankle-boots. Gloves. Top hat. Walking cane. 6 1831. British. Double-breasted green wool coat fastened with gilt buttons, inset sleeves with gathered head and flared cuffs. Yellow waistcoat. White shirt and stock. Cream trousers. Brown leather ankle-boots. White gloves. 7 1831. French. Mid-calf-length single-breasted wool tweed greatcoat, large collar and wide revers, inset sleeves with gathered head and flared cuffs, hip-level flap pockets. Single-breasted green embroidered waistcoat, high button fastening. Red silk scarf. Monocle on ribbon worn around neck. Cream trousers. Ankle-boots. Top hat. Walking cane.

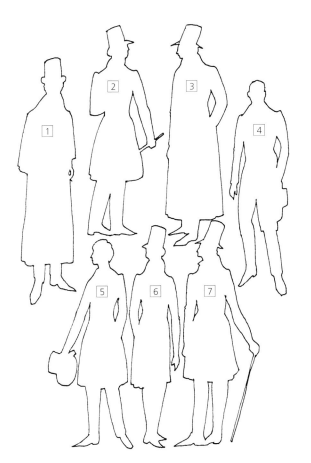

Day Wear 1832–1836

1 1832. British. Mid-calf-length single-breasted brown wool greatcoat, shoulder-wide shawl collar, wrist-length cape, waist-level flap pockets, covered buttons. White shirt and stock. Brown striped trousers. Black ankle-boots. Black top hat. Leather gloves. 2 1833. German. Knee-length striped wool coat, vertical pockets concealed in back skirt pleats, gathered inset sleeves. White shirt, high collar points. Black stock. White trousers, inset stripe on outside leg. Ankle-boots. Top hat. Gloves. Walking cane. 3 1833. German. Mid-calf-length single-breasted brown wool coat, large black velvet shawl collar matching covered buttons, tight sleeves with gathered head, hip-level diagonal welt pockets. Green coat. White shirt and stock. Blue trousers. White stockings. Black patent-leather pumps with bow trim. Black top hat. Yellow gloves. 4 1834. British. Single-breasted black wool tailcoat worn open, tight sleeves with gathered head, large collar and wide revers. Single-breasted striped silk waistcoat, shawl collar. White shirt, pleated front, turned-down points. White cravat. White trousers. Black ankle-boots. Black top hat. 5 1834. British. Single-breasted knee-length black wool coat, large collar and wide revers, tight sleeves with gathered head, hip-level flap pockets. Double-breasted yellow silk waistcoat. White shirt. Red silk cravat. Striped trousers. Ankle-boots. Top hat. Gloves. 6 1834. British. Knee-length blue wool tweed coat, high collar, back pleats, tight sleeves with gathered head. Beige trousers, inset stripe on outside leg. Ankle-boots. Top hat. Leather gloves. 7 1836. British. Knee-length fitted black wool coat, inset sleeves with gathered head, pockets concealed in back skirt pleats, high collar points. Pink silk cravat. White trousers, inset stripe on outside leg. Ankle-boots worn with spurs. Short yellow leather gauntlets. Top hat. Walking cane.

Day Wear 1836–1840

1 1836. German. Mid-calf-length single-breasted brown wool coat, fastening with single button at waist-level, worn open; outsized black velvet collar and wide revers, tight sleeves with narrow cuffs. Double-breasted brown wool tailcoat. Striped waistcoat. White frilled and pleated shirt. White stock. Fitted grey wool trousers. Ankle-boots. Black top hat. Yellow gloves. 2 1836. German. Knee-length single-breasted blue wool coat worn open, tight sleeves, large collar and wide revers, full skirts. Single-breasted yellow waistcoat, shawl collar. White ruffled shirt. White and blue spotted cravat. Fitted grey striped trousers. Black ankle-boots. Grey top hat. Yellow gloves. Walking cane. 3 1836. German. Knee-length edge-to-edge green wool topcoat fastening with hooks and bars under decorative braid frogging; fur collar, cuffs and trimming. Red stock. White cloth trousers with stirrups. Ankle-boots. Black top hat. Grey gloves. Walking cane. 4 1837. British. Knee-length double-breasted grey cloth overcoat, braid trimming, tight sleeves with sewn cuffs, hip-level flap pockets. Blue stock. Striped trousers. Ankle-boots. Top hat. Gloves. 5 1837. American. Thigh-length double-breasted unfitted cloth coat, outsized shawl collar, large self-fabric buttons, hip-level diagonal piped pockets, deep cuffs. Green scarf. Flesh-coloured trousers. Ankle-boots. Brown top hat. Yellow gloves. 6 1840. American. Thigh-length unfitted grey cloth topcoat, grey velvet collar, centre-back pleat, diagonal pockets, sleeve hem and upper back parts decorated with braid. Tight grey cloth trousers with stirrups. Ankle-boots. Brown top hat. Yellow gloves. Walking cane. 7 1840. British. Double-breasted knee-length fitted green wool coat, cut away front skirt, tight cuffless sleeves. Grey waistcoat. White shirt and stock. Fitted pale yellow trousers. Black ankle-boots. Black top hat. Yellow leather gloves. Walking cane.

Day Wear 1840–1842

1 1840. British. Knee-length black wool coat, back cut into two panels without a waist seam, each seam ends in a pleat from the waist, marked with a covered button, matching three buttons on hem of central seam. Fitted striped trousers with stirrups. Ankle-boots. Top hat. Gloves. 2 1840. British. Knee-length single-breasted black wool coat with buttons to hem, worn open; narrow sleeves; full skirts with four diagonal flap pockets. Single-breasted red wool waistcoat, shawl collar. White shirt and stock. Fitted checked wool trousers with stirrups. Black ankle-boots. Top hat. 3 1841. German. Fitted single-breasted striped brown wool coat buttoning from waist to under collar, diagonal piped breast pocket, red silk handkerchief, two matching pockets in hem of front skirts, tight sleeves with narrow stitched cuffs. White frilled shirt. White stock. Fitted trousers with stirrups. Ankle-boots. Top hat. Gloves. 4 1841. British. Knee-length double-breasted light brown cloth topcoat, short top-stitched shoulder cape under velvet shawl collar, matching deep turned-back sleeve cuffs and covered buttons, diagonal hip-level flap pockets. White shirt and stock. Tight brown trousers. Black ankle-boots. Black top hat. Grey gloves. 5 1842. British. Double-breasted black cloth coat; black velvet collar, sleeve cuffs and covered buttons; plaited silk braid trim between buttons; red silk handkerchief in piped breast pocket; diagonal hip-level flap pockets. Tight beige wool trousers with inset braid on outside leg. Ankle-boots with pointed toes. Black silk top hat. Yellow gloves. Walking cane. 6 1842. British. Mid-calf-length green wool tweed cape, short shoulder cape under long pointed collar, bound slit openings. Black coat. Blue waistcoat. Red scarf. Beige trousers with stirrups. Ankle-boots. Walking cane. 7 1842. British. Knee-length grey wool edge-to-edge coat fastening under black velvet collar with two covered buttons, short shoulder cape, flared sleeves. Tight grey trousers with stirrups. Ankle-boots, square toes. Black hat. Yellow gloves. Walking cane.

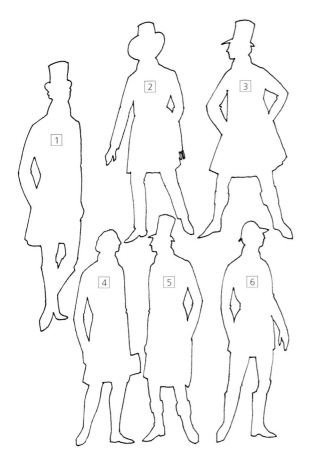

Sports Wear 1830–1842

[1] 1830. British. Riding. Single-breasted green wool coat, fastening with gilt buttons, matching buttons on wrists of fitted sleeves, narrow collar and revers. Red wool waistcoat. White frilled and pleated shirt. Yellow stock. Cream and white striped breeches. Long black boots, gold tassel trim, pointed toes. Black top hat. Yellow gloves. [2] 1834. German. Shooting. Short single-breasted brown cloth coat, fastening with tiny buttons from waist to under high collar, tight sleeves, hip-level flap pockets. White and red spotted scarf. Brown trousers, leather insert from knee to hem. Stirrups. Short boots. Straw hat, high crown, wide brim, worn over striped scarf. Leather game bag. White gloves. [3] 1839. British. Hunting. Knee-length unfitted blue cloth coat, fastening with gilt buttons from below waist to under wide black velvet collar, matching velvet turned-back sleeve cuffs, hip-level diagonal welt pockets, quilted red silk lining. Single-breasted waistcoat. Stock. Cream and white trousers. Long black leather boots, brown cuffs. Spurs. Black top hat. White gloves. [4] 1839. British. Dress riding. Double-breasted green wool coat, self-fabric buttons, tight cuffless sleeves, flap pockets set into waist seam. Yellow waistcoat. White frilled shirt, high points. Red stock. Fitted white trousers. Short boots worn with spurs. Silk top hat. Leather gloves. [5] 1840. German. Hunting. Single-breasted red wool coat, worn open; fastening with gilt buttons, matching buttons on wrist of tight sleeves; black velvet collar; diagonal hip-level flap pockets. Buckled leather waist-belt. White waistcoat. Black stock. White breeches. Long black leather boots, brown cuffs, pointed toes. Silk top hat. Leather gloves. [6] 1842. British. Hunting. Single-breasted red wool coat, fastening from waist to under stand collar with gilt buttons, matching buttons on tight sleeves, breast pockets and waist-level flap pockets. Buckled leather belt. White ribbed cloth breeches. Leather boots worn with spurs. Black velvet cap, large visor. Yellow leather gloves.

Evening and Court Wear 1830–1842

[1] 1830. English. Court. Single-breasted blue silk coat worn open, dark blue velvet stand collar, matching deep turned-back sleeve cuffs and large covered buttons, hip-level flap pockets, all edges piped with gold silk satin. White and cream striped silk waistcoat. White ruffled shirt. White stock. Yellow silk satin knee breeches. White silk stockings. Black pumps trimmed with buckles. Black bicorn hat. White gloves. [2] 1834. American. Opera wear. Mid-calf-length silk cape gathered from fitted shoulder yoke, cape fastens with two buttons under large velvet collar. White stock tied into large bow. White pantaloons. White silk stockings. Black silk pumps with buckle trim. Black silk top hat. White silk gloves. [3] 1836. German. Opera wear. Mid-calf-length brown velvet cape lined with red silk, fastening with gold cords from under large pointed collar. Black coat. White and gold embroidered waistcoat. Frilled and pleated shirt. White stock. Cream pantaloons. Striped silk stockings. Black silk pumps with gilt buckles. [4] 1837. German. Court. Velvet coat, embroidered stand collar and sleeve cuffs, matching waist-level flap pockets and large buttons. Collarless white brocade waistcoat. White ruffled shirt. White stock. Black striped silk breeches. White silk stockings. Black pumps, pointed toes. Black bicorn hat. Leather gloves. [5] 1838. German. Evening. Single-breasted grey cloth coat worn open, tight cuffless sleeves. White striped silk low-cut waistcoat, shawl collar. White frilled and pleated shirt. White silk stockings. Black silk pumps. Black bicorn hat. White gloves. [6] 1842. German. Evening. Single-breasted black cloth tailcoat worn open, tight cuffless sleeves, wide revers. Low-cut collarless gold brocade waistcoat. White shirt, high collar points. Black leather pumps, pointed toes. Leather gloves.

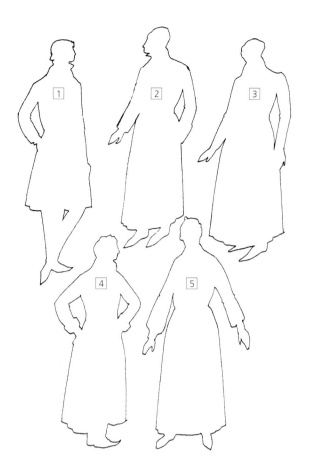

Dressing Gowns 1830–1840

1 1830. American. Double-breasted knee-length dressing gown of white silk patterned with leaves and flowers, plain yellow silk collar, edges bound in orange silk to match sleeve hems. Loose-fitting trousers match gown. White shirt, turned-down collar points. Green silk scarf. Yellow leather slippers, curled and pointed toes. Multi-coloured striped knitted silk cap, tassel trim. 2 1830. German. Ankle-length wrapover multi-coloured fine wool dressing gown, wide shawl collar, deep turned-back sleeve cuffs. Wide tie-belt. White shirt, turned-down collar points. Red silk scarf. Red velvet brimless cap trimmed with gold braid. Striped silk stockings. Yellow leather slippers, pointed toes. 3 1832. British. Double-breasted ankle-length velvet dressing gown, narrow shawl collar with self piping, self-covered buttons, narrow sleeves with gathered head, full gathered skirts. White shirt and stock. White stockings. Red leather slippers with pointed toes. 4 1835. British. Mid-calf-length blue wool dressing gown, wide collar and turned-back sleeve cuffs piped with yellow, fitted body, full gathered skirts. White pantaloons. White stockings. Red leather mules, curled and pointed toes. 5 1840. French. Ankle-length wrapover collarless silk brocade dressing gown, full sleeves gathered into narrow wrist cuffs; red silk cord belt matching edges of open pockets, side vents, wrapover and sleeve hems. Patterned silk scarf. Green velvet brimless cap trimmed with gold braid and a pompon. Red leather slippers, pointed toes.

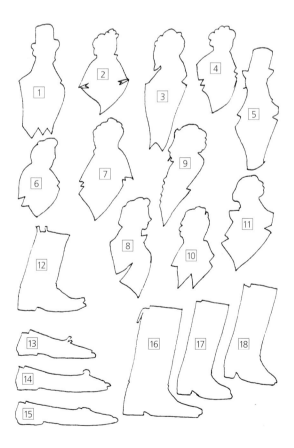

Accessories and Hairstyles 1830–1842

1 1830. American. Silk top hat, curled brim. Red silk stock tied into large bow. Shirt with ruffled frill. Green silk embroidered waistcoat. 2 1831. French. Curled hair. Long shaped side-whiskers. White muslin shirt and stock. Cloth waistcoat. 3 1831. British. Curled hair. Long side-whiskers and chin beard. Silk scarf. Cloth waistcoat. 4 1834. German. Curled hair and shaved side-whiskers. Blue silk scarf. Double-breasted waistcoat. 5 1834. British. Grey beaver top hat. Black stock. Shirt with turned-down collar points. Waistcoat with collar and revers. 6 1834. German. Long hair, side-whiskers and short beard. Green silk scarf. Shirt with turned-down collar. 7 1835. French. Curled hair and side-whiskers. Black silk cravat tied into large bow. Shirt, ruffled front, long collar points. 8 1839. British. Long hair and side-whiskers dressed onto face. Red silk stock. 9 1840. British. Curled hair with side parting, shaped side-whiskers, tiny under-lip beard, moustache. White muslin shirt, ruffled frill, high collar points. White muslin stock. 10 1841. French. Curled hair dressed onto the face, side parting. Red silk stock tied into large bow. High collar points. 11 1842. British. Curled hair, side parting, long side-whiskers dressed onto face. Dark-blue silk cravat. Collar points turned down. 12 1830. British. Short black leather riding boots, lined in red. 13 1830. British. Brown leather shoes lined with fine green leather, ribbon-bow fastening. 14 1830. British. Black patent-leather evening pumps lined with red silk, ribbon-bow trim. 15 1830. British. Black patent-leather evening pumps lined with red silk, ribbon-and-buckle trim. 16 1835. British. Black patent-leather riding boots, cream leather cuffs, low heels. 17 1842. British. Black patent-leather boots, red leather uppers, low heels. 18 1840. British. Black patent-leather boots, green leather uppers, high heels.

1843

1843

1844

1844

1845

1848

1849

Day Wear 1849

1849 1849 1849 1849

1849 1849 1849 1849

1849

1849

1850

1850

1850

1850

1850

1850

1852

1852

1853

1853

1854

1854

1855

1843

1843

1844

1849

1850

1852

1855

Sports Wear 1843–1850

1843

1846

1849

1849

1850

1850

1850

1850

1850

1852

1852

1853

1854

1855

Negligee 1843–1851

1843

1845

1849

1849

1850

1851

1856

1857

1858

1859

1859

1859

1861

Day Wear 1862–1864

1862

1862

1862

1863

1863

1864

1864

1864

1864

1864

1865

1865

1865

1865

Day Wear 1866–1868

1866

1866

1866

1867

1867

1867

1868

1868

1856

1859

1859

1860

1860

1864

1868

1860

1864

1856

1868

1865

1860

1861

1856

1868

1863

1856

1856

1856

1858

1858

1860

1860

1860

1861

1861

1858

1865

1865

1864

1863

1864

1865

1865

1866

1868

1867

1867

1868

Day Wear 1843–1849

1 1843. British. Double-breasted blue wool tailcoat, large collar and wide revers, tight sleeves with sewn cuffs. Green waistcoat. White shirt. Blue stock. Narrow trousers. Black ankle-boots. 2 1843. British. Brown wool tweed tailcoat, low waist seam, pockets concealed in side-back pleats, tight sleeves with sewn cuffs. Light brown wool trousers. Black leather ankle-boots. White leather gloves. 3 1843. British. Knee-length double-breasted green checked wool topcoat, high stand collar with strap fastening, covered buttons, cuffless sleeves, hip-level diagonal welt pockets. Narrow cream wool trousers. Black ankle-boots. Black silk top hat. Leather gloves. Walking cane. 4 1845. British. Double-breasted fitted grey cloth coat; black velvet collar, revers and sleeve cuffs; hip-level welt pockets. Black top hat. Leather gloves. 5 1845. British. Single-breasted knee-length blue cloth coat worn open, single-button fastening on waist, outsized blue velvet collar and matching chest-wide revers, tight cuffless sleeves, hip-level diagonal bound pockets. Double-breasted silk waistcoat, shawl collar. Collarless white silk under-waistcoat. Red silk scarf. Tight striped trousers. Ankle-boots, square toes, high heels. Black top hat. Leather gloves. 6 1848. British. Fitted yellow wool coat, tight cuffless sleeves, low waist seam, pockets concealed in back pleats. Tight brown and beige wool trousers. Ankle-boots, high heels. Black top hat. White leather gloves. Walking cane. 7 1849. British. Single-breasted thigh-length blue wool jacket, edges bound with yellow braid, small collar and narrow revers, tight cuffless sleeves, hip-level bound pockets. Orange wool waistcoat with yellow bindings. White shirt, turned-down collar. Blue scarf. Tight grey cloth trousers. White stockings. Black pumps, pointed toes.

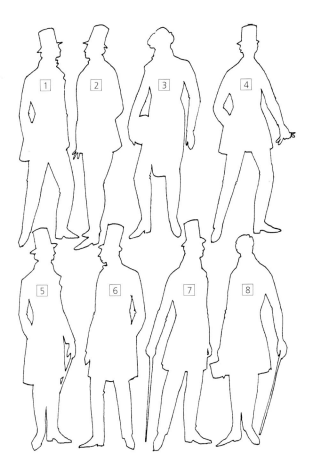

Day Wear 1849

1 1849. British. Single-breasted grey wool jacket, tight sleeves with narrow sewn cuffs, hip-level bound pockets. Collarless single-breasted yellow wool waistcoat, edges bound with orange braid. White under-waistcoat. White shirt. Blue silk cravat. Fitted grey wool trousers. White stockings. Black leather pumps. Black top hat. Leather gloves. 2 1849. British. Fitted brown wool jacket cut without centre-back or waist seams, tight cuffless sleeves. Fitted beige trousers, braid trim on outside leg. Black ankle-boots and top hat. Leather gloves. 3 1849. British. Single-breasted black cloth tailcoat worn open, tight cuffless sleeves. Embroidered single-breasted waistcoat, high button fastening, narrow shawl collar. White shirt, turned-down collar. Red stock. Fitted grey cloth trousers. Black ankle-boots, pointed toes. Black silk top hat lined with red silk. Leather gloves. 4 1849. British. Single-breasted blue wool coat, large collar, wide revers, tight sleeves with narrow sewn cuffs. Double-breasted cream waistcoat, wide shawl collar. Red silk scarf. Fitted grey wool trousers. Black ankle-boots. Black top hat. Leather gloves. 5 1849. British. Single-breasted green cloth topcoat, single-button fastening on waist, large collar and wide revers, diagonal hip-level pocket. Single-breasted beige cloth coat, high button fastening, rounded collar and revers. White shirt. Red silk cravat. Fitted pale-green trousers. Ankle-boots, square toes. Top hat. Leather gloves. Cane. 6 1849. British. Single-breasted knee-length beige wool topcoat, notched shawl collar, top-stitched edges, welt breast pocket, silk handkerchief, hip-level bound pockets, tight sleeves with turned-down cuffs. White shirt. Red cravat. Fitted grey cloth trousers. Ankle-boots, square toes. Black silk top hat. Leather gloves. Cane. 7 1849. British. Single-breasted grey cloth coat, large collar and wide revers, tight sleeves with sewn cuffs. Single-breasted embroidered green silk waistcoat. White shirt. Blue stock. Grey trousers, red stripe. Ankle-boots. Top hat. Gloves. Cane. 8 1849. British. Double-breasted knee-length coat, top-stitched edges, tight cuffless sleeves, hip-level pockets. Brown stock. Black boots. Black top hat.

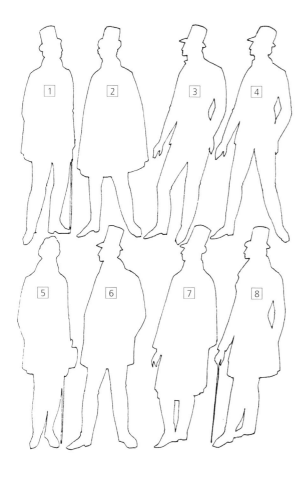

Day Wear 1849–1850

1 1849. British. Single-breasted unfitted grey wool topcoat, strap-and-button fastening, large flat collar with rounded edges, top-stitching, tight cuffless sleeves, diagonal hip-level welt pockets. Cream and green checked cloth trousers. Ankle-boots, square toes. Grey beaver top hat. 2 1849. British. Knee-length grey and beige checked wool cape, black velvet collar, concealed front opening, top-stitched detail. Tight flesh-coloured trousers. Black ankle-boots, square toes. Black top hat. 3 1850. British. Fitted single-breasted beige wool jacket, top-stitched edges, narrow collar and rounded revers, breast pocket, welt pocket, silk handkerchief, hip-level flap pockets, tight cuffless sleeves. Yellow single-breasted waistcoat, collar and revers, flap pockets, braided edges. Blue cravat. Flesh-coloured trousers, red stripe on outside leg. Black shoes worn with buttoned spats. Black top hat. Leather gloves. 4 1850. British. Fitted single-breasted cloth jacket, high button fastening, small collar and narrow revers, vertical pockets set into side panel seams, tight cuffless sleeves. White shirt. Red cravat. White trousers. Black shoes worn with buttoned spats. Stiffened grey felt hat, domed crown, curled brim. Leather gloves. 5 1850. British. Knee-length double-breasted wool overcoat, large collar and wide revers with rounded edges, sleeves with turned-back cuffs, breast pocket, welt pocket, silk handkerchief. White shirt, turned-down collar. Green scarf. Fitted grey cloth trousers. Ankle-boots. Top hat. Walking cane. 6 1850. British. Short blue wool tweed topcoat, blue silk shawl collar matching covered buttons and bound edges. Red scarf. Fitted beige trousers. Black ankle-boots. Black top hat. 7 1850. British. Knee-length unfitted sleeveless green cloth topcoat, wrist-length split cape, deep vent in back seam. Beige and cream checked trousers. Black ankle-boots. Dark-blue silk top hat. Leather gloves. 8 1850. British. Short double-breasted wool topcoat, large collar and wide revers, breast pocket, welt pocket, matching pockets low in skirts, cuffless sleeves. Double-breasted green coat, shawl collar. Purple silk scarf. Cream trousers. Ankle-boots. Top hat. Leather gloves. Walking cane.

Day Wear 1852–1855

1 1852. British. Unfitted single-breasted topcoat, button fastening to under collar, decorative top-stitching, cuffless raglan sleeves, diagonal hip-level welt pockets. Narrow cream wool trousers. Black ankle-boots. Black silk top hat. Leather gloves. Walking cane. 2 1852. British. Double-breasted hip-length wool tweed cape, large collar and wide revers, top-stitched detail, waist-level bound slit openings. Blue cravat. Narrow black trousers. Black ankle-boots, square toes. Black silk top hat. Leather gloves. Walking cane. 3 1853. British. Knee-length double-breasted black cloth frock-coat, high button fastening, narrow collar and revers, top-stitched detail, tight sleeves with sewn cuffs. Black and grey striped trousers. Black ankle-boots. Black top hat. Leather gloves. Walking cane. 4 1853. British. Short single-breasted black cloth frock-coat worn open, tight sleeves with turned-back cuffs. Single-breasted cloth waistcoat, shawl collar. White shirt. Red cravat. White cloth trousers. White stockings. Black pumps, ribbon bow trim. Top hat. Leather gloves. 5 1854. British. Knee-length double-breasted unfitted cloth topcoat, wrist-length cape from under large collar, top-stitched detail. Tight beige cloth trousers. White stockings. Black pumps. Black top hat. Leather gloves. Walking cane. 6 1854. British. Short single-breasted cloth coat, velvet collar, narrow revers, self-fabric buttons, breast welt pocket, matching hip-level pockets, tight cuffless sleeves with button trim. Green scarf. White trousers. Black ankle-boots. Black stiffened felt bowler hat. Leather gloves. Walking cane. 7 1855. British. Double-breasted knee-length unfitted blue cloth coat with red lining, large collar and wide revers bound with dark blue braid to match all edges and hems of flared sleeves. White cloth trousers, inset stripe on outside leg. Ankle-boots. Top hat. Leather gloves. Walking cane.

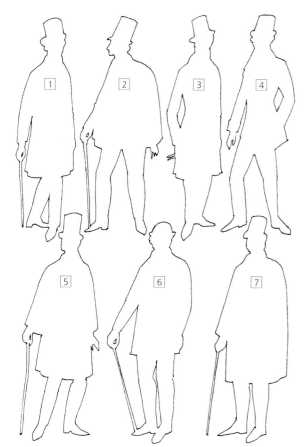

Evening Wear 1843–1855

1 1843. British. Single-breasted black tailcoat worn open, large collar and wide revers, tight sleeves with sewn cuffs. Single-breasted white silk waistcoat, shawl collar, welt pockets, pearl buttons, embroidered borders. White muslin ruffled shirt. White stock. Light-grey pantaloons. White stockings. Black pumps, buckled trim. White gloves. 2 1843. British. Single-breasted black cloth tailcoat worn open, black velvet collar, wide revers. Collarless cream silk waistcoat, embroidered borders. White muslin ruffled shirt. Cream silk cravat. Blue silk breeches. Grey stockings. Black silk pumps. White gloves. 3 1844. British. Single-breasted black cloth coat worn open, large collar and wide revers, tight cuffless sleeves. Collarless white striped silk waistcoat. White ruffled shirt, high collar points. Black silk cravat. Tight black cloth pantaloons. White stockings. Black pumps. 4 1849. British. Double-breasted black cloth tailcoat, M-notch collar and wide revers, tight cuffless sleeves with button trim. Single-breasted blue silk brocade waistcoat, shawl collar. White muslin pleated shirt, high collar points. White silk cravat. Tight black pantaloons. Silk stockings. Black pumps, ribbon-bow trim. Black silk top hat. White gloves. 5 1850. British. Single-breasted dark green cloth tailcoat worn open, tight sleeves with sewn cuffs, top-stitched, M-notch collar and wide revers. Single-breasted black waistcoat, shawl collar. Collarless yellow silk under-waistcoat. Black silk scarf. Dark-grey pantaloons. White stockings. Black pumps, square toes. 6 1852. British. Black suit. Silk embroidered waistcoat, shawl collar. Pleated white muslin shirt, high collar points. White cravat. Knee-length brown silk cape lined in red silk, large collar and wide revers. White stockings. Black pumps. Black top hat. White gloves. 7 1855. British. Double-breasted blue cloth tailcoat, M-notch collar. Single-breasted yellow silk brocade waistcoat, shawl collar. Tight black cloth trousers. White silk stockings. Black pumps. Black top hat. White gloves.

Sports Wear 1843–1850

1 1843. British. Riding. Single-breasted brown wool tailcoat worn open, long collar and wide revers, tight sleeves with narrow cuffs. Double-breasted striped yellow waistcoat, wide revers. Black silk stock. White corded cotton trousers with stirrups. Short boots. Top hat. 2 1846. British. Cricket. White muslin shirt, rolled-up sleeves, stand collar covered with red and white spotted scarf. White cotton trousers. Black leather belt. Short boots. Top hat. 3 1849. British. Riding. Single-breasted green wool coat fastened high on chest with loop and buttons. Collarless light green cloth waistcoat, welt pockets. White shirt, high collar points. Blue stock. White trousers. Ankle-boots. Leather gloves. 4 1849. British. Hunting. Single-breasted green wool jacket, tight sleeves with narrow cuffs, various flap pockets. Pink cloth waistcoat buttons under high shawl collar. Shirt with turned-down collar. Red stock. Wide white cotton trousers with buttons from hem to knee. Short boots worn with spats. Black cap, large visor. 5 1850. British. Riding. Double-breasted green checked wool coat, green velvet collar, top-stitched detail, covered buttons. White shirt, turned-down collar. Cravat. Tight cream and white trousers. Short boots worn with spurs. Top hat. Gloves. 6 1850. British. Hunting. Short single-breasted red wool coat, gilt buttons, top-stitched edges, breast flap pocket, tight cuffless sleeves with gilt button trim. Green stock tied into bow. Tight white trousers. Long cuffed boots worn with spurs. Green velvet peaked cap. Leather gloves. 7 1850. British. Hunting. Single-breasted red wool jacket, gilt buttons, blue velvet collar and revers matching sleeve cuffs, breast welt pocket, silk handkerchief. Buckled leather waistbelt and bag. White shirt. Blue and white spotted scarf. White cotton trousers. Short boots worn with spats. Yellow cloth peaked cap. Leather gloves.

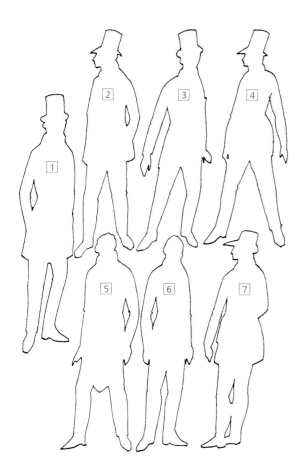

Sports Wear 1850–1855

1 1850. British. Riding. Double-breasted wool frock-coat, large collar and wide revers, tight cuffless sleeves, low waist seam. Waistcoat. White shirt. Green cravat. Checked trousers. Short brown leather boots worn with spurs. Brown silk top hat. 2 1850. British. Walking. Short single-breasted cloth frock-coat, long collar and narrow revers, breast pocket with silk handkerchief, tight cuffless sleeves. Lilac waistcoat. White shirt. Red scarf. Striped trousers. Ankle-boots. Green beaver top hat. Leather gloves. 3 1852. British. Riding. Double-breasted fitted green cloth tailcoat with shawl collar, tight sleeves with sewn cuffs. Yellow waistcoat. White shirt. Green cravat. White trousers. Ankle-boots. Top hat. Gloves. 4 1852. British. Riding. Double-breasted blue cloth tailcoat, pearl buttons, narrow collar and revers, tight cuffless sleeves with button trim. Yellow waistcoat. Pink cravat. White and grey checked trousers. Short black boots worn with spurs. Brown top hat. Yellow leather gloves. 5 1853. British. Riding. Double-breasted blue cloth tailcoat, buttons to under large collar, breast welt pocket. Red scarf. Green waistcoat. White cloth trousers. Ankle-boots. Leather gloves. 6 1854. British. Shooting. Single-breasted brown wool jacket worn open; top-stitched collar, revers and various flap pockets; tight cuffless sleeves. Single-breasted waistcoat, shawl collar. White shirt, high collar points. Blue cravat. Cream and white striped cotton trousers. Short boots worn with buttoned spats. 7 1855. British. Shooting. Short green wool jacket with back pleats. White striped cotton trousers covered by knee-high canvas gaiters, buttoning from ankle to knee on outside leg. Short boots. Straw hat, shallow flat-topped crown, wide brim edged with blue ribbon. Canvas and leather bag. Leather gloves.

Negligee 1843–1851

1 1843. French. Knee-length edge-to-edge collarless purple velvet coat, fastening from neck to waist with loops and buttons; round neckline, front edges, hemline, side slits, vertical hip-level pockets and wide flared sleeves decorated with gold mesh and braids. Shirt with unstiffened turned-down collar. Silk scarf. Tight ankle-length pantaloons. Silk stockings. Fine leather slippers, curled and pointed toes. Brimless purple velvet cap trimmed with gold braids and long tassel. 2 1845. French. Mid-calf-length single-breasted dressing gown, scalloped shawl collar, front wrapover and turned-down sleeve cuffs, strap-and-button fastening, buttoned belt. Shirt with unstiffened turned-down collar. Silk scarf. Silk stockings. Slippers with pointed toes. 3 1849. British. Mid-calf-length single-breasted collarless red corded velvet dressing gown, dark red velvet bound edges trimmed with gold braid, matching vertical hip-level pockets. Shirt with unstiffened turned-down collar. Black silk scarf. White silk stockings. Black slippers. 4 1849. British. Ankle-length wrapover padded and quilted pink silk dressing gown, wide shawl collar, edges bound with dark pink silk, matching hems of tight sleeves and rouleau belt. Muslin shirt. Blue silk scarf, fringed edges. Red leather slippers. Brimless velvet cap trimmed with gold braid and single gold tassel. 5 1850. British. Ankle-length wrapover blue corded velvet dressing gown, wide quilted silk shawl collar, matching sleeve cuffs, edges trimmed with gold silk cord, matching waistbelt with tassel trim. Shirt with unstiffened collar. Green silk scarf. Red slippers. Brimless embroidered velvet cap with gold tassel trim. 6 1851. French. Hip-length edge-to-edge dark red velvet jacket, blue quilted silk shawl collar and narrow cuffs, plain blue silk bindings, matching diagonal bound pockets, braid-and-button fastening, braid decoration and trimming. Shirt with unstiffened collar. Patterned silk scarf. Blue cotton trousers, braid trim on outside leg. Yellow leather mules, pointed and curled toes. Brimless black velvet cap trimmed with gold braid and long tassel.

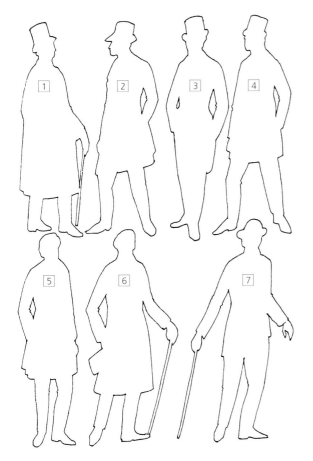

Day Wear 1856–1861

1 1856. German. Mid-calf-length unfitted green and brown tweed topcoat with centre-back inverted box pleat, large detachable hood and flared sleeves. Grey trousers, inset stripe on outside leg. Ankle-boots. Top hat. Gloves. Walking cane. 2 1857. French. Single-breasted knee-length coat, long collar and narrow revers, inset sleeves with turned-back buttoned cuffs. Double-breasted waistcoat, notched shawl collar. Pleated shirt, stiffened stand collar. Bow-tie. Fitted trousers. Shoes worn with spats. Felt hat, high crown, wide brim. 3 1858. British. Double-breasted wool coat worn open; collar, revers and flap pockets bound with silk braid. Single-breasted waistcoat, shawl collar, braided edges. Shirt with turned-down collar. Wide bow-tie. Narrow fitted trousers. Ankle-boots. Top hat. 4 1859. British. Thigh-length single-breasted unfitted grey and white striped wool coat, high fastening to under small collar and narrow revers, breast patch pocket, silk handkerchief, matching hip-level pockets. Shirt with wide turned-down collar. Red cravat. Narrow trousers. Ankle-boots. Top hat. Gloves. 5 1859. German. Single-breasted knee-length blue cloth coat, black velvet collar, wide revers. Single-breasted grey and yellow checked silk waistcoat, shawl collar. White shirt with stand collar. Blue bow-tie. Narrow fitted trousers. Ankle-boots. 6 1859. British. Knee-length brown wool coat, concealed fly front opening, brown velvet collar, narrow revers, cuffless sleeves, hip-level bound pockets. White shirt. Black bow-tie. Narrow trousers. Ankle-boots. Top hat. Gloves. Walking cane. 7 1861. American. Single-breasted brown wool jacket fastening with single button under wide revers, cuffless sleeves, breast bound pocket, matching hip-level pockets. Red cloth waistcoat. Shirt with wide turned-down collar. Silk scarf. Narrow fitted trousers. Leather ankle-boots. Brown stiffened felt bowler hat. Leather gloves. Walking cane.

Day Wear 1862–1864

1 1862. German. Knee-length single-breasted grey tweed coat, long collar and wide revers, sleeves with stitched cuffs. Single-breasted waistcoat, high fastening to under narrow roll collar. Fitted trousers in matching fabric. Shirt with stand collar. Narrow bow-tie. Ankle-boots. Grey stiffened felt hat, wide brim, shallow crown. 2 1862. German. Long single-breasted blue cloth coat, small collar and narrow revers, sleeves with stitched cuffs, button detail, breast welt pocket, hip-level flap pockets set into seam. Narrow fitted checked wool trousers. Ankle-boots. Shirt with turned-down collar. Narrow bow-tie. Black silk top hat. White kid leather gloves. 3 1862. French. Knee-length single-breasted grey tweed overcoat, high button fastening, top-stitched detail, matching breast welt pockets, single silk handkerchief, hip-level welt pockets, inset sleeves with narrow cuffs. Striped trousers. Ankle-boots. Leather gloves. 4 1863. British. Single-breasted grey wool jacket, edges trimmed with braid, matching collar and revers, stitched cuffs and hip-level flap pockets. Single-breasted red cloth waistcoat, shawl collar. Shirt with stand collar. Black cravat. Narrow fitted striped cloth trousers. Ankle-boots. Top hat. Leather gloves. 5 1863. British. Knee-length single-breasted cloth overcoat, high button fastening, cuffless sleeves, hip-level welt pockets. Grey top hat. Leather gloves. 6 1864. British. Single-breasted brown wool jacket, fastening with single button under narrow collar, braided edges match hip-level pockets and stitched sleeve cuffs. Trousers in matching fabric. Ankle-boots. Brown felt bowler hat. Leather gloves. 7 1864. British. Single-breasted grey cloth frock-coat, high fastening under small collar and narrow revers, top-stitched detail, cuffless sleeves, low waist seam. Red waistcoat. Shirt with small stand collar. Black cravat. Striped trousers. Ankle-boots. Top hat.

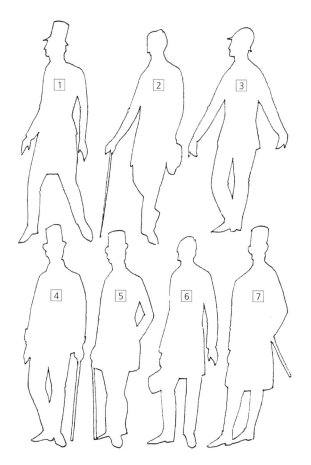

Day Wear 1864–1865

1 1864. British. Single-breasted green cloth frock-coat, narrow collar and revers, narrow sleeves with stitched cuffs, hip-level flap pockets set into seam. Double-breasted yellow and green checked silk waistcoat, wide shawl collar. Shirt with stiffened stand collar. Green silk bow-tie. Fitted narrow beige cloth trousers. Ankle-boots, square toes. Black silk top hat. Leather gloves. 2 1864. German. Single-breasted grey cloth coat, fastening under small collar and revers, matching welt breast pockets, hip-level flap pockets set into seam, sleeves with stitched cuffs. Blue waistcoat. White shirt, turned-down collar. Blue cravat. White and grey checked trousers. Ankle-boots, square toes. Felt hat, shallow flat-topped crown trimmed with ribbon and bow, straight brim. Leather gloves. Walking cane. 3 1864. German. Waisted wool jacket, braided edges matching hip-level flap pockets and sewn cuffs, back vent and side pleats, button trim. Fitted trousers, braid set into outside leg. Ankle-boots. Stiffened brown felt bowler, narrow curled brim. Leather gloves.
4 1865. British. Double-breasted hip-length grey wool coat, edges trimmed with fur matching small collar, deep cuffs and flap pockets. Narrow fitted trousers. Ankle-boots, square toes. Top hat. Leather gloves. Walking cane. 5 1865. British. Double-breasted cloth frock-coat, black silk collar and revers, narrow sleeves with stitched cuffs. Single-breasted waistcoat, high fastening under shawl collar. Striped wool trousers. Ankle-boots. Top hat. Leather gloves. Walking cane. 6 1865. British. Double-breasted black wool tweed frock-coat, top-stitched detail, single breast welt pocket, cuffless sleeves. Black trousers, ankle-boots and top hat. Grey gloves. 7 1865. British. Wool frock-coat, top-stitched panel seams, back vent with knife pleat on each side, stitched cuffs. Narrow grey cloth trousers. Ankle-boots. Top hat with wide ribbon band. Yellow leather gloves. Walking cane.

Day Wear 1866–1868

1 1866. German. Single-breasted fur-trimmed brown wool coat, braid buttons, loops and straps, hip-level flap pockets. Shirt with stand collar. Silk cravat. Narrow checked wool trousers. Ankle-boots, square toes. Stiffened brown felt bowler hat, shallow crown, ribbon band and bow, narrow curled brim. Leather gloves. 2 1866. British. Mid-calf-length blue checked wool overcoat, collar trimmed with fur, matching sleeve cuffs. Beige trousers. Black leather ankle-boots. Top hat. Leather gloves. 3 1867. German. Single-breasted grey wool coat, fastening by two buttons under high stand collar, stitched sleeve cuffs with button detail, single breast flap pocket, matching hip-level pockets. Pale grey trousers. Ankle-boots. Top hat, wide band. Grey leather gloves. Walking cane. 4 1867. British. Single-breasted black cloth coat worn open, wide shawl collar, cuffless sleeves. Single-breasted blue and black brocade waistcoat, high fastening to under small shawl collar. Shirt with turned-down collar. Cravat. Narrow pale-grey trousers. Black boots. Top hat. Leather gloves. Walking cane. 5 1867. British. Mid-calf-length green wool tweed overcoat with detachable hood, wide sleeves with stitched cuffs, hip-level flap pockets, buttoned half-belt. Grey trousers. Black boots, pointed toes. Stiffened brown felt hat, high domed crown trimmed with wide ribbon band and bow, narrow curled brim. Leather gloves. Walking stick.
6 1868. German. Single-breasted wool jacket, small collar and wide revers, top-stitched edges, single breast buttoned-flap pocket, matching hip-level pockets, stitched cuffs, button detail. Narrow trousers in matching fabric. Single-breasted red wool waistcoat, small shawl collar. White shirt, turned-down collar. Silk necktie. Black shoes worn with spats. Black bowler hat. Grey gloves. 7 1868. German. Short double-breasted blue cloth jacket, large collar with rounded edges, matching revers, stitched cuffs, hip-level flap pockets. Shirt with turned-down collar. Green silk necktie. Grey trousers. Ankle-boots, square toes. Grey top hat, wide dark-grey band. Yellow leather gloves.

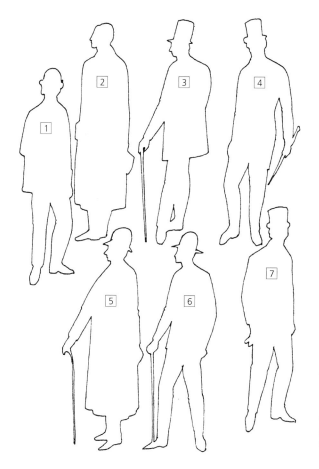

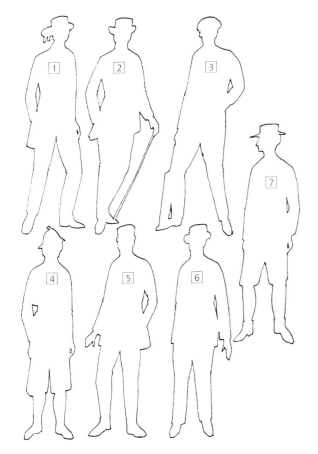

Sports and Leisure Wear 1856–1868

1 1856. American. Fishing. Single-breasted blue cloth jacket, breast welt pockets, button trim, hip-level buttoned flap pockets, cuffless sleeves. Single-breasted yellow cloth waistcoat, shawl collar. Shirt with turned-down collar. Lilac scarf. Grey and white striped trousers. Blue and white striped cotton stockings. Black leather pumps. Straw hat, shallow flat-topped crown trimmed with ribbon, wide curled brim. 2 1859. American. Country wear. Single-breasted brown checked wool jacket, roll collar, large hip-level patch pockets. Fitted trousers in matching fabric. Single-breasted green cloth waistcoat, shawl collar. White shirt with narrow turned-down collar. Blue silk scarf. Ankle-boots. Straw hat, striped ribbon trim. Walking stick. 3 1859. British. Cricket. White and cream spotted cotton shirt, turned-down collar. Red bow-tie. Narrow fitted cream cloth trousers worn with leather waist-belt. White canvas ankle-boots. Cream wool sectioned peaked cap. 4 1860. British. Shooting. Single-breasted cream linen tweed Norfolk jacket, buttoned from waist to under collar, box pleats from mid-shoulder to waist, buttoned belt, large hip-level patch pockets, cuffless sleeves. Gathered knee breeches in matching fabric. Yellow ribbed wool stockings. Two-tone lace-up ankle-boots. Brown wool deerstalker hat. 5 1860. British. Sailing. Single-breasted checked cloth jacket, diagonal hip-level welt-pockets. Yellow checked cloth waistcoat. White shirt. Blue scarf. Grey trousers. Ankle-boots. Stiffened felt cap, small visor. 6 1864. British. Cricket. Single-breasted striped cotton jacket, fastening by single button under narrow revers, small collar, hip-level piped pockets. Shirt with turned-down collar. Necktie. Cream cotton trousers worn with leather belt. Canvas ankle-boots. Stiffened straw hat, blue ribbon band. 7 1868. British. Country wear. Single-breasted cream linen jacket, fastening by single button under rounded collar, cuffless sleeves, hip-level flap pockets. Knee breeches in matching fabric. Green waistcoat. Shirt. Necktie. Beige ribbed wool stockings. Elastic-sided leather ankle-boots. Stiffened straw boater, shallow flat-topped crown, straight flat brim, striped ribbon trim.

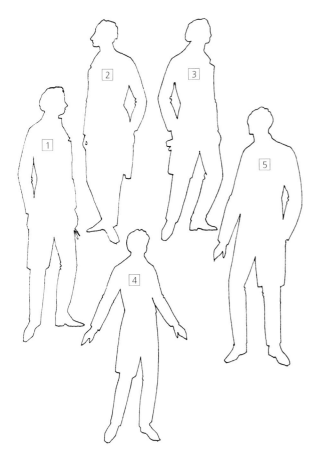

Evening Wear 1856–1868

1 1856. French. Double-breasted black cloth tailcoat worn open, long collar and wide revers, top-stitched detail, sewn cuffs. Narrow fitted trousers in matching fabric. Single-breasted blue silk brocade waistcoat, narrow shawl collar. White silk collarless under-waistcoat. White muslin shirt, stiffened stand collar. White silk stock tied into large bow. Black shoes, square toes. 2 1860. German. Single-breasted blue cloth tailcoat worn open, long collar and double-breasted revers, cuffless sleeves, button trim. Black cloth trousers. Single-breasted low-cut silk waistcoat, shawl collar. White shirt, stand collar. White bow-tie. Black shoes. White gloves. 3 1864. British. Single-breasted black wool tailcoat worn open, narrow collar and double-breasted revers, stitched cuffs. Trousers in matching fabric. White shirt, stand collar. Narrow bow-tie. Single-breasted low-cut black brocade waistcoat, shawl collar. Black shoes. White gloves. 4 1865. American. Double-breasted black cloth tailcoat worn open; stitched collar, revers and cuffs. Narrow fitted ankle-length trousers in matching fabric. White silk stockings. Black patent-leather pumps, ribbon bow trim. Single-breasted black silk collarless waistcoat. White tucked muslin shirt, stand collar. Bow-tie. 5 1868. British. Double-breasted black cloth tailcoat worn open, collar and revers faced with black silk, top-stitched detail, stitched cuffs. Narrow fitted trousers in matching fabric. Double-breasted low-cut silk waistcoat, shawl collar. White frilled muslin shirt, stiffened stand collar. White bow-tie. White gloves. Black shoes.

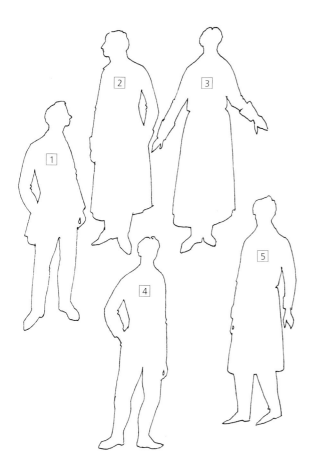

Negligee and Underwear 1856–1868

1 1856. British. Single-breasted velvet lounging jacket, fastening with loops and buttons, long shawl collar covered in black silk, matching sleeve cuffs, button detail, cord edging trim. Double-breasted grey silk velvet waistcoat, wide revers and narrow collar, top-stitched edges. White shirt, high stiffened stand collar. Black silk cravat, stick pin. Grey trousers. White stockings. Red leather slippers, pointed toes. 2 1860. French. Double-breasted mid-calf-length blue wool dressing gown, notched shawl collar bound with multi-coloured embroidered silk, matching buttons, hip-level flap pockets and wide sleeve cuffs. White shirt. Blue cravat. Striped trousers. Black shoes. 3 1861. British. Ankle-length orange silk dressing gown, single-button fastening under padded and quilted shawl collar, quilting repeated on wide cuffs and hip-level welt pockets, patterned quilting on front wrapover and around hemline, edges piped with dark orange silk, matching rouleau belt, tassel ends. Stand collar. Cravat. Black shoes. 4 1863. British. Hip-length collarless knitted white wool vest with front buttoning strap opening, full length inset sleeves with open underarm gusset, stitched cuffs and button trim. Ankle-length drawers in matching knitted fabric, front strap opening, tight legs end in wide knitted rib on ankle. 5 1868. British. Knee-length single-breasted green checked wool dressing gown, fastening with two large covered buttons, shawl collar, turned-back sleeve cuffs and hip-level patch pockets edged with green cord, matching waist-cord with tasseled ends. Spotted silk scarf. Grey trousers. Black shoes.

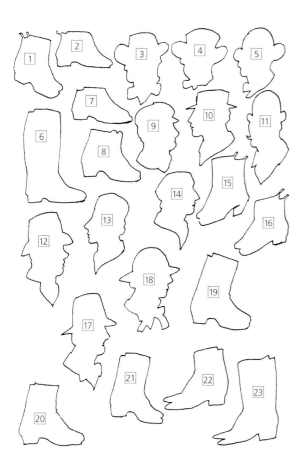

Accessories 1856–1868

1 1856. Two-tone grey leather lace-up ankle-boots with toecaps.
2 1856. Two-tone black and white leather elastic-sided ankle-boots.
3 1856. Brown felt hat, shallow crown, narrow band, wide curled brim. Cravat tied into bow. 4 1858. Yellow straw hat, shallow flat-topped crown, striped silk band, wide curled brim. Bow-tie. 5 1858. Brown stiffened felt hat, high domed crown, petersham band, wide curled brim. One-sided bow-tie. 6 1858. Knee-length cream felt gaiters, buttons on outside edge, top-stitched detail. Stirrups. 7 1860. Short grey leather lace-up boots, low heels. 8 1860. Brown leather lace-up ankle-boots, pointed toecaps, low heels. 9 1860. Green tweed eight-section cap, narrow front visor, back visor turned up and sewn, button trim. 10 1861. Stiffened natural straw hat, high flat-topped crown, wide striped ribbon band, straight brim. 11 1861. Grey stiffened felt bowler hat, wide petersham band, narrow curled brim. 12 1863. Stiffened natural straw hat, high flat-topped crown, wide pink ribbon band, curled brim. 13 1864. Black brimless fur hat. 14 1865. Brimless black velvet smoking hat, multi-coloured embroidered band. 15 1865. Black leather elastic-sided boots with toecaps, high heels, low button fastening. 16 1865. Brown leather elastic-sided boots. 17 1866. Grey felt hat, high flat-topped crown, wide silk band, curled brim. 18 1864. Brown felt hat, brown velvet ribbon band, narrow downturned brim. 19 1865. Beige leather lace-up ankle-boots, high stacked heels. 20 1867. Brown leather boots, high heels, toecaps, buttoned beige suede uppers. 21 1867. Black leather boots, side-button fastening, high stacked heels, shaped toecaps. 22 1868. Grey leather lace-up ankle-boots with grey patent-leather toecaps, high stacked heels. 23 1868. Tan leather and black patent leather mid-calf-length riding boots, elasticated front vent, pointed toes, high heels.

1869

1869

1869

1869

1869

1869

1869

1870

1871

1873

1874

1874

1874

1874

1876

1876

1876

1876

1876

1877

1878

1878

1880

1880

1881

1869

1869

1872

1873

1874

1876

1880

Evening Wear 1869–1881

1869

1872

1873

1874

1875

1877

1881

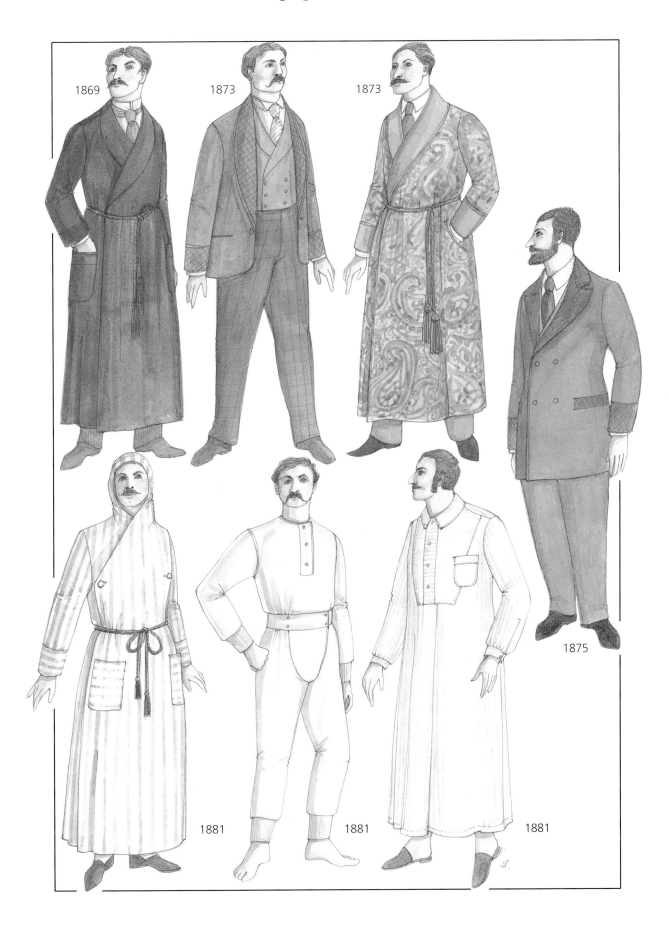

1869

1873

1873

1875

1881

1881

1881

1869

1869

1871

1873

1873

1875

1876

1876

1877

1878

1881

1876

1879

1881

1880

1880

1881

1882

1884

1884

1885

1885

1885

1885

1885

1885

1885

1886

1887

1888

1889

1889

1889

1889

1889

1889

1889

1889

1890

1890

1892

1890

1892

1893

1894

1882

1888

1888

1888

1885

1889

1889

1889

1891

1894

Evening Wear 1882–1894

1882

1886

1888

1890

1894

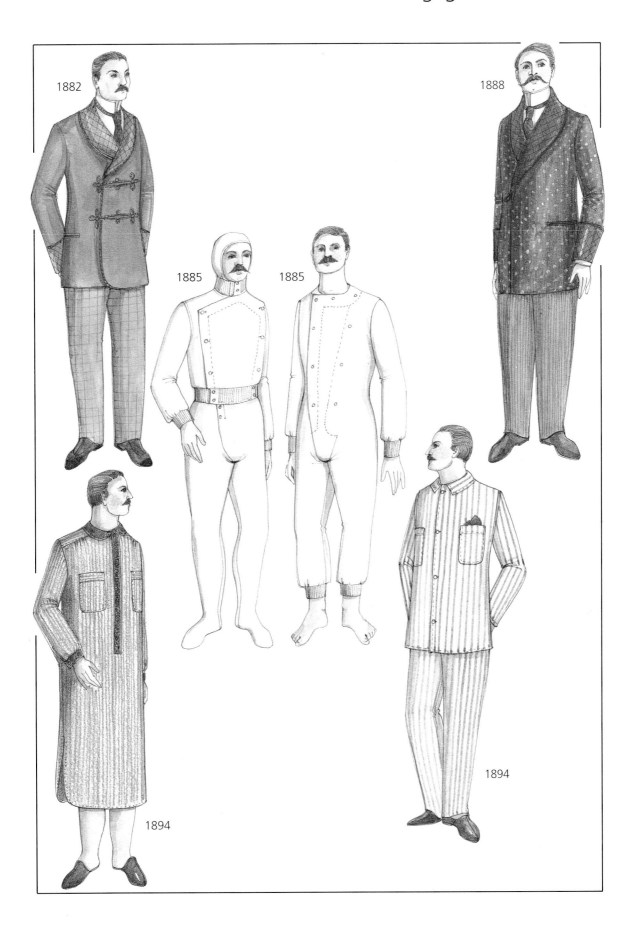

1882

1888

1885

1885

1894

1894

1882

1885

1885

1887

1890

1894

1894

1882

1890

1890

1891

1891

1891

1892

1894

1894

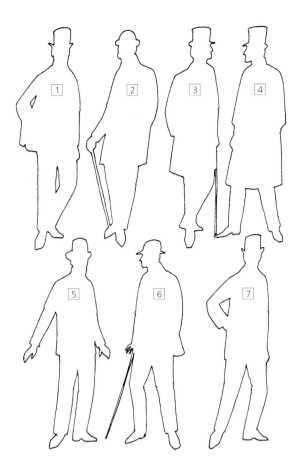

Day Wear 1869

1 1869. British. Short double-breasted grey tweed coat, black velvet collar, welt pockets and bound edges, matching stitched cuffs and side vents. Shirt with turned-down collar. Green silk necktie. Fitted brown cloth trousers. Ankle-boots. Top hat, wide ribbon band. 2 1869. British. Double-breasted green cloth overcoat, velvet collar and stitched cuffs, edges bound with black braid, matching flap pockets. Checked cloth trousers. Black leather ankle-boots. Brown felt bowler hat. Leather gloves. Walking cane. 3 1869. British. Double-breasted light brown wool overcoat, black velvet collar, top-stitched edges, hip-level flap pockets, narrow stitched cuffs, self-covered buttons. Shirt with turned-down collar. Cravat. Grey and black striped trousers. Black leather boots, square toes. Black top hat. Leather gloves. Walking cane. 4 1969. British. Single-breasted knee-length green wool overcoat, wrist-length cape in matching fabric and lined with red wool, covered buttons, top-stitched edges. Grey and black checked cloth trousers. Black boots. Black top hat. Leather gloves. 5 1869. British. Double-breasted grey wool jacket, small collar and wide revers, single breast welt pocket, hip-level flap pockets, button-trimmed cuffless sleeves. Narrow trousers in matching fabric. White stand collar. Pink silk necktie. Black boots, pointed toes. Grey felt hat, tall crown, narrow brim, wide petersham ribbon band. 6 1869. British. Grey wool tweed two-piece suit: single-breasted jacket, small collar and wide revers, buttoned-down flap pockets, stitched edges, stitched cuffs with button trim; narrow trousers. Single-breasted red cloth waistcoat, high button fastening to under shawl collar. White shirt. Blue necktie. Black shoes worn with white spats. Black bowler hat. Leather gloves. Walking cane. 7 1869. British. Short double-breasted blue cloth coat, collar with wide rounded revers, hip-level flap pockets and stitched sleeve cuffs edged with petersham braid. White shirt. Green necktie. Grey trousers. Black boots. Black top hat. Leather gloves.

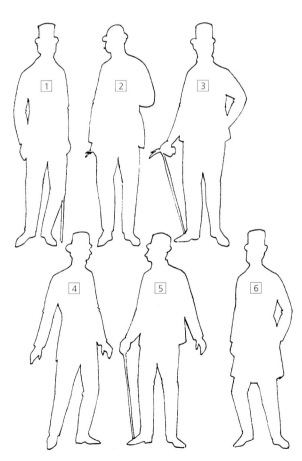

Day Wear 1870–1874

1 1870. British. Single-breasted tweed coat, black velvet collar, wide rounded revers, waist-level flap pockets, covered buttons, cuffless sleeves. Double-breasted yellow waistcoat. White shirt, turned-down collar. Black cravat. Light brown checked cloth trousers. Black boots. Black top hat. Leather gloves. 2 1871. German. Two-piece wool suit: single-breasted jacket, single-button fastening under narrow revers, small collar, stitched cuffs trimmed with buttons, hip-level flap pockets; narrow trousers. White shirt. Blue silk necktie. Single-breasted pink cloth waistcoat. Black shoes worn with white spats. Brown bowler hat. Leather gloves. 3 1873. British. Two-piece blue checked wool suit: short double-breasted jacket, braid trim on collar, revers and single breast welt pocket, hip-level welt pockets, side vents and stitched cuffs; narrow trousers. White shirt. Yellow silk cravat. Black boots. Black top hat. Leather gloves. Walking stick. 4 1874. British. Two piece brown striped wool suit: single-breasted cutaway jacket, large collar, double-breasted revers, stitched sleeve cuffs with button trim; narrow trousers. Single-breasted grey cloth waistcoat. White shirt, wing collar. Blue silk necktie. Black boots. Black felt hat, high flat-topped crown, narrow curled brim. Leather gloves. 5 1874. British. Short double-breasted green wool tweed topcoat, small revers, stand collar, top-stitched detail, single breast welt pocket, silk handkerchief, hip-level welt pockets, stitched sleeve cuffs with decorative buttoned straps. Beige cloth trousers. Black leather boots. Brown felt hat, high flat-topped crown, narrow curled brim. Leather gloves. Walking cane. 6 1874. British. double-breasted cloth frock-coat, self-covered buttons, wide revers, top-stitched detail, stitched cuffs. Yellow cloth waistcoat. White shirt, stand collar. Black ribbon bow-tie. Grey and black striped trousers. Black leather ankle-boots, pointed toes. Black top hat. Leather gloves.

Day Wear 1874–1876

1 1874. British. Knee-length blue wool tweed frock-coat, blue velvet collar, stitched cuffs, low waist seam, vertical button-trimmed pockets concealed in side-back pleats, central vent. Grey cloth trousers. Black leather boots. Black silk top hat. Leather gloves. Walking cane. 2 1876. German. Two-piece brown striped wool suit: single-breasted jacket with small collar and wide revers, stitched cuffs trimmed with self-covered buttons; narrow trousers. Double-breasted pink waistcoat, wide shawl collar. White shirt. Large silk bow-tie. Black boots. Black top hat. Leather gloves. Walking cane. 3 1876. British. Ankle-length double-breasted cloth overcoat, elbow-length shoulder cape lined with red quilted silk, large collar, stitched cuffs, buttoned waist-belt, diagonal hip-level welt pockets. Grey trousers. Black boots. Black felt bowler, stiffened crown, curled brim. 4 1876. British. Ankle-length double-breasted brown wool overcoat, high button fastening to under wide revers, large collar, narrow turned-back sleeve cuffs, hip-level flap pockets, top-stitched detail. Grey striped trousers. Black boots, pointed toes. Black felt hat, high crown, curled brim. Leather gloves. 5 1876. German. Knee-length black cloth coat, concealed buttoned-fly opening, narrow collar and revers, stitched cuffs, hip-level welt pockets. White shirt, wing collar. Blue silk necktie. Blue and grey checked wool trousers. Black boots. Black silk top hat. Leather gloves. 6 1876. German. Double-breasted angle-fronted grey wool tailcoat, top-button fastening under wide revers, flap pockets set into waist seam, small ticket-pocket on right side only, stitched cuffs. Grey waistcoat. White shirt, stand collar. Narrow blue bow-tie. Narrow grey and black checked cloth trousers. Black leather ankle-boots. Black top hat, wide petersham ribbon band. Leather gloves. Walking cane, silver top.

Day Wear 1877–1881

1 1877. German. Knee-length single-breasted wool overcoat, wide collar and small revers, large self-covered buttons, hip-level patch pockets, small ticket-pocket on right side only, stitched cuffs, top-stitched detail. White shirt, stand collar. Narrow ribbon bow-tie. Brown and black checked cloth trousers. Black leather boots. Black stiffened-felt bowler hat, narrow curled brim. Leather gloves. 2 1878. British. Single-breasted brown wool tailcoat, buttoned from high-waist position to under deep collar, self-covered buttons, stitched cuffs. Yellow waistcoat. Beige and grey striped trousers, flared hems. Black boots. Black top hat. Leather gloves. Walking stick. 3 1878. British. Knee-length double-breasted blue cloth frock-coat, wide revers, stitched cuffs, top-stitched detail. White shirt, stand collar. Pink silk cravat. Cream cloth trousers, flared hems. Black boots. Black top hat, wide petersham ribbon band. Leather gloves. Walking cane. 4 1880. British. Single-breasted grey cloth tailcoat, black velvet collar, fastening with self-covered buttons from high waist position to under narrow revers, two breast flap pockets matching the pockets set into waist seam, small ticket-pocket on right side only, stitched cuffs with button trim. Blue waistcoat. White shirt, stand collar. Red cravat. Grey cloth trousers. Black boots. 5 1880. German. Single-breasted green cloth coat, fastening with single self-covered button on low waistline, rounded collar, long rounded revers, tight sleeves with stitched cuffs. Leather gloves. Single-breasted grey silk waistcoat, shawl collar. White shirt, stand collar. Yellow silk cravat. Tight grey cloth trousers. Black boots worn with white spats. Black top hat. 6 1881. British. Three-piece brown wool suit: long single-breasted jacket, high fastening, narrow collar and revers, single breast welt pocket, hip-level bound pockets, cuffless sleeves with button trim; single-breasted waistcoat, high fastening with self-fabric buttons, narrow shawl collar; narrow trousers. White shirt, wing collar. Yellow silk necktie. Black boots worn with spats. Black bowler hat. Walking cane.

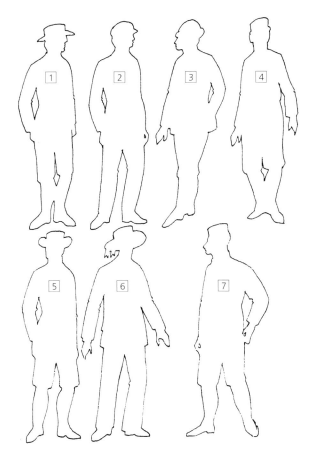

Sports and Leisure Wear 1869–1880

1 1869. British. Country wear. Two-piece wool suit: single-breasted jacket, top-stitched strap opening, self-covered buttons from below waist to under deep collar, matching waist-belt, shoulder to waist box pleats, large hip-level patch pockets; knee breeches. White shirt. Green stock. Brown wool ribbed stockings. Leather boots with canvas uppers. Straw hat, flat-topped crown, wide blue ribbon band, wide brim. 2 1869. British. Cricket. Two-piece cream linen suit: single-breasted jacket fastened with one button under narrow collar and revers, braided edges matching patch pockets and stitched sleeve cuffs; narrow trousers. White shirt, turned-down collar. Necktie. Lace-up canvas boots, leather trim. Blue and cream peaked cap. 3 1872. British. Country wear. Two-piece wool suit: single-breasted jacket, fastening with self-fabric buttons from waist to under wide revers, hand-stitched edges matching flap pockets and sleeve hems; breeches gathered into band under knee. Striped shirt. Cravat. Short brown leather boots worn with beige leather buttoned gaiters. Brown bowler hat. Leather gloves. 4 1873. British. Football. Striped knitted-cotton shirt, white cotton stand collar and sleeve cuffs. Black cotton breeches, elasticated waist and hems. Knitted stockings. Two-tone leather lace-up ankle-boots. Felt pillbox hat. 5 1874. British. Shooting. Two-piece suit: double-breasted coat, top-stitched collar and revers, matching all edges, sleeve cuffs and hip-level patch pockets, two diagonal breast welt pockets; cartridge belt; knee breeches. Short leather boots worn with long leather gaiters. Brown felt hat, wide blue ribbon band, large brim. 6 1876. British. Yachting. Two-piece white linen suit: long edge-to-edge jacket with double-breasted button detail, long wide revers, small collar, top-stitched edges, matching sleeve cuffs and hip-level flap pockets; tight trousers, flared hems. Black leather ankle-boots. Black stiffened and laquered straw boater, blue ribbon band and tails. 7 1880. British. Bicycling. Two-piece suit: single-breasted fitted jacket, fastening from low waist to stand collar, welt pockets; knee breeches. Knitted stockings. Lace-up ankle-boots. Pillbox hat. Leather gloves.

Evening Wear 1869–1881

1 1869. German. Double-breasted tailcoat worn open, small collar, wide revers, self-fabric buttons, tight cuffless sleeves; tight trousers in matching fabric. Single-breasted white silk waistcoat, scooped neckline, narrow shawl collar. White shirt, tucked front, turned-down collar. Black ribbon bow-tie. Black shoes. Black top hat. White gloves. 2 1872. British. Double-breasted tailcoat worn open, small collar, wide revers, narrow stitched cuffs; tight trousers in matching fabric, shiny ribbon braid on outside seam. Single-breasted black silk waistcoat, scooped neckline, narrow shawl collar, welt pockets. White shirt, ruffled front, high winged collar. White bow-tie. Black shoes. 3 1873. British. Two-piece black wool suit; double-breasted jacket worn open, wide revers, M-notch collar, stitched cuffs, self-fabric button trim; fitted trousers. Single-breasted white silk waistcoat, low neckline, shawl collar, two welt pockets. White shirt, high wing collar. Black ribbon bow-tie. Black shoes. White gloves. 4 1875. German. Two-piece suit: double-breasted jacket worn open, narrow collar and revers, fitted sleeves with stitched cuffs; tight trousers. White waistcoat, low neckline, shawl collar. White shirt, turned-down collar, single row of ruffles on opening. White silk tie. Black shoes. Black silk top hat. White gloves. 5 1877. German. Two-piece suit: double-breasted jacket worn open, long collar, wide revers, cuffless sleeves with button trim; tight trousers. Double-breasted white silk waistcoat, low neckline, narrow shawl collar. White shirt, rounded turned-down collar. Black tie. Black shoes. White gloves. 6 1874. British. Two-piece black wool suit: fitted jacket, back panels end in two pleats and central vent, stitched cuffs with self-fabric button trim; narrow trousers, ribbon braid covering outside seams. Black shoes. White gloves. 7 1881. American. Two-piece informal dinner suit: double-breasted jacket, quilted collar and revers, single breast welt pocket, hip-level flap pockets, stitched sleeve cuffs; narrow trousers, ribbon braid covering outside seams. White shirt, tucked front, high stand collar. Black silk bow-tie. Black shoes. Black top hat. White gloves. Walking cane.

Negligee and Underwear 1869–1881

1 1869. British. Ankle-length wrapover blue wool dressing gown, deep shawl collar, inset sleeves with narrow turned-back cuffs, hip-level patch pockets, cord belt with tassel ends. White shirt. Yellow tie. Grey trousers. Leather slippers. 2 1873. British. Single-breasted pink velvet breakfast jacket, single-fastening with self-fabric button on low waistline, plain quilted pink silk shawl collar and cuffs, hip-level bound pockets. Double-breasted grey cloth waistcoat, shawl collar. White shirt, turned-down wing collar. Grey and white striped silk necktie. Blue and grey checked cloth trousers. Black boots. 3 1873. British. Ankle-length wrapover patterned-silk dressing gown, plain silk shawl collar and cuffs, cord waist-belt with large tassel ends. White shirt. Green silk necktie. Grey trousers. Red leather slippers, curled and pointed toes. 4 1881. American. Ankle-length double-breasted blue and white striped cotton bathrobe with hood, fastening with two chest-level self-fabric buttons, stitched cuffs, large hip-level patch pockets, blue cord belt with tassel ends. Red leather slippers, pointed toes. 5 1881. British. Collarless cream knitted-cotton vest, buttoned strap opening, long inset sleeves with ribbed cuffs, long cream knitted-cotton drawers, buttoned waistband, side-front flap opening, tight legs with ribbed cuffs around ankles. 6 1881. British. Ankle-length blue and white striped cotton unfitted nightshirt; shirt collar, front panel and buttoned cuffs cut with horizontal stripes; body, sleeves and single breast patch pocket cut with vertical stripes. Leather mules. 7 1875. British. Double-breasted green velvet breakfast jacket, self-fabric buttons, large quilted silk collar and wide revers, matching stitched cuffs and hip-level welt pockets. Grey waistcoat. White shirt. Red necktie. Grey trousers. Black shoes.

Accessories and Hairstyles 1869–1881

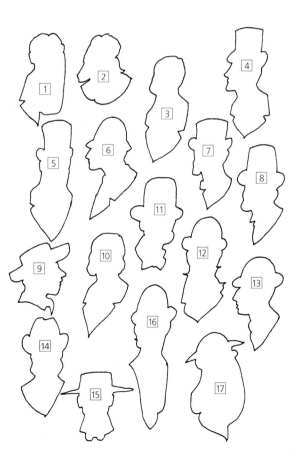

1 1869. Short hair with central parting, short side-whiskers, curled moustaches. Monocle. Wing collar with ribbon bow-tie. 2 1869. Hair with central parting, long side-whiskers. Monocle. 3 1871. Short hair with side parting, moustaches join long side-whiskers. Stand collar, asymmetric bow-tie. 4 1873. Tall black silk top hat, straight sides, curled brim. Short hair, full beard, moustaches. 5 1873. Tall waisted grey-beaver top hat, wide curled brim. Short hair, chest-length square-cut beard worn with trimmed moustaches. 6 1875. Sectioned wool tweed hat, turned-down brim, self-fabric band and bow trim. Short hair, no side-whiskers, long moustaches. 7 1876. Waisted black silk top hat, curled brim. Long waved hair. Side-whiskers. 8 1876. Straw hat with tall flat-topped crown trimmed with deep petersham ribbon band, wide curled brim. Short hair, long side-whiskers and trimmed moustaches. 9 1881. Straw hat, shallow crown, deep silk ribbon band, wide upturned brim. Short hair, curled moustaches. 10 1876. Sleek hair with side parting, long curled side-whiskers joined to clipped moustaches. 11 1877. Straw hat, tall flat-topped crown, wide silk ribbon band, broad brim trimmed with matching ribbon. Curled hair, long side-whiskers. 12 1878. Bowler hat, high hard crown, curled brim. Short hair, full beard with central parting on chin, long curled wide moustaches. 13 1879. Grey felt bowler hat, low hard crown trimmed with petersham band and bow, matching edge of curled brim. Short hair, long side-whiskers, trimmed moustaches. 14 1881. Grey felt hat, high crown with central crease, wide ribbon band, brim edged with matching ribbon. 15 1880. Stiffened straw hat, low flat-topped crown, petersham ribbon band, straight flat brim. Short hair, no side-whiskers, curled moustaches. 16 1880. Black bowler hat, high hard crown, deep ribbon band, wide curled brim. 17 1881. Grey felt bowler hat, shallow crown, wide sharply curled brim, plain ribbon band. Pince-nez. Short hair, long side-whiskers.

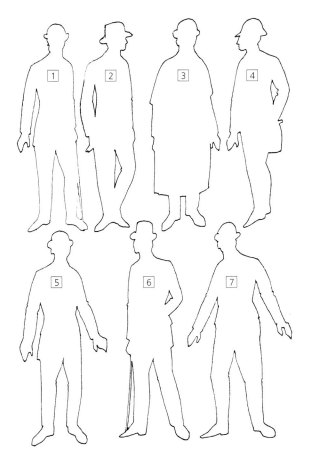

Day Wear 1882–1885

1 1882. British. Two-piece suit: single-breasted jacket, small collar, narrow lapels, stitched sleeve cuffs, hip-level welt pockets, piped breast pocket and waist-level ticket pocket, cut-away front skirts, edges and details bound with wool braid; narrow trousers. White shirt. Red silk cravat. Brown bowler hat. Brown shoes. Leather gloves. Walking cane. 2 1884. German. Double-breasted black wool jacket, high fastening to under small lapels, tight sleeves with stitched cuffs, hip-level piped pockets, cut-away front skirts, edges and detail bound with black wool braid. Grey and black striped trousers. White shirt. Blue and white striped silk cravat. Black felt hat. Black leather boots. Leather gloves. 3 1884. German. Mid-calf-length checked wool topcoat, elbow-length bias-cut shoulder cape, matching stitched sleeve cuffs and diagonal hip-level flap pockets. White shirt. Green necktie. Grey bowler hat. Black boots. Leather gloves. 4 1885. German. Three-piece grey wool suit: single-breasted jacket, cut-away front skirts, high fastening to under narrow lapels, flap pockets set into hip-level seam, single waist-level ticket pocket, shaped stitched sleeve cuffs with button detail; single-breasted waistcoat; narrow trousers. White shirt. Yellow bow-tie. Black bowler hat. Ankle-boots. Leather gloves. 5 1885. British. Two-piece green wool tweed suit: single-breasted jacket, self-fabric buttons, high fastening to under narrow lapels, breast pocket, hip-level flap pockets, stitched sleeve cuffs, all edges and detail bound with black braid; narrow trousers. White shirt with pointed collar. Green wool tie. Bowler hat. Ankle-boots. Leather gloves. 6 1885. British. Double-breasted jacket, high fastening to under wide lapels, hip-level flap pockets, stitched cuffs, top-stitched detail. Grey striped trousers. White shirt. Red silk cravat. Straw hat. Brown leather ankle-boots. Leather gloves. Cane. 7 1885. British. Two-piece brown striped cloth suit: single-breasted jacket, high fastening to under narrow lapels, breast pocket with silk handkerchief, hip-level flap pockets, cuffless sleeves, button trim on wrist; narrow trousers. White shirt. Yellow silk necktie. Brown bowler. Two-tone brown leather boots.

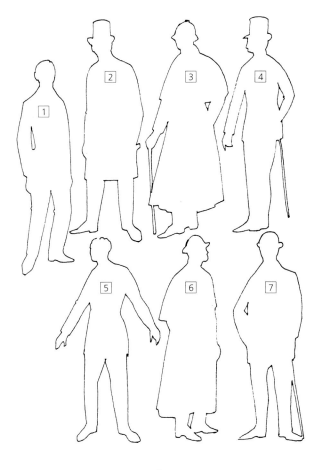

Day Wear 1885–1889

1 1885. British. Two-piece grey wool suit: single-breasted jacket, self-fabric buttons, high front fastening to under narrow lapels, single breast pocket, narrow sleeves with stitched cuffs, cut-away front, braided edges; single-breasted waistcoat; narrow trousers. White shirt, stand collar. Tie with large knot. Black leather shoes, pointed toecaps. 2 1885. British. Knee-length single-breasted grey wool topcoat, fly fastening to under small lapels, breast pocket, hip-level flap pockets, fitted sleeves with stitched cuffs. White shirt with wing collar. Black silk cravat. Black and grey striped trousers. Black boots. Black top hat. Grey gloves. 3 1885. American. Mid-calf-length wrapover checked cloth topcoat, elbow-length shoulder cape, single-button fastening under brown velvet collar, buckled leather waist-belt, diagonal hip-level pockets. Narrow trousers. Brown boots. Tweed cap, front and back peaks, earflaps tied on top. Leather gloves. Walking cane. 4 1886. German. Two-piece suit: fitted jacket, back cut in panels, flap pockets set into low waist seam, back vent and side pleats, button trim, cuffless sleeves; narrow trousers. Black top hat. Black boots. White gloves. Walking cane. 5 1887. British. Fitted single-breasted green wool jacket, self-fabric buttons, high fastening to under small collar and lapels, breast pocket with red silk handkerchief, low waist seam, cut-away front skirts, cuffless sleeves. Single-breasted waistcoat. Narrow grey striped cloth trousers. White shirt. Black cravat. Black leather buttoned boots, pointed toecaps, white uppers. 6 1888. British. Mid-calf-length single-breasted wool topcoat, elbow-length shoulder cape, self-fabric buttons, high fastening to under small lapels, hip-level flap pockets; saddle decoration on edges, hem and detail. Brown trousers. White shirt. Green tie. Bowler hat. Leather and canvas button boots. Leather gloves. 7 1889. British. Short single-breasted grey cloth coat; fly fastening, hip-level flap pockets, breast and ticket pockets, collar, lapels, cuffless sleeve hems, edges and hem decorated with rows of saddle-stitching. White shirt, stand collar. Blue and white striped silk necktie. Grey checked cloth trousers. Black bowler hat. Black boots. Leather gloves. Walking cane.

Day Wear 1889

1 1889. British. Single-breasted knee-length frock-coat, high button fastening to under narrow lapels, tight sleeves with stitched cuffs, button detail, flap pockets set into low waist seam, breast pocket, silk handkerchief. Narrow grey striped trousers. White shirt, stand collar. Striped silk cravat. Black bowler hat. Suede and leather button boots. Grey gloves. 2 1889. British. Mid-calf-length wool tweed topcoat, fly fastening, wrist-length shoulder cape, fly fastening to single button under collar, edges bound with black wool braid. Black trousers. Black hat, high crown, wide brim. Black cloth and leather button boots. Grey leather gloves. 3 1889. British. Double-breasted knee-length, black cloth frock-coat, self-fabric buttons, silk faced lapels, tight sleeves with stitched cuffs, button detail, breast pocket. Black striped trousers. White shirt, wing collar. Black tie. Black silk top hat. Black leather boots, patent toecaps. Grey gloves. Walking cane. 4 1889. German. Long double-breasted wool topcoat, high button fastening to under large fur collar, matching deep fur cuffs, breast and hip-level flap pockets, saddle-stitched decoration. Checked trousers. White shirt. Black cravat. Top hat, wide band. Black leather button boots. Leather gloves. 5 1889. British. Knee-length wool topcoat, fly fastening to under narrow lapels, cuffless sleeves with button-and-strap decoration on wrists, breast pocket, silk handkerchief, ticket pocket, hip-level flap pockets. Checked trousers. White shirt. Tie, large knot. Bowler hat, high crown. Brown boots. Leather gloves. 6 1889. British. Two-piece striped wool suit: single-breasted jacket, self-fabric buttons to under narrow lapels, cuffless sleeves, button decoration at wrist, breast and hip-level flap pockets, ticket pocket, double row of saddle-stitching on edges and detail; narrow trousers. White shirt, wing collar. Silk tie, large knot. Bowler hat, wide crown. Canvas and leather boots. Leather gloves. Walking cane. 7 1889. British. Two-piece grey checked wool suit: single-breasted jacket, high fastening to under narrow lapels, patch pockets; narrow trousers. White shirt. Pink tie. Black bowler. Black boots. Leather gloves.

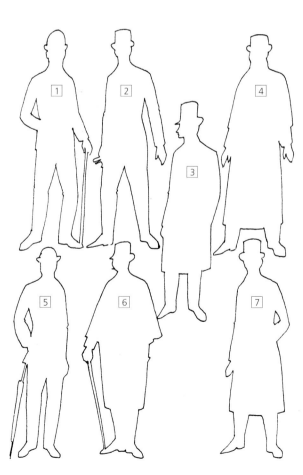

Day Wear 1890–1894

1 1890. British. Single-breasted wool tweed jacket, high fastening to under narrow lapels, breast and hip-level flap pockets, cuffless sleeves trimmed on wrist with three buttons, saddle-stitched decoration. Single-breasted collarless checked wool waistcoat, high fastening. White shirt, stand collar. Green silk cravat. Grey striped trousers. Checked cloth bowler hat, high crown, wide brown ribbon band. Brown leather boots. 2 1890. British. Double-breasted coat, high fastening to under narrow lapels, breast pocket with silk handkerchief, cut-away front skirts, saddle-stitched edges. Tight black striped trousers. White shirt. Black cravat. Black silk top hat. Black boots, patent-leather toecaps. Leather gloves. 3 1890. British. Double-breasted grey wool topcoat, breast and hip-level flap pockets, saddle-stitched edges and detail. Narrow trousers. White shirt. Green cravat. Black silk top hat. Black boots. Grey leather gloves. 4 1892. British. Mid-calf-length double-breasted wool tweed topcoat, single-breasted elbow-length shoulder cape, turned-up collar fastened with buttoned flap, top-stitched edges. Narrow trousers. Black felt hat, shallow flat-topped crown, curled brim. Black leather boots. Grey leather gloves. 5 1892. British. Two-piece brown wool tweed suit: single-breasted jacket, high fastening to under narrow lapels, breast pocket, ticket and hip-level flap pockets, cuffless sleeves, button trim; narrow trousers. Yellow waistcoat. White shirt, wing collar. Red and white spotted cravat. Brown leather and canvas boots. Brown bowler, shallow crown. Rolled umbrella. 6 1893. German. Knee-length single-breasted wool tweed topcoat, high fastening to under narrow lapels, wrist-length shoulder cape, top-stitched edges. Checked wool trousers. White shirt. Striped tie. Top hat. Black leather boots. Leather gloves. Walking cane. 7 1894. German. Long double-breasted fitted striped wool frock-coat, high fastening, wide lapels, cuffed sleeves with button detail, breast pocket, flap pockets set into waist seam. Striped cloth trousers. White shirt, stand collar. Black silk tie. Silk top hat, low crown. Black boots, patent-leather toecaps. Grey leather gloves.

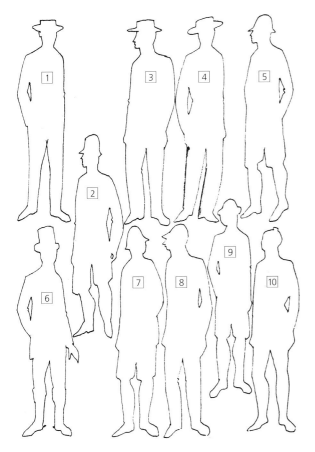

Sports and Leisure Wear 1882–1894

1 1882. French. Seaside. Two-piece striped suit: single-breasted jacket, high fastening under stand collar; breast, ticket and hip-level welt pockets; stitched cuffs; narrow trousers. Straw boater. Canvas and leather shoes.
2 1885. British. Shooting. Two-piece tweed suit: single-breasted jacket, narrow lapels, flap pockets, leather shoulder patches; knee breeches. Tweed hat, hard crown, front and back peaks. Boots, buttoned gaiters. Leather gloves. 3 1888. British. Seaside. Two-piece suit: double-breasted jacket, small collar, wide lapels, breast pocket, hip-level flap pockets, narrow trousers. Shirt, wing collar. Tie. Straw boater. Canvas and leather shoes. Leather gloves. 4 1888. British. Tennis. Single-breasted striped jacket, patch pockets, stitched cuffs. White flannel trousers. White shirt. Striped tie. Straw boater. White cotton gloves. 5 1888. British. Country. Two-piece checked wool suit: single-breasted jacket, box pleat from shoulder to hem, buttoned belt, large patch pockets, knee breeches with buttoned cuffs. Black leather boots, canvas uppers. Knitted socks. Tweed hat, front and back peaks, earflaps. 6 1889. British. Hunting. Fitted single-breasted red wool coat, cut away front skirts, flap pockets. Tight breeches. Long boots, spurs. Shirt, wing collar. Red tie. Black silk top hat. Leather gloves. 7 1889. British. Bicycling. Two-piece wool suit: single-breasted jacket, stand collar, breast and hip-level welt pockets, knee breeches, saddle-stitched detail. Leather shoes. Knitted socks. Tweed hat, front and back peaks, earflaps. Leather gloves. 8 1889. British. Cricket. Two-piece striped suit: short single-breasted jacket, flap pockets; narrow trousers. Matching belt and peaked cap. Shirt. Striped tie. Black and white leather shoes. 9 1891. German. Country. Two-piece wool tweed suit: single-breasted jacket, box pleat from shoulder to hem, buttoned belt, cuffless sleeves; knee breeches with buttoned cuffs. Canvas and leather boots. Knitted socks. Tweed hat, shallow crown, curled brim. Leather gloves. 10 1894. American. Bathing. Two-piece blue and red knitted-cotton bathing suit: fitted top with short sleeves and V-neckline trimmed with red; tight breeches. Matching cap. Rubber shoes.

Evening Wear 1882–1894

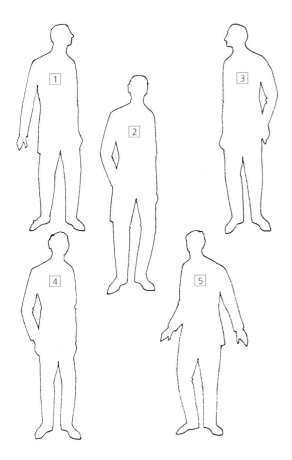

1 1882. British. Evening dress, formal. Two-piece fine black wool suit: double-breasted tailcoat worn open, long roll collar faced with black satin, narrow sleeves with stitched cuffs, button trim; narrow trousers. Single-breasted white cotton piqué waistcoat, low-cut neckline with roll collar. White muslin starched-front shirt, high stand collar. Narrow white cotton piqué bow-tie. White stockings. Black patent-leather pumps, petersham bow trim. White kid gloves. 2 1886. British. Evening dress, formal. Two-piece fine black wool suit: double-breasted tailcoat worn open, small collar, wide lapels faced with black silk; narrow trousers. White single-breasted waistcoat, low-cut neckline, roll collar. White starched-front shirt, high stand collar. White bow-tie. White stockings. Black patent-leather pumps, petersham bow trim. 3 1888. British. Lounge dress, informal. Three-piece ribbed black wool suit: double-breasted jacket worn open, roll collar; narrow trousers. White starched-front shirt, wing collar. White bow-tie. Black patent-leather button boots, suede uppers.
4 1890. American. Lounge dress, informal. Two-piece black wool suit: single-breasted jacket worn open, roll collar faced with black satin, hip-level bound pockets, stitched sleeve cuffs, button trim; narrow trousers. Single-breasted white cotton piqué waistcoat, low neckline, roll collar. White starched-front shirt, stand collar. Black silk bow-tie. White stockings. Black patent-leather pumps, petersham bow trim. 5 1894. British. Lounge dress, informal. Double-breasted black velvet jacket, braid trim and loop-and-button fastening, roll collar faced with black silk, hip-level welt pockets, cuffless sleeves, button trim. Narrow black wool trousers. Single-breasted white cotton piqué waistcoat, low-cut neckline, roll collar, welt pockets. White cotton starched-front shirt, stand collar. White silk bow-tie. Black patent-leather button boots, suede uppers. White kid gloves.

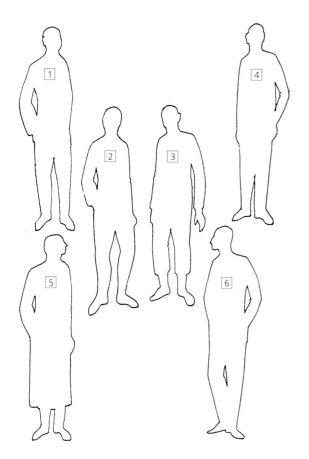

Underwear and Negligee 1882–1894

1 1882. British. Double-breasted blue velvet smoking jacket, braid trim, loop-and-button fastening, wide quilted black silk shawl collar, matching sleeve cuffs, hip-level bound pockets, jacket edges piped with twisted two-tone silk cord. Narrow grey checked trousers. White shirt, high stand collar. Red and black spotted tie. Black leather button boots. 2 1885. British. Two-piece knitted cream wool sleepsuit: waist-length double-breasted hooded top, inset sleeves gathered into ribbed cuffs, matching collar and waistband; fitted drawers with integral feet, side-front button fastening. 3 1885. British. Collarless double-breasted all-in-one cream knitted-wool combinations, inset sleeves gathered into ribbed cuffs; matching ankle-length drawers. 4 1888. British. Long double-breasted dark red and white spotted silk morning jacket, single loop-and-button fastening, large quilted red silk shawl collar, matching sleeve cuffs, hip-level pockets and edges piped with red satin. Grey and black striped trousers. White shirt, high stand collar. Blue and grey striped tie. Black leather elastic-sided boots. 5 1894. American. Mid-calf-length red and white striped wool flannel nightshirt, large breast-level patch pockets, narrow shoulder yoke, inset sleeves gathered into plain red flannel buttoned cuffs, matching peter-pan collar and front strap opening, all edges and side vents decorated with saddle-stitching. Red leather mules. 6 1894. British. Two-piece blue and white striped cotton pyjama suit: single-breasted jacket, buttoned to under collar, breast-level patch pockets, one with silk handkerchief, cuffless sleeves, jacket edges and detail decorated with saddle-stitching; unfitted trousers. Red leather slippers.

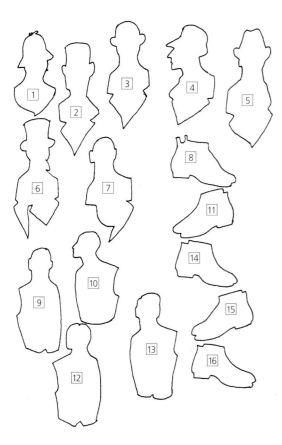

Accessories 1882–1894

1 1882. Tweed hat cut in four sections, front and back visor, earflaps. Stand collar. Bow-tie. Long side-whiskers and moustache. 2 1885. Black silk top hat, high waisted crown, curled brim. Wing collar. Patterned silk cravat. Pin. Trimmed moustache. 3 1885. Grey bowler hat, wide crown, curled brim, black petersham ribbon band. Stand collar, striped silk necktie. Small trimmed moustache. 4 1887. Checked tweed hat, low crown, soft curled brim. Wing collar, tweed tie. Cleanshaven. 5 1890. Grey felt homburg hat, high crown, wide petersham ribbon band, matching trim on curled brim. Trimmed moustache and beard. Wing collar. Spotted silk necktie. 6 1894. Top hat, shallow waisted crown, curled brim, matching hat band. Stand collar, patterned silk cravat, pin. Moustache and chin beard. 7 1894. Monocle on long ribbon. Short hair, cleanshaven. Wing collar, striped slik scarf threaded through gold ring. 8 1882. Ankle-length black leather elastic-sided boots, small heels. 9 1890. Double-breasted checked wool waistcoat, high fastening with jet buttons to under lapels, welt pockets. Stand collar, green silk cravat. 10 1891. Double-breasted checked green wool waistcoat, high fastening with jet buttons to under lapels, stand collar, welt pockets. Stand collar, red silk cravat. 11 1890. Beige canvas spats, side-button fastening, elasticated strap under foot, top-stitched edges. Black leather boots. 12 1892. Collarless single-breasted orange silk waistcoat, high fastening, welt pockets. Stand collar, knotted tie. 13 1894. Single-breasted striped silk waistcoat, high fastening to under narrow lapels, long collar, welt pockets. Wing collar, striped silk necktie. 14 1891. Grey wool spats, side-button fastening, buckled strap under foot. Black leather boots. 15 1891. Green and black leather cycling boots, front lacing to top of small toecaps, low heels. 16 1894. Brown leather laced boots, polished toecaps, low heels.

1895 1895 1895 1895

1895 1895 1895 1895

Day Wear 1897–1900

1897

1898

1899

1899

1899

1899

1899

1900

1900

1900

1902

1904

1905

1905

1906

1907

Sports and Leisure Wear 1895–1901

1895

1895

1897

1897

1901

1901

1901

Sports and Leisure Wear 1902–1907

1902

1902

1905

1906

1906

1907

1907

Evening Wear 1895–1907

1895

1898

1899

1902

1899

1907

1895

1899

1900

1907

1905

1905

Footwear 1895–1907

1895

1897

1899

1899

1899

1899

1900

1900

1900

1900

1901

1902

1905

1905

1905

1907

1905

1906

1907

1907

1907

1907

1908

1908

1908

1908

1909

1909

1909

Day Wear 1910–1915

1910

1910

1911

1911

1912

1914

1915

1915

1916

1917

1917

1917

1917

1918

Day Wear 1918–1920

1918

1919

1919

1920

1920

1920

1908

1910

1910

1918

1920

1920

Evening Wear 1908–1920

1908

1908

1910

1917

1917

1920

1908

1912

1915

1913

1913

1917

1920

1908

1908

1909

1910

1910

1912

1915

1915

1917

1918

1918

1920

1914

1912

1917

1918

1919

1918

1920

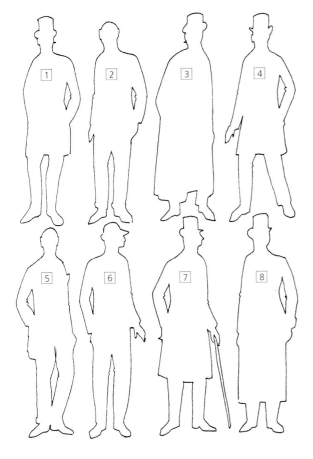

Day Wear 1895

1 1895. American. Black wool frock-coat, small collar, wide lapels, breast pocket, stitched cuffs. Double-breasted silk waistcoat, shawl collar. Grey striped wool trousers. White shirt, stand collar. Green bow-tie. Black top hat. Leather boots with pointed toes. **2** 1895. American. Two-piece cream linen suit: single-breasted jacket, narrow lapels, cuffless sleeves, patch pockets; narrow trousers with turn-ups and central crease. Leather belt. Striped cotton shirt, stiff white collar. Spotted bow-tie. Lace-up shoes, pointed toes. **3** 1895. American. Mid-calf-length wrapover wool overcoat; large black astrakhan collar, cuffs and matching lining; hip-level pockets. Double-breasted green wool frock-coat. Grey striped trousers. Black top hat. Boots with patent-leather toecaps. **4** 1895. American. Single-breasted blue wool frock-coat, wide lapels faced with silk, stitched cuffs, button trim, breast pocket, hip-level flap pockets. Single-breasted black silk waistcoat, shawl collar, welt pockets, watchchain. Narrow trousers, central crease. White shirt, stand collar. Blue tie. Top hat. Button boots, patent-leather toecaps. **5** 1895. British. Single-breasted jacket, small collar, wide lapels, breast pocket with handkerchief, stitched cuffs, button trim. Wide cummerbund. White shirt, stiff collar. Striped tie. Tie-clip. Tight checked wool trousers, turn-ups and central crease. Elasticated boots. **6** 1895. British. Three-piece checked beige wool suit: single-breasted jacket, cut-away front, high fastening under wide lapels, breast pocket, ticket pocket, hip-level flap pockets, cuffless sleeves, button trim; single-breasted waistcoat; tight trousers, central crease. White shirt, wing collar. Red tie. Tweed hat. Elastic-sided boots. **7** 1895. British. Double-breasted knee-length topcoat, velvet collar and cuffs, breast pocket, ticket pocket, hip-level flap pockets, saddle-stitched detail. Tight trousers. Shirt with wing collar. Bow-tie. Top hat. Lace-up shoes. Gloves. Walking cane. **8** 1895. British. Mid-calf-length double-breasted black striped wool topcoat, wide lapels, silk facings, cuffed sleeves, diagonal hip-level flap pockets. Shirt with stand collar. Striped cravat. Striped trousers. Silk top hat. Button boots, patent-leather toecaps. Leather gloves.

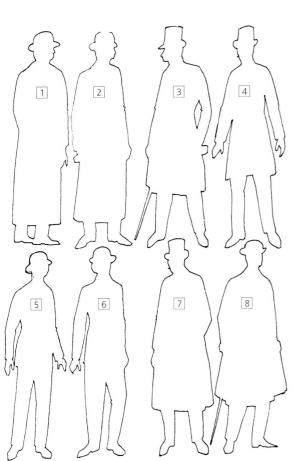

Day Wear 1897–1900

1 1897. British. Mid-calf-length beige checked wool overcoat with hood, buttoned half-belt set into top-stitched panel seams, centre-back vent, wide sleeve cuffs. Striped trousers. Bowler hat. Elastic-sided boots. **2** 1898. British. Mid-calf-length double-breasted wool tweed overcoat, buttoning to under braid-trimmed collar, matching front edges, flap pockets and turned-back cuffs. Tweed trousers. Bowler hat. Gloves. **3** 1899. British. Knee-length double-breasted frock-coat, wide lapels, silk facings, matching covered buttons, tight sleeves, stitched cuffs, waist seam. Single-breasted waistcoat in matching fabric. Narrow trousers. Shirt with stiff collar. narrow tie. Top hat. Shoes with pointed toecaps. Gloves. Walking cane. **4** 1899. British. Single-breasted grey cloth morning coat, three-button fastening, narrow lapels, cut-away front, stitched cuffs, button trim. Single-breasted waistcoat in matching fabric. Grey striped trousers, central crease. Top hat. Black leather button boots, pointed, patent-leather toecaps and trim. **5** 1899. British. Three-piece brown tweed suit: single-breasted jacket, high fastening to under lapels, hip-level flap pockets, cuffless sleeves; single-breasted collarless waistcoat; narrow trousers, central crease. White shirt with stiff collar. Silk tie. Brown bowler hat, petersham ribbon trim. Brown leather lace-up, pointed shoes. **6** 1899. British. Three-piece tweed suit: double-breasted jacket, high fastening, wide lapels, breast pocket, hip-level flap pockets, cuffless sleeves, button trim, top-stitched detail; single-breasted collarless waistcoat; narrow trousers, central crease. White shirt, stand collar. Silk cravat. Bowler hat. Leather lace-up shoes, pointed toes. **7** 1899. British. Single-breasted knee-length checked wool overcoat, fly fastening, narrow lapels, stitched cuffs, button trim, hip-level flap pockets. Narrow trousers. Top hat. Button boots, patent-leather trim. **8** 1900. British. Single-breasted unfitted knee-length wool tweed overcoat, fly fastening, hip-level flap pockets, turned-back cuffs, top-stitched detail. Narrow trousers. Bowler hat. Brown leather button boots, pointed toes. Cane.

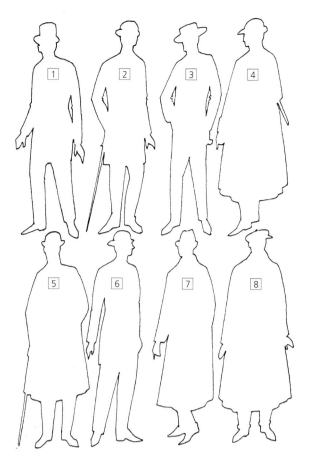

Day Wear 1900–1907

1 1900. British. Single-breasted dark grey wool morning coat, breast pocket, stitched cuffs, button trim. Double-breasted grey silk waistcoat, wide shawl collar, self-fabric buttons. White shirt, stand collar. Striped tie. Top hat. Shoes, pointed toes. Grey gloves. 2 1900. British. Short single-breasted wool coat, fly fastening to under narrow lapels, breast pocket, ticket pocket matching hip-level flap pockets, top-stitched detail. White shirt, wing collar. Silk bow-tie. Narrow trousers, central crease, turn-ups. Bowler hat. Shoes, pointed toes. Grey leather gloves. 3 1902. British. Two-piece striped wool suit: single-breasted jacket, high fastening, patch pockets and cuffless sleeves with button trim; narrow trousers, central crease, turn-ups. Leather belt. White cotton shirt, stiff collar. Bow-tie. Straw boater. Shoes, pointed toes. Gloves. 4 1904. British. Long wool overcoat, centre-back inverted box pleat, set-in sleeves with deep cuffs, hip-level patch-and-flap pockets, top-stitched seams and detail. Narrow trousers, central crease, turn-ups. Bowler hat. Shoes, pointed toes. Gloves. Cane. 5 1905. German. Long single-breasted wool tweed overcoat, high fastening to under narrow lapels, cuffless sleeves with buttoned strap, hip-level patch-and-flap pockets, top-stitched seams and detail. Narrow trousers, central crease, turn-ups. Bowler hat. Shoes, pointed toes. Leather gloves. Cane. 6 1905. German. Two-piece dark grey cloth suit: angle-fronted morning coat, high double-breasted fastening, single-breasted fastening on waist seam, cuffless sleeves, button trim; narrow trousers, central crease. Cotton shirt, stiff collar. Tie. Bowler hat. Shoes, pointed toes. Grey gloves. 7 1906. British. Mid-calf-length checked wool overcoat, buttoned belt set into side panel seams, cuffless sleeves, button trim, back vent, top-stitched detail. Narrow trousers. Brown felt homburg hat. Button boots, pointed toes. Leather gloves. 8 1907. British. Mid-calf-length double-breasted unfitted wool overcoat, wide lapels, large collar, cuffless raglan sleeves, buttoned strap, hip-level vertical pockets, top-stitched detail. Narrow trousers. Checked wool cap, large visor. Two-tone leather shoes, pointed toes. Gloves.

Sports and Leisure Wear 1895–1901

1 1895. British. Punting. Collarless white cotton top, round neckline and front opening bound and trimmed in red, matching hems of short sleeves. Knee-length white cotton trousers, buttoned waistband, fly fastening, hems trimmed to match top. Knitted stockings. Lace-up leather shoes. 2 1895. British. Bathing. Two-piece blue striped cotton bathing suit: single-breasted collarless jacket, wide neckline, front opening and short sleeves faced with white cotton; self-fabric buckled belt; knee-length drawers, hems faced to match jacket. Rubber beach shoes. 3 1897. American. Bicycling. Two-piece brown striped wool suit: double-breasted jacket, high fastening, cuffless sleeves, diagonal hip-level flap pockets; wide knee breeches. White shirt, wing collar. Red tie. Knee-high knitted stockings. Leather shoes. Bowler hat. Gloves. 4 1897. American. Bicycling. Two-piece wool suit: single-breasted jacket, high fastening, cuffless sleeves, patch pockets, inverted box pleat detail; knee breeches. White shirt, soft collar. Blue scarf. Knitted yellow wool V-neck pullover. Brown knee-high stockings. Leather lace-up shoes. Small red wool peaked cap. 5 1901. British. Cricket. Single-breasted blue cloth jacket, cuffless sleeves, hip-level bound pockets. White shirt, soft collar. Blue and yellow striped tie. Matching cummerbund. Cream trousers, central crease. Small blue peaked cap, embroidered emblem. Leather shoes. 6 1901. British. Touring. Two-piece brown wool tweed suit: single-breasted jacket, high fastening, narrow lapels, box pleat from middle shoulder to waist, buttoned belt, stitched cuffs, button detail, hip-level flap pockets, top-stitched edges and detail; wide breeches, deep buttoned cuffs. White shirt, wing collar. Narrow tie. Knee-high stockings. Brown leather ankle-boots, pointed toes. Brown tweed cap. Leather gloves. Walking stick. 7 1901. British. Swimming. Two-piece knitted green cotton swimming costume: hip-length sleeveless top, low round neckline and armholes bound in yellow, hem decorated with bands of black ribbon and piped in yellow; knee-length drawers with hems matching top. Black rubber beach shoes.

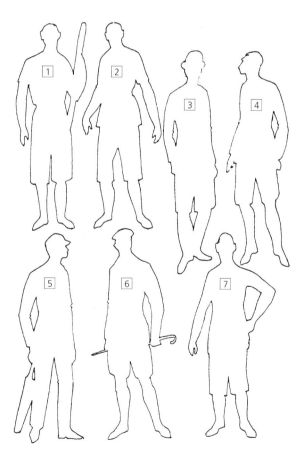

Sports and Leisure Wear 1902–1907

1 1902. British. Tennis. Two-piece cream linen suit: single-breasted jacket, high fastening, cuffless sleeves, breast pocket, hip-level flap pockets; narrow trousers, central crease. Leather belt. White cotton shirt, stiff collar. Striped tie. Straw boater, wide ribbon band. Canvas and leather shoes, pointed toes. 2 1902. British. Country wear. Two-piece brown checked wool suit: single-breasted jacket, high fastening, wide yoke, inset sleeves gathered into buttoned cuff, belt, button fastening, large hip-level patch-and-flap pockets; wide breeches, deep buttoned cuffs. White shirt, soft collar worn without a tie. Long gaiters worn with boots and knitted stockings. Tweed hat, front and back visors. Leather gloves. 3 1905. American. Golf. Two-piece grey flannel suit: single-breasted jacket, high fastening, cuffless sleeves, patch-and-flap pockets, box pleat detail; narrow breeches. White shirt, stand collar. Narrow tie. Knee-high stockings. Ankle-boots. Brown felt hat. 4 1906. British. Shooting. Two-piece tweed suit: single-breasted jacket, high fastening, leather yoke, patch pockets with buttoned flaps, belt, button fastening; knee breeches, wide buttoned cuffs. Knee-high stockings. Long lace-up leather boots, pointed toes. 5 1906. British. Swimming. One-piece sleeveless blue wool swimming costume, low round neckline, scooped armholes, short legs with piped edges. 6 1907. British. Football. Knitted black cotton shirt, white cotton collar, buttoned-strap opening, long inset sleeves with ribbed cuffs, emblem embroidered in yellow on left side of chest. Knee-length black cotton shorts, wide waistband, fly opening. Small black cap trimmed with yellow braid. Knee-high socks. Black leather lace-up ankle-boots. 7 1907. American. Skating. Two-piece, checked wool suit: long double-breasted jacket, high fastening, cuffless sleeves, breast pocket, large hip-level patch pockets; knee breeches tucked into knitted socks with decorative cuffs. White shirt, stiff collar. Spotted tie. Felt cap. Leather ankle-boots.

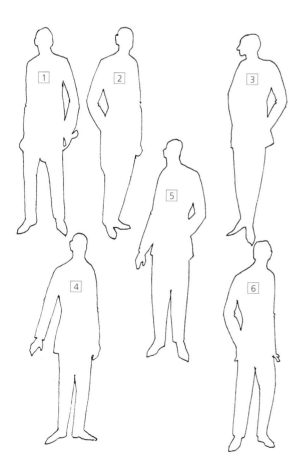

Evening Wear 1895–1907

1 1895. American. Three-piece evening suit: double-breasted tailcoat worn open, wide lapels faced with silk, matching covered buttons, stitched cuffs, button trim; single-breasted waistcoat, low neckline, shawl collar, pointed hemline; narrow trousers, central crease. White starched-front shirt, wing collar. White bow-tie. Black leather button boots, suede uppers. White gloves. 2 1898. British. Two-piece evening suit: double-breasted tailcoat worn open, wide lapels faced with silk, cuffless sleeves, button trim; narrow trousers, central crease, side seams covered with ribbon braid. Single-breasted white piqué waistcoat, low neckline, shawl collar. White starched-front shirt, stand collar. White bow-tie. Button boots. 3 1899. British. Two-piece informal evening suit: single-breasted jacket worn open, single button, wide lapels faced with silk, piped pockets, cuffless sleeves; narrow trousers, central crease, side seams covered with ribbon braid. Single-breasted white silk waistcoat, low neckline, shawl collar, pearl buttons. White starched-front shirt, stand collar. White bow-tie. Black pumps, bow trim, pointed toes. 4 1899. British. Two-piece informal evening suit: single-breasted jacket worn open, single button, roll collar faced with silk, stitched sleeve cuffs, button trim, diagonal hip-level piped pockets; narrow trousers, central crease. Single-breasted white piqué waistcoat, low neckline, shawl collar, welt pockets. Watchchain. White starched-front shirt, wing collar. Black bow-tie. Pumps, ribbon trim. Silk stockings. 5 1902. German. Two-piece informal evening suit: single-breasted jacket, lapels faced with silk, cuffless sleeves, button trim, flap pockets; narrow trousers, central crease. Double-breasted cream silk waistcoat, low neckline, shawl collar. Matching bow-tie. White starched-front shirt, high stand collar. Pumps, bow trim. Silk stockings. 6 1907. German. Two-piece informal evening suit: double-breasted tailcoat worn open, roll collar faced with silk, cuffless sleeves, button trim; narrow trousers, central crease, side seams covered with ribbon braid. Single-breasted white silk waistcoat, low neckline, shawl collar, pearl buttons. White starched-front shirt, stand collar. White bow-tie. Button boots. White gloves.

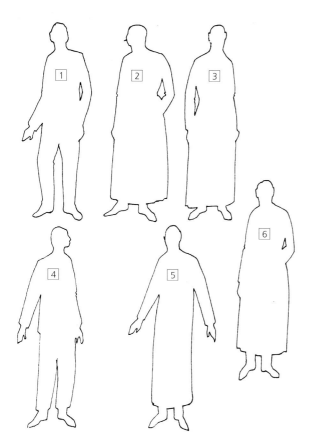

Nightwear and Negligee 1895–1907

1 1895. British. Two-piece red and grey striped cotton pyjama suit: single-breasted jacket, fastening to under shirt collar with pearl buttons, long inset sleeves with stitched hems, breast patch pocket; unfitted trousers, cord waist. Red leather slippers, pointed toes. 2 1899. British. Ankle-length single-breasted green wool dressing gown, corded edges and detail on short roll collar, patch pockets and sleeve cuffs, matching tasseled waist-belt. Brown leather slippers, pointed toes. 3 1900. British. Ankle-length double-breasted, multi-coloured patterned-silk dressing gown, roll collar, belt and stitched cuffs piped with plain blue silk, matching covered buttons, diagonal hip-level welt pockets. Yellow and white spotted silk scarf. Red leather mules, pointed toes. 4 1905. British. Two-piece white-green-and-grey striped cotton pyjama suit: double-breasted jacket with single row of buttons, shirt collar, inset sleeves with stitched cuffs, breast patch pocket, piped edges and detail; unfitted ankle-length trousers, cord waist. Brown leather slippers. 5 1905. American. Ankle-length blue and white striped cotton nightshirt, stand collar, narrow yoke, short strap opening, inset sleeves with cuffs, breast patch pocket, short vent in side skirts, top-stitched edges. Black leather slippers. 6 1907. British. Mid-calf-length single-breasted blue and pink striped silk dressing gown, lapels faced with plain purple silk and bound with lilac, matching asymmetric flaps of patch pockets, asymmetric sleeve cuffs, fringed belt and covered buttons, monogrammed breast pocket. Black leather slippers.

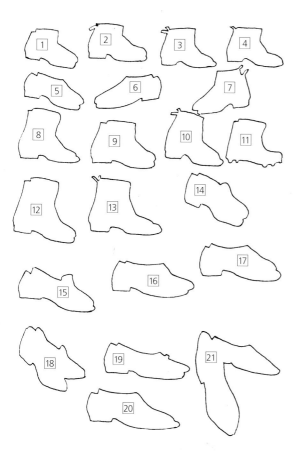

Footwear 1895–1907

1 1895. Leather shoes worn with short grey felt spats, side-button fastening, securing strap under foot. 2 1897. Black leather ankle boots, side-front-button fastening, hard toecaps. 3 1899. Two-tone brown leather front-lacing boots, ribbon laces, hard toecaps. 4 1899. Light brown leather ankle-boots, side-button fastening, hard toecaps. 5 1899. Light brown soft leather front-lacing shoes, ribbon laces, no toecaps, white kid lining. 6 1899. Black patent-leather front-lacing shoes, ribbon laces, pointed toecaps. 7 1900. Short black patent-leather front-lacing boots, ribbon laces, pointed toecaps. 8 1900. Short cream buckskin front-lacing cricket boots. 9 1900. Ankle-length brown leather cycling boots, cream leather pipings, metal clasp fastenings. 10 1901. Short brown cloth-topped front-lacing boots, ribbon laces, hard toecaps. 11 1902. Ankle-length canvas and rubber front-lacing sports boots. 12 1905. Black patent-leather boots with white canvas side-buttoned uppers, no toecaps. 13 1905. Black leather front-lacing ankle-length boots, ribbon laces, patterned cloth part-uppers, pointed toecaps. 14 1905. Light brown leather front-lacing shoes, fine laces, rounded toes, no toecaps, grey kid lining. 15 1905. Blue cloth carpet slippers, edges bound with contrasting cloth, rubber soles and heels. 16 1906. Tan leather front-lacing brogues, fine leather laces, thick soles, no toecaps, kid lining. 17 1907. Cream leather front-lacing sports shoes, fine laces, shaped strap over instep, hard toecap, brogue detail, kid lining. 18 1907. Red leather house slippers, red cloth bindings, thin leather soles and low heels. 19 1907. Black patent-leather evening pumps, low-cut fronts trimmed with large petersham ribbon bows, thin leather soles and low heels, pointed toes, no toecaps. 20 1907. Brown leather brogues, leather laces, kid lining, thick soles, no toecaps. 21 1907 Brown leather brogues, front lacing, leather laces, kid lining, thick soles, hard toecaps.

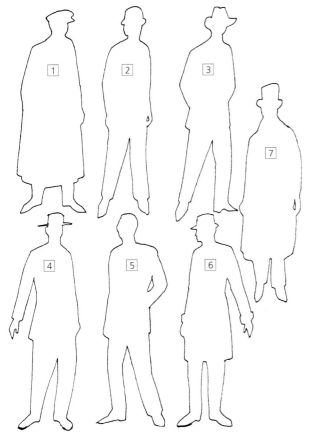

Day Wear 1908–1909

1 1908. British. Mid-calf-length unfitted brown and green checked wool overcoat, wrapover front fastening on right shoulder, deep collar, cuffless sleeves, buttoned strap above wrist, diagonal welt pockets in front panel. Brown checked wool trousers. Large cap, wide visor. Brown leather shoes, pointed toes. Leather gloves. 2 1908. British. Three-piece suit: single-breasted jacket, three-button fastening, narrow lapels, breast pocket, hip-level flap pockets, cuffless sleeves; collarless single-breasted waistcoat, welt pockets; narrow trousers, central crease, wide turn-ups. Shirt with stiff collar. Bow-tie. Bowler hat. Shoes, pointed patent-leather toecaps and trim. 3 1908. American. Single-breasted jacket, three-button fastening, narrow lapels, small collar, padded shoulders, breast pocket, large hip-level patch pockets, cuffless sleeves. Narrow trousers, central crease, wide turn-ups. Brown felt hat, wide brim. 4 1908. British. Three-piece brown wool suit: single-breasted jacket, three-button fastening, cuffless sleeves, breast pocket, hip-level flap pockets; collarless single-breasted waistcoat; narrow trousers, central crease. Shirt with stiff collar, rounded corners. Silk tie. Straw boater, high crown, wide band, straight brim. Leather shoes. 5 1909. American. Two-piece checked suit, double-breasted jacket, wide lapels, cuffless sleeves, padded shoulders, breast pocket, hip-level flap pockets; narrow trousers, central crease. Shirt with stiff collar. Red silk tie. Lace-up leather shoes. 6 1909. British. Knee-length single-breasted grey flannel overcoat, fly fastening, narrow lapels, sleeves with narrow cuffs, flap pockets. Narrow trousers, central crease. Shirt with stand collar. Silk tie. Homburg hat, wide petersham ribbon band. Lace-up leather shoes, patent-leather trim. Leather gloves. 7 1909. British. Knee-length double-breasted wool overcoat, large astrakhan collar, cuffless sleeves, flap pockets, top-stitched detail. Narrow trousers, central crease. Shirt with stiff collar. Silk tie. Black silk top hat. Black leather button boots, pointed patent-leather toecaps. Leather gloves.

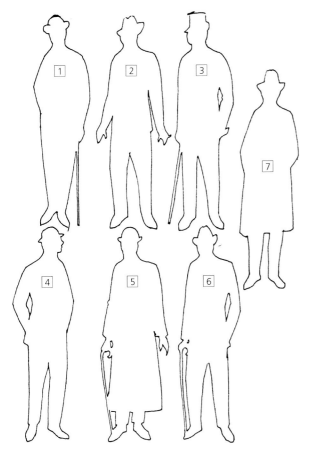

Day Wear 1910–1915

1 1910. British. Three-piece wool suit: single-breasted jacket, three-button fastening, stitched sleeve cuffs, button detail, flap pockets; collarless single-breasted waistcoat, narrow trousers, central crease. Blue and white striped cotton shirt, white wing collar and cuffs. Blue tie. Bowler hat worn at an angle. Black shoes, grey spats. Walking cane. 2 1910. American. Two-piece green and black checked wool suit: short single-breasted jacket, two-button fastening, flap pockets, cuffless sleeves, single-button trim; narrow ankle-length trousers, central crease, turn-ups. Green and white striped cotton collar-attached shirt. Yellow tie. Trilby. Leather lace-up shoes. 3 1911. British. Single-breasted tailcoat, fastening with single button, breast pocket, silk handkerchief, cuffless sleeves, button trim. Collarless single-breasted waistcoat. Narrow striped trousers, central crease. White shirt, stiff collar. Spotted silk tie. Top hat. Black shoes, grey spats. Grey gloves. Walking cane. 4 1911. German. Three-piece blue cloth suit: single-breasted jacket, three-button fastening, flap pockets, cuffless sleeves; collarless single-breasted waistcoat; narrow trousers, central crease, turn-ups. Shirt with stiff collar. Green silk tie. Black bowler hat. Black shoes, grey spats. 5 1912. American. Mid-calf-length double-breasted wool overcoat, wide lapels. Large collar, deep sleeve cuffs, flap pockets, top-stitched detail. Cotton shirt. Striped silk tie. Two-tone lace-up boots. Leather gloves. Walking stick. 6 1914. British. Three-piece brown wool suit: single-breasted jacket, three-button fastening, breast pocket, flap pockets, stitched sleeve cuffs, collarless single-breasted waistcoat; narrow trousers, central crease, turn-ups. Brown trilby hat. Brown leather lace-up brogued shoes. Walking stick. 7 1915. British. Knee-length single-breasted overcoat, fly fastening, breast pocket with silk handkerchief, flap pockets, stitched sleeve cuffs. White cotton collar-attached shirt. Striped silk tie. Narrow ankle-length trousers, central crease, turn-ups. Brown trilby hat. Black shoes, grey spats. Leather gloves. Walking stick.

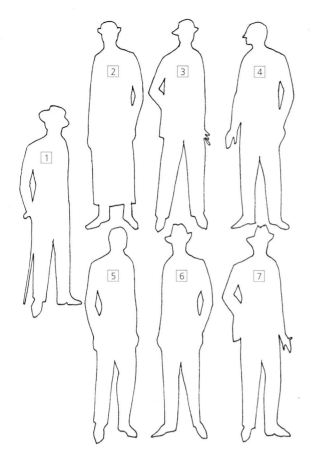

Day Wear 1915–1918

1 1915. French. Three-piece grey linen suit: single-breasted jacket, three-button fastening, breast pocket with silk handkerchief, hip-level flap pockets, cuffless sleeves, button trim; collarless single-breasted waistcoat; narrow trousers, central crease. White collar-attached shirt. Blue silk tie. Straw boater, wide ribbon band, straight brim. Button boots with pointed toes. Gloves. Walking stick. 2 1916. American. Mid-calf-length single-breasted green wool overcoat, wide lapels, buttoned belt, inset sleeves with narrow cuffs, outsized patch pockets. Shirt with stand collar. Red silk tie. Narrow trousers. Bowler hat. Lace-up shoes. Gloves. 3 1917. American. Three-piece brown wool tweed suit: single-breasted jacket, three-button fastening, patch pockets with buttoned flaps; collarless single-breasted waistcoat; narrow trousers, central crease, turn-ups. Shirt with stiff collar. Silk tie. Brown felt trilby hat, deep band, wide brim. Leather shoes, pointed toes. 4 1917. American. Three-piece blue cloth suit, single-breasted jacket, three-button fastening, patch pockets, cuffless sleeves; collarless single-breasted waistcoat, four welt pockets; narrow trousers, central crease. White cotton collar-attached shirt. Yellow silk tie. Black leather lace-up shoes, pointed toes. 5 1917. American. Two-piece blue cloth suit: single-breasted jacket, three-button fastening, cuffless sleeves, four patch pockets with box pleats and buttoned flaps; narrow trousers, central crease, turn-ups. White shirt, stand collar. Red bow-tie. Black lace-up shoes, pointed toes. 6 1917. British. Three-piece suit: double-breasted jacket, breast pocket, hip-level flap pockets, cuffless sleeves; collarless single-breasted waistcoat; narrow trousers, central crease. Shirt with wing collar. Silk tie. Homburg hat. Black leather lace-up shoes. 7 1918. British. Three-piece light brown wool suit: single-breasted jacket, two-button fastening, breast pocket, hip-level flap pockets, cuffless sleeves; collarless single-breasted waistcoat, welt pockets; narrow trousers, central crease. White cotton collar-attached shirt. Pink silk tie. Brown felt trilby hat, deep petersham band, wide brim. Brown leather button boots.

Day Wear 1918–1920

1 1918. American. Mid-calf-length double-breasted black cloth overcoat, fur lining, matching collar, inset sleeves with wide cuffs, breast pocket, hip-level flap pockets. Silk scarf. White cotton collar-attached shirt. Blue silk tie. Narrow trousers. Bowler hat. Suede button boots, patent-leather toecaps. 2 1919. German. Two-piece blue cloth suit: double-breasted fitted jacket, wide lapels, small collar, breast pocket with silk handkerchief, hip-level flap pockets, cuffless sleeves, button trim; narrow trousers, central crease. Brown bowler hat. Lace-up shoes. Gloves. 3 1919. German. Knee-length single-breasted brown cloth topcoat, wide pointed lapels, cuffless raglan sleeves, buttoned strap at wrist, belt with self-fabric buckle, hip-level diagonal welt pockets. White cotton collar-attached shirt, button detail. Blue tie. Narrow grey flannel trousers, central crease. Brown felt trilby hat. Lace-up shoes. Gloves. Walking stick, horn handle. 4 1920. French. Three-piece grey and black striped cloth suit: single-breasted jacket, single-button fastening, long pointed lapels, breast pocket with silk handkerchief, flap pockets, cuffless sleeves, three-button trim; collarless single-breasted waistcoat; narrow ankle-length trousers, central crease, turn-ups. Shirt, wing collar. Silk tie. Straw boater. Two-tone button boots, grey spats. 5 1920. British. Three-piece dark grey wool suit: single-breasted fitted jacket, two-button fastening, breast pocket, silk handkerchief, flap pockets, cuffless sleeves, single-button trim; collarless single-breasted waistcoat; narrow ankle-length trousers, central crease, turn-ups. White shirt with wing collar. Blue silk tie. Grey homburg hat, grey petersham band. Two-tone leather shoes. Walking cane. 6 1920. British. Mid-calf-length double-breasted wool overcoat, high fastening, wide lapels, inset two-piece cuffed sleeves and hip-level flap pockets with top-stitched detail. White shirt, stiff collar. Blue silk tie. Narrow wool trousers, central crease, turn-ups. Brown wool tweed cap. Brown leather lace-up shoes, pointed toecaps.

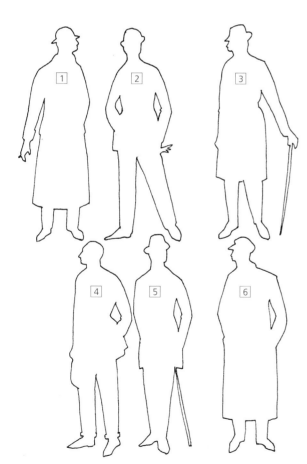

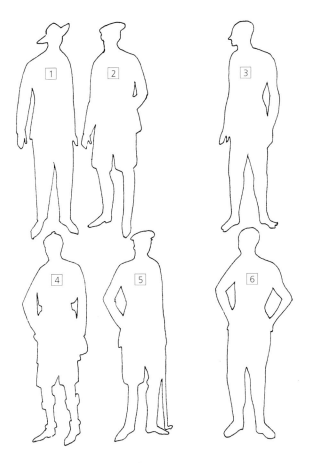

Sports and Leisure Wear 1908–1920

1 1908. British. Tennis. Single-breasted grey cotton jacket, two-button fastening, breast patch pocket, flap pockets, cuffless sleeves. White cotton shirt, stiff collar. Red bow-tie. Ankle-length grey cotton trousers, central crease, turn-ups. Dark grey canvas belt with self-fabric buckle. Fine natural straw hat, wide brim swept up on one side. Cream canvas sports shoes.
2 1910. British. Motoring. Three-piece brown wool tweed suit: single-breasted jacket, three-button fastening, narrow lapels, small collar, four patch-and-flap pockets, sleeve cuffs and edges with top-stitched decoration; collarless single-breasted waistcoat; wide breeches, button-fastening on knee. White shirt, starched collar. Green wool tie. Knee-high brown leather gaiters worn with lace-up leather shoes. Brown tweed cap. Leather gauntlets. 3 1910. American. Bathing. Hip-length fitted sleeveless green knitted-cotton top; low scooped neckline, armholes, and hem of thigh-length drawers bound in white. 4 1918. German. Climbing. Long wrapover waterproofed cotton jacket, wide lapels, large collar, buckled self-fabric belt, outsized patch-and-flap pockets, cuffless sleeves. Ribbed wool pullover, high polo-neck collar, wide cuffs turned over jacket sleeves. Breeches at knee-level and tucked into knitted socks with patterned cuffs. Ankle socks. Leather boots. Knitted brimless hat. Fur-lined leather mittens. 5 1920. British. Golfing. Two-piece green wool tweed suit: single-breasted jacket, three-button fastening, four patch pockets with buttoned flaps, inset sleeves with narrow cuffs, top-stitched edges and detail; wide breeches tucked into high stockings. White cotton collar-attached shirt. Linked pin. Brown wool tweed tie. Green wool tweed cap. Long buttoned spats worn over elastic-sided boots. 6 1920. American. Bathing. Hip-length sleeveless blue and white knitted-wool top, low neckline and armholes bound in yellow, yellow cloth belt, white trim, white plastic buckle, fitted trunks. Blue canvas beach shoes trimmed with white.

Evening Wear 1908–1920

1 1908. British. Mid-calf-length edge-to-edge black wool overcoat, outsized fur collar, matching cuffs and lining, hip-level welt pockets. Double-breasted white cotton piqué waistcoat, low neckline, roll collar. White starched-front shirt, wing collar. White bow-tie. Black silk top hat. Black suede and leather button boots. 2 1908. British. Three-piece black cloth evening suit: double-breasted tailcoat, worn open, wide silk-faced lapels, cuffless sleeves, single-button trim; single-breasted collarless waistcoat; narrow trousers, satin ribbon on outside seam, central crease. White starched-front shirt. White bow-tie. Silk top hat. Leather button boots, patent-leather toecaps. White kid gloves. 3 1910. American. Two-piece black cloth dinner suit: single-breasted jacket, single-button fastening, satin-faced roll collar, breast pocket, silk handkerchief, flap pockets, cuffless sleeves, button trim; narrow trousers, satin stripe on outside seam, central crease. White starched-front shirt, wing collar. Narrow black ribbon bow-tie. Patent-leather pumps, bow trim, pointed toes. Silk stockings. 4 1917. American. Three-piece black cloth dinner suit: single-breasted jacket, single-button fastening, double-breasted lapels faced with silk, cuffless sleeves; single-breasted collarless waistcoat, satin-covered buttons; narrow trousers, central crease. White starched-front shirt, wing collar. Black satin bow-tie. Button boots. Kid gloves. Walking cane. 5 1917. American. Two-piece black cloth evening suit: double-breasted tailcoat, worn open, wide lapels faced with satin, cuffless sleeves; narrow trousers, central crease. Single-breasted white cotton piqué waistcoat, narrow roll collar, pearl buttons. White starched-front shirt. White bow-tie. Black patent-leather pumps, bow trim. Silk stockings. Top hat. Gloves. Walking cane. 6 1920. British. Three-piece black wool dinner suit: single-breasted jacket, high single linked-button fastening, satin-covered buttons, matching double-breasted lapels, hip-level diagonal piped pockets, cuffless sleeves, button trim; single-breasted collarless waistcoat, satin-covered buttons; narrow trousers, satin ribbon trim on outside seam, central crease. White starched-front shirt, wing collar. Black bow-tie. Pumps with bow trim. Silk stockings.

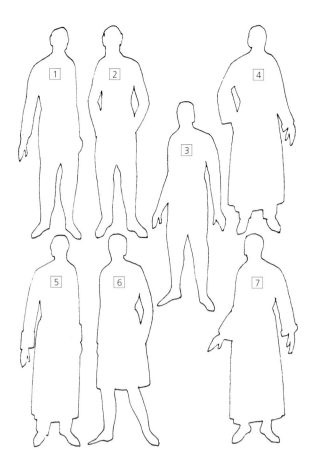

Underwear and Negligee 1908–1920

1 1908. British. Collarless all-in-one knitted-cotton combination vest and drawers, strap opening from bound neckline to crotch, rubber buttons, full-length inset sleeves, ribbed cuffs, matching cuffs on ankle-length drawers. 2 1912. British. All-in-one knitted-wool combination vest and drawers, narrow stand collar, double-breasted, fastening with two rubber buttons at high chest-level, buttoned fly from waist to crotch, full-length inset sleeves, ribbed cuffs, matching cuffs on ankle-length drawers. 3 1915. British. Collarless knitted-wool vest, strap opening from bound neckline to above waist, rubber buttons, short inset sleeves, ribbed cuffs, mid-calf-length drawers, buttoned waistband, asymmetric fly opening, narrow ribbed cuffs. Wool socks. 4 1913. French. Ankle-length wrapover brown cloth dressing gown, long roll collar, wide cuffless dolman sleeves, hip-level patch pockets, thick self-fabric rouleau tie-belt. Double-breasted green cloth waistcoat. White scarf. Black slippers, bow trim. 5 1913. American. Mid-calf-length wrapover yellow-gold-and-cream patterned-silk dressing gown, long quilted plain silk roll collar, matching cuffs, twisted silk cord with tassel ends. White shirt. Blue tie. Black leather slippers. 6 1917. American. Knee-length wrapover, green and yellow checked cotton bathrobe, waist-length roll collar with piped edges, matching patch pockets and sleeve cuffs, wide self-fabric tie-belt. 7 1920. American. Ankle-length wrapover lilac-purple-and-white patterned-silk dressing gown, waist-length plain purple silk roll collar, matching trim on patch pockets, narrow sleeve cuffs and wide tie-belt with tassel ends. White shirt. Black and grey silk tie. Black leather mules.

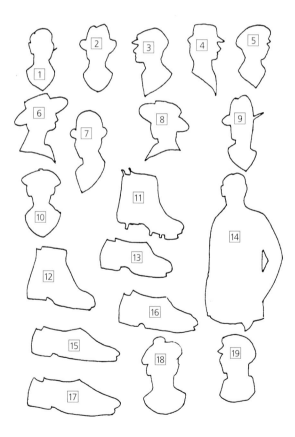

Accessories 1908–1920

1 1908. Short hair, waxed moustaches. White shirt, stiff collar; silk tie; tie pin. 2 1908. Grey felt homburg hat, wide petersham ribbon band, matching binding on curled brim. 3 1909. Grey wool tweed peaked cap. 4 1910. Brown felt trilby hat, wide petersham ribbon band, narrow curled brim. White cotton collar-attached shirt, buttoned collar points. 5 1910. Brown cloth peaked cap cut in four sections. Striped shirt, plain white collar. 6 1912. Natural straw boater, shallow crown with striped ribbon band, wide flat brim. 7 1915. Black bowler hat, hard crown, wide petersham band, narrow curled brim. Striped shirt, plain white collar; green bow-tie. 8 1915. Natural straw boater, shallow crown trimmed with yellow and white striped ribbon band and bow, flat brim. 9 1917. Brown felt trilby, deep petersham ribbon band, wide upturned brim, edge bound with petersham. 10 1918. Sectioned grey cloth peaked cap. Shirt and tie worn with collar pin. 11 1918. Ankle-length light brown leather football boots, hard toecaps, thick soles with leather studs. 12 1914. Ankle-length black leather lace-up boots, red kid lining. 13 1912. Brown suede lace-up shoes, thick soles, hard toecaps. 14 1920. Collarless single-breasted knitted-wool cardigan, high fastening with horn buttons, full-length sleeves with ribbed cuffs, matching hem, edges and hip-level welt pockets. 15 1918. Yellow leather sandals, strap-and-buckle fastening, kid lining, low heels, pointed toes. 16 1917. White canvas lace-up sports shoes, leather trim, rubber soles. 17 1919. Black patent-leather lace-up shoes, ribbon laces, low heels, pointed toes. 18 1918. Yellow and green hand-knitted wool tam o'shanter, pompon decoration. 19 1920. Black wool peaked cap. Polo-neck pullover.

1921

1921

1921

1922

1923

1924

1925

1925

1926

1926

1927

1927

1927

1927

1928

1928

1929

1929

1930

1930

1930

Day Wear 1931–1933

1931

1931

1932

1932

1932

1933

1933

1921

1922

1928

1930

1931

1932

1933

1933

1933

Evening Wear 1921–1933

1921

1928

1928

1929

1930

1933

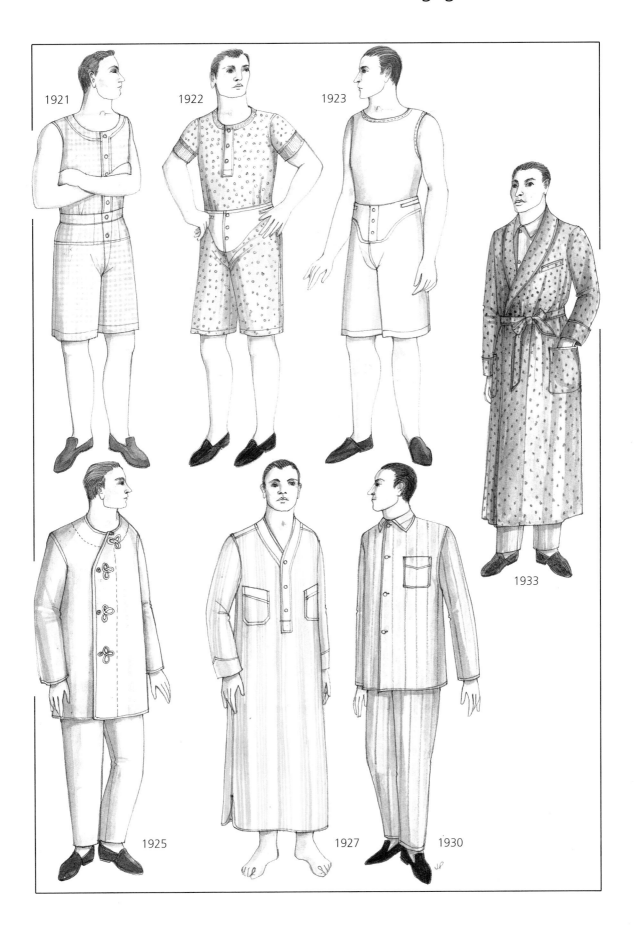

1921

1922

1923

1933

1925

1927

1930

1921

1923

1925

1925

1928

1928

1930

1933

1928

1933

1928

1933

1933

1933

1934

1934

1935

1935

1935

1935

1936

Day Wear 1936–1940

1936

1937

1938

1938

1939

1939

1940

1940

1941

1941

1942

1944

1945

1945

Day Wear 1946

1946   1946   1946   1946

1946   1946   1946

1934

1935

1936

1935

1937

1941

1946

Evening Wear 1934–1946

1935

1938

1940

1934

1936

1945

1946

1934

1935

1943

1944

1937

1946

1934

1938

1945

1934

1945

1935

1946

1946

1938

1945

1934

1939

1939

1939

1944

1945

1940

1946

1940

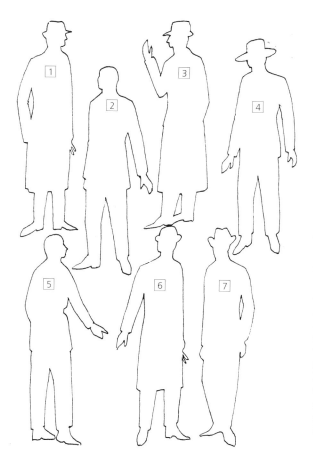

Day Wear 1921–1925

1 1921. American. Long double-breasted overcoat, wide lapels, large collar, chest-level flap pockets, diagonal hip-level welt pockets. Narrow ankle-length trousers with turn-ups. Cotton shirt. Wool tie. Black trilby hat. Black leather lace-up shoes. Black gloves. 2 1921. American. Single-breasted light brown cloth jacket with double-breasted lapels, breast pockets with red silk handkerchief, hip-level welt pockets, buttoned belt, narrow sleeves with stitched cuffs. Ankle-length trousers with turn-ups. White cotton collar-attached shirt, collar pin. Yellow silk tie. Two-tone leather shoes. 3 1921. American. Long grey wool overcoat with buttoned half-belt set into side-back panel seams, centre-back vent from waist, large patch-and-flap pockets, top-stitched edges and seams. Narrow trousers with turn-ups. Black trilby hat. Black and grey leather brogues. 4 1922. French. Double-breasted blue and grey striped cotton jacket with wide lapels, patch pockets with button trim. Narrow ankle-length cream flannel trousers with turn-ups. White cotton shirt with buttoned-down collar. Orange silk tie. Straw boater with wide blue and white striped ribbon band. Two-tone leather brogues. 5 1923. British. Belted cotton jacket with box pleats from shaped shoulder yoke to hem, central vent, large patch pockets. Narrow ankle-length trousers with turn-ups. Two-tone leather and suede brogues. 6 1924. British. Fitted double-breasted grey wool overcoat with wide lapels, breast pocket with silk handkerchief, diagonal hip-level welt pockets, narrow sleeves with three-button trim. Narrow ankle-length trousers with turn-ups. White collar-attached shirt. Red silk tie. Black bowler hat. Black leather shoes. Leather gloves. 7 1925. American. Double-breasted linen tweed jacket with wide lapels, breast pocket with silk handkerchief, flap pockets, fitted sleeves with three-button trim. Cream linen trousers with turn-ups. White collar-attached shirt. Black and cream striped bow-tie. Cream straw hat, high crown, wide brim, cream satin band. Two-tone leather shoes.

Day Wear 1925–1927

1 1925. British. Unfitted knee-length brown wool overcoat, high single-breasted fly fastening, narrow lapels, small collar, breast pocket, hip-level flap pockets, sleeve hem trimmed with four buttons. Narrow trousers with turn-ups. Collar-attached shirt with collar pin. Narrow tie. Trilby hat with wide band. Lace-up shoes. Leather gloves. 2 1926. British. Green wool overcoat with back vent from under waist-level buttoned half-belt, two-piece sleeves with four-button trim, large patch-and-flap pockets. Narrow trousers with turn-ups. Trilby hat with wide brim. Two-tone leather shoes. Leather gloves. 3 1926. British. Single-breasted blue cloth jacket with two-button fastening, narrow lapels, breast pocket with silk handkerchief, diagonal hip-level flap pockets. Single-breasted yellow cloth waistcoat. Wide grey flannel trousers with turn-ups. Blue and white striped shirt with white collar and cuffs. Orange tie. Light brown trilby hat. Black leather shoes. Walking stick. 4 1927. British. Three-piece light brown single-breasted suit: fitted jacket with wide lapels, breast pocket, hip-level flap pockets, narrow sleeves; collarless single-breasted waistcoat; wide trousers with turn-ups. Cotton shirt with buttoned collar points. Green striped tie. Brown leather shoes. 5 1927. British. Formal morning wear. Single-breasted black cloth frock-coat with single-button fastening, wide lapels, narrow sleeves. Collarless single-breasted grey cloth waistcoat. Narrow grey and black striped trousers, no turn-ups. White shirt worn with wing collar. Black tie. Top hat. Shoes worn with buttoned spats. Black gloves. 6 1927. British. Two-piece double-breasted suit: fitted jacket with wide lapels, narrow sleeves with single-button trim, breast pocket with silk handkerchief, hip-level flap pockets; narrow trousers with turn-ups. Blue and white striped shirt with buttoned collar points. Red tie. Black bowler. Black shoes. 7 1927. German. Double-breasted overcoat with wide lapels, waist-level half-belt at back, breast pocket with silk handkerchief, diagonal flap pockets. Narrow trousers with turn-ups. Red and white striped shirt. Red tie. Grey trilby hat. Elastic-sided boots worn with buttoned spats. Mock-bamboo walking stick. Leather gloves.

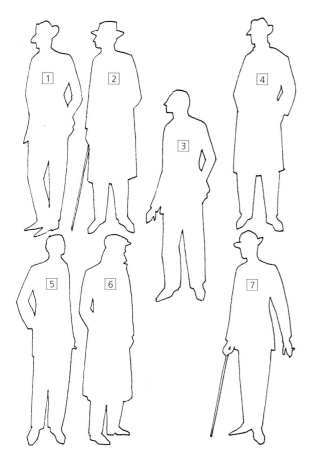

Day Wear 1928–1930

1 1928. American. Three-piece light brown suit: single-breasted jacket with wide lapels; double-breasted waistcoat with wide shawl collar and welt pockets; trousers pleated from the waist, cut straight from knee-level, turn-ups. Collar-attached shirt. Narrow tie. Cream felt trilby hat with wide ribbon band, brim turned up at one side. Leather shoes with pointed toecaps. 2 1928. British. Single-breasted grey wool overcoat, wide lapels, inset sleeves with split cuffs, button trim, large patch-and-flap pockets, top-stitched edges and detail. Straight-cut trousers with turn-ups. Collar-attached shirt. Striped tie. Trilby hat. Two-tone leather brogues. Leather gloves. Walking stick. 3 1929. British. Single-breasted checked wool jacket, double-breasted lapels, breast pocket with spotted silk handkerchief. Matching tie. Cream flannel trousers pleated from waist, cut straight from knee-level, turn-ups. Two-tone leather brogues. 4 1929. American. Wrapover knee-length grey wool coat, wide lapels, raglan sleeves with turned-back shaped cuffs, self-fabric belt with black leather buckle, diagonal welt pockets. Straight trousers with turn-ups. Collar-attached shirt. Narrow tie with small knot. Checked wool scarf. Black trilby hat. Two-tone brogues. 5 1930. British. Double-breasted black wool jacket with flap pockets, breast pocket with silk handkerchief. Cream trousers cut straight from knee, turn-ups. Collar-attached shirt. Tie with small knot. Leather brogues, pointed toecaps. 6 1930. British. Single-breasted brown wool overcoat, large collar, wide lapels, belt with self-covered buckle, vertical welt pockets, top-stitched edges and detail. Straight-cut trousers, turn-ups. Collar-attached shirt. Narrow tie. Striped wool scarf. Wool cap. Leather shoes. 7 1930. British. Formal city wear. Double-breasted black wool jacket, breast pocket with silk handkerchief, hip-level bound pockets. Straight-cut striped trousers, no turn-ups. White shirt. Striped tie. Bowler hat. Black leather shoes worn with buttoned spats. Grey kid gloves. Walking stick.

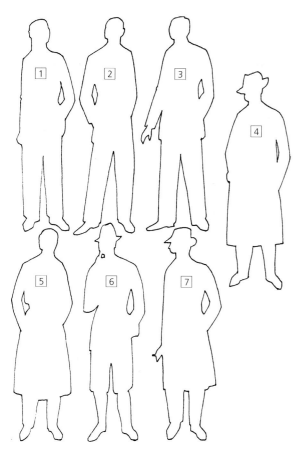

Day Wear 1931–1933

1 1931. American. Three-piece light brown wool suit: single-breasted jacket with three-button fastening, wide lapels, breast pocket and hip-level flap pockets, narrow sleeves, three-button trim; collarless single-breasted waistcoat; straight-cut trousers with turn-ups. Collar-attached shirt. Patterned tie. Leather shoes. 2 1931. American. Three-piece blue striped suit: single-breasted jacket with two-button fastening, wide lapels, breast pocket with silk handkerchief, hip-level flap pockets; collarless single-breasted waistcoat; straight-cut trousers with turn-ups. Cotton shirt with long collar points. Pink and grey spotted silk tie. Black leather brogues. 3 1932. American. Three-piece green tweed suit: single-breasted jacket with two-button fastening, two breast patch pockets, matching hip-level pockets, narrow sleeves, button trim; collarless single-breasted waistcoat; straight-cut trousers with turn-ups. White collar-attached shirt. Yellow tie. 4 1932. British. Double-breasted striped wool overcoat, large collar, wide lapels, inset sleeves with buttoned cuffs, breast pocket, vertical hip-level welt pockets. Straight-cut trousers with turn-ups. Collar-attached shirt. Narrow tie with small knot. Grey trilby hat with black band. Black shoes. 5 1932. British. Double-breasted weatherproofed-cotton raincoat with raglan sleeves, single-button trim, large collar and wide lapels, belt with leather buckle, diagonal welt pockets. Straight-cut trousers with turn-ups. Collar-attached shirt. Striped tie. Brown leather shoes. 6 1933. British. Three-piece checked wool country suit: fitted single-breasted jacket with three-button fastening, breast pocket and hip-level flap pockets; collarless single-breasted waistcoat; wide knee breeches pleated from waist. Striped cotton collar-attached shirt. Wool tie. Long wool stockings. Leather shoes. 7 1933. British. Double-breasted weatherproofed-cotton raincoat, large collar, wide lapels, deep yoke, buttoned shoulder flaps, matching wrist-level straps, wide belt with leather buckle, shaped welt pockets with button trim, top-stitched edges and detail. Straight-cut trousers with turn-ups. Broad striped cotton collar-attached shirt. Patterned tie. Trilby hat with wide brim. Lace-up leather shoes.

Beachwear 1921–1933

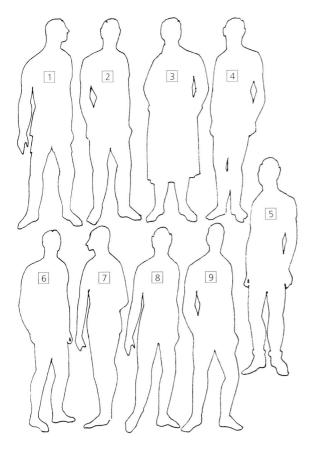

1 1921. American. Sleeveless collarless blue knitted-cotton bathing costume, fastening on each shoulder with two rubber-covered buttons; neckline, armholes, hem of skirt and drawers bound with plain white knitted cotton; drawers attached to top on waistline. Yellow-blue-and-white rubber beach shoes. 2 1922. British. Red-white-and-blue sleeveless, knitted-cotton bathing costume, main body parts cut with vertical stripes, hip-level band cut horizontal, short knickers joined to vest top on hip seam. 3 1928. American. Mid-calf-length wrapover white cotton-towelling beach robe, shawl collar; sleeve cuffs, hem, sleeve head and patch pockets with top-stitched decoration; red and blue cord belt with tassel ends. 4 1930. American. Black knitted-cotton bathing trunks, wide waistband, elasticated white cotton belt, white band set into each side seam. 5 1931. American. Collarless, beige knitted-cotton T-shirt, short inset sleeves with narrow band, matching high round neckline, single breast patch pocket. Red cotton shorts, deep waistband, buckled leather belt, side hip pockets, buttoned flap pocket set into waist seam, right side only. Ankle socks. Lace-up canvas shoes. 6 1932. American. White knitted-cotton vest, scooped neckline, low-cut armholes and cut-away sides bound with self-fabric. Blue knitted-cotton swimming trunks, deep waistband, elasticated white cotton belt, decorative hip-level buttoned flap from side seams. Blue and white rubber beach shoes. 7 1933. British. Brown knitted-cotton swimming costume, scooped armholes, wide back straps. 8 1933. British. Black knitted-cotton swimming costume, scooped neckline and low armholes form narrow shoulder straps, cut-away side panels. 9 1933. British. Blue knitted-cotton swimming costume, scooped neckline and armholes, wide shoulder straps, buttoned hip-level belt with yellow stripe, diagonal brown and yellow stripe across upper chest.

Evening Wear 1921–1933

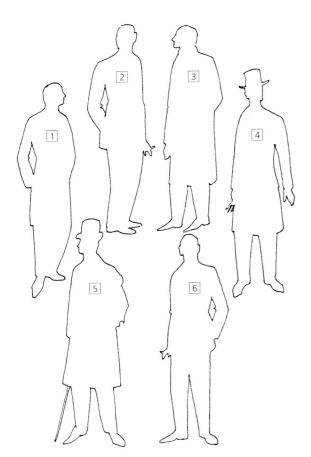

1 1921. American. Two-piece formal evening suit: double-breasted tailcoat worn open, wide lapels faced with silk satin, matching covered buttons; straight-cut trousers pleated at waist, no turn-ups. Single-breasted white piqué waistcoat, low round neckline with roll collar, pearl buttons. White starched-front shirt, wing collar. White piqué bow-tie. Fine black leather button boots. 2 1928. British. Two-piece black wool dinner suit: single-breasted jacket with double-breasted silk satin lapels, matching covered buttons, high waist linked fastening and piped pockets; straight-cut trousers pleated from waist, black satin ribbon stripe on outside seams, no turn-ups. Single-breasted black silk waistcoat. White shirt, wing collar. Black silk bow-tie. Black leather elastic-sided boots. 3 1928. British. Knee-length black wool single-breasted overcoat with fly fastening to under wide silk lapels, matching covered buttons on inset sleeves, breast pocket with white silk handkerchief, hip-level flap pockets. Trousers with satin ribbon stripe. Spotted silk scarf. Black shoes. White gloves. 4 1929. British. Knee-length black wool double-breasted fitted overcoat with wide silk lapels, breast pocket with silk handkerchief, hip-level flap pockets. Black wool trousers. White silk scarf. Black silk top hat. Black shoes. White gloves. 5 1930. British. Sleeveless black wool opera coat with fly fastening to under double-breasted silk lapels, wrist-length cape in matching fabric, lined with red silk. Black wool suit. White shirt, wing collar. White bow-tie. Black silk top hat. Black shoes. White gloves. Walking cane. 6 1933. American. Two-piece black wool dinner suit: single-breasted jacket with double-breasted silk lapels, matching covered buttons, breast pocket with white silk handkerchief, hip-level flap pockets; straight-cut trousers. White cotton piqué shirt, wing collar. Black silk bow-tie. Black shoes.

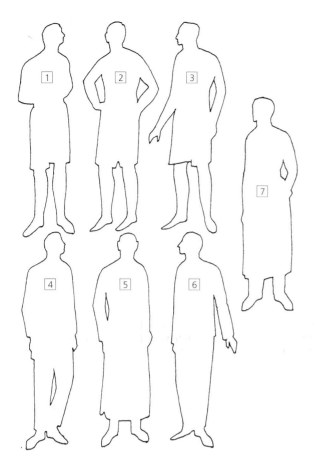

Underwear and Negligee 1921–1933

⊡ 1921. American. Sleeveless checked cotton vest with low round neckline, bound to match single-breasted buttoned opening, knee-length drawers in matching fabric with wide buttoned waistband, top-stitched hip-yoke. Brown wool carpet slippers with rubber soles. ⊡ 1922. American. Collarless lightweight cotton-mesh vest, short sleeves with ribbed hems to match edge of round neckline, plain cotton strap opening wtih rubber buttons, knee-length drawers in matching fabric with narrow waistband and shaped yoke in plain cotton, front fastening with rubber buttons, top-stitched hems. Black leather slippers. ⊡ 1923. American. Sleeveless white knitted-cotton vest with wide round neckline, bound and top-stitched to match armholes, knee-length drawers in matching fabric, shaped hip yoke in plain cotton with adjustable side straps, front fastening with rubber buttons, top-stitched hems. Brown leather slippers. ⊡ 1925. American. Blue silk pyjamas, collarless double-breasted jacket with single row of pearl buttons edged with rouleau motifs, matching bound edges, round neckline and hems, ankle-length trousers in matching fabric. Blue leather slippers. ⊡ 1927. American. Ankle-length striped cotton nightshirt, neckline and combined strap opening in plain cotton, matching shaped sleeve cuffs, shoulder yokes and trim on patch pockets, top-stitched detail. ⊡ 1930. British. Pink-blue-and-white striped cotton pyjamas, single-breasted patch pocket, cuffless sleeves, top-stitched detail, ankle-length trousers in matching fabric. Black leather slippers. ⊡ 1933. British. Mid-calf-length blue and red spotted silk wrapover dressing gown with long roll collar, single breast pocket, hip-level patch pockets, inset sleeves with turned-back cuffs, self-fabric tie-belt, all edges piped with plain blue silk. Pink-green-and-white striped cotton pyjamas. Red leather slippers.

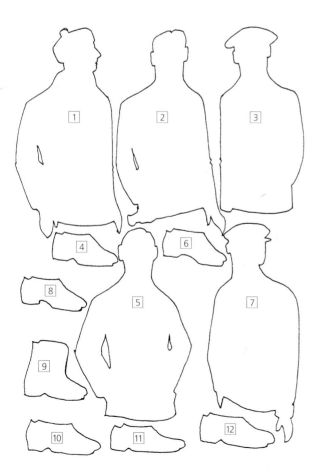

Footwear and Knitwear 1921–1933

⊡ 1921. American. Knitted beige wool sweater with large shawl collar, chest-level multi-coloured patterned band, deep ribbed welt on hem of sweater matching cuffs of inset sleeves. White collar-attached shirt. Striped tie. Knitted brimless hat trimmed with a pompon. ⊡ 1923. American. White knitted-cotton tennis sweater with round neckline, V-shaped bands of red and blue from each shoulder to a point on mid-chest, matching narrow bands above ribbed sleeve cuffs. White flannel shirt with long collar points, worn open. ⊡ 1925. British. Multi-coloured patterned knitted-wool sweater with low round neckline, long inset sleeves with ribbed cuffs, matching hip-level pockets. White cotton collar-attached shirt. Patterned yellow silk tie. Large brown peaked cap. ⊡ 1925. American. Brown leather brogues. ⊡ 1928. British. Brown knitted-wool cardigan with high fastening under large shawl collar, leather buttons, inset sleeves with cuffs, hip-level pockets. White shirt with long collar points. Checked wool tie. ⊡ 1993. French. Two-tone suede leather shoes. ⊡ 1928. American. Patterned V-neck knitted-wool sweater, long inset sleeves with decorative cuffs, matching hemline. White cotton shirt worn with stiff collar. Red and pink striped silk tie. Sectioned green wool peaked cap. ⊡ 1930. French. Blue and white leather shoes, no toecaps. ⊡ 1928. American. White canvas sports boots trimmed with red, moulded rubber soles, ribbed toecaps, padded ankle patches. ⊡ 1933. British. Black and white kid leather brogues. ⊡ 1933. British. Brown and white kid leather brogues with pointed toecaps. ⊡ 1933. American. White leather brogues trimmed with brown suede.

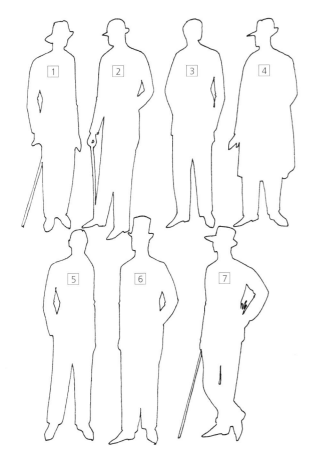

Day Wear 1934–1936

1 1934. British. Two-piece double-breasted cream wool suit: jacket with wide top-stitched lapels, matching patch pockets and stitched sleeve cuffs; straight-cut trousers with turn-ups. White cotton collar-attached shirt. Blue and white spotted silk tie. Matching handkerchief in breast pocket of jacket. White straw hat, wide black ribbon band. Two-tone leather shoes, pointed toes. Pale cream leather gloves. Walking stick.
2 1934. British. Two-piece double-breasted striped wool suit: jacket with flap pockets and cuffless sleeves; straight-cut trousers with turn-ups. Green and white striped cotton collar-attached shirt. Orange silk tie. White straw panama hat, blue ribbon band. Leather shoes. Walking stick.
3 1935. British. Double-breasted blue wool jacket with metal buttons, matching trim on cuffless sleeves, wide lapels, patch pockets. Pale grey flannel trousers with turn-ups. Patterned silk scarf. White canvas tennis shoes.
4 1935. British. Knee-length green waterproofed cloth raincoat with fly fastening, cuffless raglan sleeves and flap pockets. Straight-cut trousers. Green and white striped cotton collar-attached shirt. Green tie. Felt trilby hat, ribbon band and wide brim. Leather shoes.
5 1935. British. Three-piece two-tone brown striped wool suit: two-button single-breasted jacket with wide lapels; collarless single-breasted waistcoat; straight-cut trousers with turn-ups. White collar-attached shirt. Red and grey striped tie. Brown leather shoes.
6 1935. British. Morning suit: black frock-coat with single-button fastening, wide lapel and cuffless sleeves; collarless single-breasted grey cloth waistcoat; grey and black striped trousers, no turn-ups. White shirt, wing collar. Two-tone grey striped silk cravat. Grey top hat. Black shoes worn with spats. White kid gloves.
7 1936. British. Two-piece beige wool suit: jacket fastening with single button under wide lapels, flap pockets, cuffless sleeves; straight-cut trousers with turn-ups. White cotton collar-attached shirt. Blue silk tie. Straw boater, blue ribbon band, large side-bow trim. Leather shoes, pointed toecaps. Pale cream leather gloves. Walking stick.

Day Wear 1936–1940

1 1936. British. Two-piece double-breasted grey flannel suit: two-button fastening, wide lapels, narrow sleeves, four-button trim, breast pocket with silk handkerchief, piped pockets; wide trousers, deep turn-ups. White collar-attached shirt. Red and white striped silk tie, small knot. Grey trilby hat, wide band. Black lace-up shoes. Walking stick.
2 1937. British. Two-piece double-breasted blue and grey striped suit; three-button fastening, wide lapels, narrow sleeves with four-button trim, breast pocket with silk handkerchief, flap pockets; wide trousers, deep turn-ups. White collar-attached shirt. Plain silk tie, small knot. Trilby hat, wide band. Lace-up black leather shoes. Black leather gloves. Walking stick.
3 1938. British. Single-breasted brown checked wool overcoat, wide lapels, raglan sleeves with deep cuffs, top-stitched detail, vertical welt pockets. Collar-attached shirt. Narrow tie. Brown trilby hat. Wide trousers. Leather shoes. Leather gloves.
4 1938. British. Buttonless double-breasted wrapover dark green wool overcoat, wide lapels and large collar, wide belt with black leather buckle, welt pockets, top-stitched edges and detail. Yellow patterned silk scarf. Brown trilby hat with wide brim. Wide trousers. Lace-up leather shoes. Brown leather gloves.
5 1939. British. Two-piece single-breasted striped wool suit: high three-button fastening, wide lapels, narrow sleeves, three-button trim, breast pocket with silk handkerchief, flap pockets; wide trousers, deep turn-ups. Striped collar-attached shirt. Plain silk tie. Brown trilby hat, wide band. Lace-up leather shoes. Beige gloves. Walking stick.
6 1939. British. Knee-length single-breasted wool overcoat, fly fastening, wide lapels, two-piece sleeves with deep cuffs, large flap pockets, top-stitched edges and detail. Collar-attached shirt. Striped tie. Black trilby hat, low crown, narrow brim. Wide trousers. Lace-up shoes. Black gloves.
7 1940. British. Double-breasted fitted grey flannel overcoat, two-buttoned fastening, long wide lapels, breast pocket with silk handkerchief, diagonal piped pockets, narrow cuffless sleeves, single-button trim. Collar-attached shirt. Striped tie. Wide trousers, deep turn-ups. Black hat. Black leather lace-up shoes. Grey leather gloves. Walking stick.

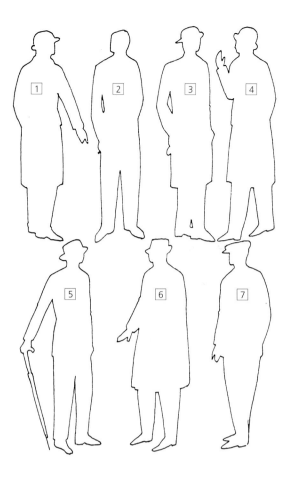

Day Wear 1940–1945

1 1940. British. Knee-length grey wool overcoat with central inverted box pleat from mid-shoulder to hem, half-belt set into side-back panel seams, hip-level flap pockets, cuffless inset sleeves with button trim. Wide trousers with turn-ups. Black bowler hat. Black leather shoes. Black leather gloves. 2 1941. British. Two-piece blue and white striped wool suit: double-breasted jacket, wide lapels, padded shoulders and patch pockets; wide trousers with turn-ups. White collar-attached shirt. Plain blue tie. Black leather shoes. 3 1941. British. Knee-length fitted black wool overcoat with double-breasted fastening, wide lapels, breast and flap pockets, narrow cuffless sleeves with three-button trim. Striped trousers with turn-ups. White collar-attached shirt. Green patterned silk tie. Bowler hat. Black leather shoes. Black leather gloves. Rolled umbrella. 4 1942. British. Knee-length unfitted grey wool overcoat with long vent from top-stitched centre-back seam, inset sleeves with decorative half-cuff, single-button trim, large patch-and-flap pockets, top-stitched detail. Wide pale grey flannel trousers, no turn-ups. Trilby hat. Black shoes. Grey gloves. 5 1944. British. Two-piece two-tone brown striped wool suit: double-breasted jacket, wide lapels, breast pocket with handkerchief, hip-level bound pockets; straight-cut trousers, no turn-ups. Grey and white striped cotton collar-attached shirt. Red silk tie. Black homburg hat. Black leather shoes. Rolled umbrella. 6 1945. British. Knee-length single-breasted unfitted overcoat, cuffless raglan sleeves, diagonal welt pockets. Trousers, no turn-ups. White collar-attached shirt. Yellow tie. Grey felt trilby hat. Black leather shoes. Grey leather gloves. 7 1945. British. Brown wool tweed jacket, high back yoke, half-belt set into side-back panel seams, cuffless sleeves with single-button trim. Beige straight-cut trousers, no turn-ups. Grey and black checked wool cap. Brown leather shoes, no toecaps.

Day Wear 1946

1 1946. British. Fitted green wool jacket with top-stitched half-belt set between side-back panel seams, two inverted box pleats from top-stitched yoke to waist seam, vent from centre-back-waist to hem, two-piece inset sleeves with single-button trim. Beige flannel trousers with turn-ups. Trilby hat. Leather shoes. 2 1946. British. Brown checked wool jacket with top-stitched yoke to waist, large patch pockets. Flannel trousers with turn-ups. Brown trilby hat. Black shoes. 3 1946. British. Single-breasted blue wool jacket with two-button fastening, breast pocket with handkerchief, bound pockets. Single-breasted collarless yellow wool waistcoat. Grey herringbone wool trousers, no turn-ups. Dark blue shirt, plain white collar. Green tie. Grey trilby hat. Black shoes. 4 1946. British. Knee-length double-breasted grey waterproofed cloth raincoat, large collar, wide lapels, raglan sleeves with buttoned straps, wide belt with leather buckle, matching leather buttons, diagonal welt pockets, top-stitched detail. Dark grey trousers. Grey and white striped collar-attached shirt. Pink and black spotted tie. Grey trilby hat. Leather shoes. Leather gloves. 5 1946. British. Single-breasted raincoat, raglan sleeves, large collar, wide lapels, belt with leather buckle, matching buttons, diagonal welt pockets, top-stitched detail. Black trousers with turn-ups. White collar-attached shirt. Red tie. Grey trilby hat. Brown lace-up shoes. Leather gloves. 6 1946. British. Knee-length raincoat, raglan sleeves, long vent in hem of centre-back seam, wide belt, top-stitched detail. Black trousers. Grey trilby hat. Brown shoes. Yellow gloves. 7 1946. British. Single-breasted blue wool jacket with flap pockets following line of diagonal yoke seam, belt with leather buckle, matching buttons, outsized patch-and-flap pockets, inset sleeves with stitched cuffs, top-stitched detail. Wide trousers with turn-ups. White collar-attached shirt. Grey and black striped tie. Lace-up shoes, no toecaps.

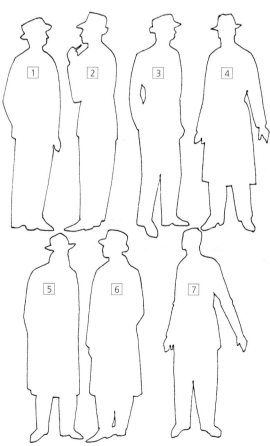

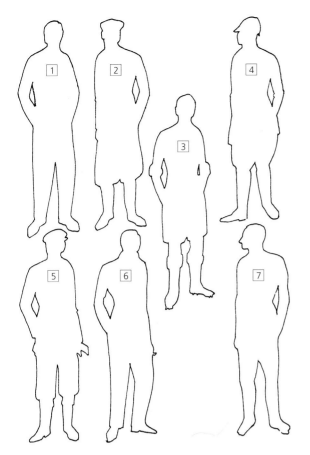

Sports and Leisure Wear 1934–1946

1 1934. American. Tennis. White knitted-cotton collar-attached shirt, short sleeves trimmed with black piping, patch pocket with embroidered crossed tennis rackets and matching black piping. Straight-cut white flannel trousers. Black leather belt with round buckle. White canvas shoes, blue leather insert. 2 1935. British. Golf. Three-piece green wool tweed suit: double-breasted jacket with two-button fastening and flap pockets; collarless single-breasted waistcoat with welt pockets; knee-length plus-fours worn with long knitted stockings. Collar-attached cotton shirt. Checked wool tie. Beige wool tweed cap. Two-tone leather brogues. 3 1935. British. Football. White cotton collar-attached shirt, long sleeves rolled to the elbow, short strap opening under open collar. Knee-length dark blue cotton drawers, elasticated waist. Knee-high white knitted wool socks banded in blue. Brown leather boots, hard toecaps, pegged soles. 4 1936. British. Riding. Long single-breasted red cloth coat, full skirts, narrow lapels, black velvet collar, single breast flap pocket, matching pockets set into waist seam, tight inset sleeves. Beige twill jodhpurs. Long black leather boots. Hard black velvet riding hat with small peak. White silk stock. Yellow gloves. 5 1937. British. Shooting. Two-piece brown wool suit: single-breasted jacket with two vertical inverted box pleats either side button fastening and between top-stitched yoke and inset belt, large bag pockets with flaps; knee-length breeches in matching fabric. Collar-attached cotton shirt. Wool tweed tie. Knee-high knitted wool socks. Leather lace-up shoes, thick soles. Checked wool cap. Brown leather gloves. 6 1941. American. Holiday wear. Cotton collar-attached shirt, cuffed sleeves, two chest-level patch pockets with buttoned flaps. Striped silk scarf worn at open neck. Straight-cut white flannel trousers, pleated from waist, turn-ups. Black leather belt with metal clasp fastening. Grey and white leather shoes. 7 1946. American. Swimwear. Blue and red knitted-cotton trunks trimmed with white piping.

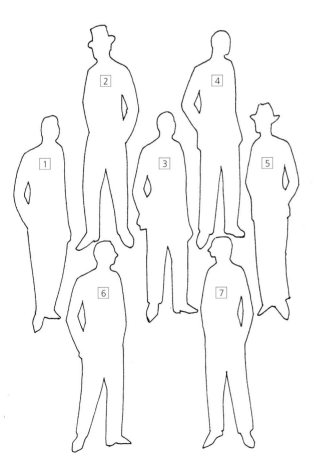

Evening Wear 1934–1946

1 1934. American. Double-breasted white cloth dinner jacket, long silk-covered roll collar, matching covered buttons, breast pocket with silk handkerchief, hip-level piped pockets. Straight-cut black cloth trousers, no turn-ups, black silk stripe on outside seams. White cotton collar-attached shirt. Black silk bow-tie. Black shoes. 2 1935. American. Double-breasted tailcoat worn open, wide silk lapels, matching covered buttons, straight-cut trousers in matching fabric, no turn-ups. Single-breasted white piqué waistcoat, wide roll collar. White starched-front shirt, wing collar. White bow-tie. Black silk top hat. Black shoes. 3 1936. American. White cloth single-breasted tuxedo, wide silk double-breasted lapels, matching covered buttons. Black straight-cut trousers, no turn-ups. Wide pleated black silk cummerbund. White collar-attached shirt. Black bow-tie. Black shoes. 4 1938. American. Two-piece black cloth evening suit: single-breasted jacket, single-button fastening, wide double-breasted silk lapels, matching covered buttons, flower worn in buttonhole of lapel, diagonal piped pockets, breast pocket with silk handkerchief; straight-cut trousers, no turn-ups, silk stripe on outer seams. White collar-attached shirt. Black bow-tie. Black homburg hat. Black shoes. 5 1940. American. Two-piece double-breasted evening suit: wide silk lapels, matching covered buttons, piped pockets, breast pocket with silk handkerchief, flower worn in buttonhole of lapel; straight-cut trousers, no turn-ups. White collar-attached shirt. Black bow-tie. Black shoes. 6 1945. American. Double-breasted pink velvet smoking jacket, wide dark pink silk roll collar, matching covered buttons and cuffs of inset sleeves, decorative braid between two-button fastening, piped pockets. Black straight-cut trousers, no turn-ups, silk braid on outer seams. White shirt, wing collar. Black bow-tie. Black shoes. 7 1946. British. Double-breasted blue velvet smoking jacket, wide black silk lapels, matching covered buttons and piped pockets, breast pocket with silk handkerchief, decorative braid between button fastening. Straight-cut black cloth trousers, no turn-ups, silk braid on outer seams. White starched-front shirt, wing collar. Black bow-tie. Black shoes.

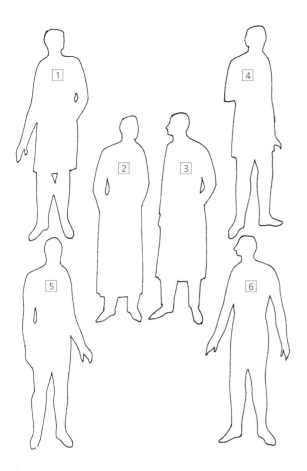

Underwear and Negligee 1934–1946

1 1934. American. Sleeveless blue and white striped cotton undershirt fastening with pearl buttons from low round neckline to hip-level curved side vents, knee-length drawers in matching fabric. Red leather slippers. 2 1943. British. Mid-calf-length wrapover blue cotton dressing gown, long roll collar piped with white cotton, matching sleeve cuffs, hip-level welt pockets, self-fabric tie-belt. Striped cotton pyjamas. Red leather slippers. 3 1944. American. Single-breasted purple silk dressing gown, roll collar faced with black silk, matching covered buttons, shaped sleeve cuffs and trim on patch pockets, silk cord tie-belt, matching trim on sleeves and pockets. Collar-attached white cotton shirt. Blue and grey striped silk tie. Black trousers. Black leather slippers. 4 1935. British. Collarless white knitted-cotton vest, short sleeves with ribbed hems, bound V-shaped neckline, matching strap opening, cloth covered buttons, drawers in matching fabric with hip yoke, strap opening with cloth-covered buttons, elasticated waistband. 5 1937. British. White knitted-wool combination vest and drawers, V-shaped neckline edged with white cotton, matching armholes and front opening, rubber buttons. Grey wool carpet slippers, leather soles. 6 1946. British. Winter underwear. Collarless knitted-wool vest, short sleeves with ribbed hems, fitted mid-calf-length drawers with ribbed cuffs, front fly opening, elasticated waistband. Black leather mules.

Accessories and Knitwear 1934–1946

1 1934. Grey felt trilby hat, narrow petersham band. White shirt. Orange and blue spotted silk tie. 2 1934. Green felt trilby hat, wide dark green petersham band and bow. 3 1938. Light grey felt homburg hat, broad black petersham band and brim binding. Pale blue and dark blue striped silk tie. 4 1945. Cream felt trilby hat, turned-down brim, broad cream petersham band. Blue, beige and white striped silk tie. 5 1945. Brown felt trilby hat, high crown, broad petersham band, wide brim. Green and pale grey striped silk tie. 6 1938. White fine straw hat, high domed crown, turned-down brim, broad blue petersham band. Blue and white striped cotton shirt. Blue and red spotted silk tie. 7 1935. Brown wool tweed peaked cap. Large red-white-and-pink striped bow-tie. 8 1946. Waist-length double-breasted sleeveless hand-knitted brown wool waistcoat. Yellow, white and pink striped cotton shirt. Orange wool tie. 9 1946. Waist-length single-breasted sleeveless hand-knitted green wool waistcoat. White cotton shirt. Red silk tie. 10 1934. Brown and white leather lace-up shoes. 11 1939. Orange leather open sandals, buckle-and-strap fastening, crepe soles. 12 1939. Waist-length hand-knitted red wool polo-neck sweater. 13 1945. Waist-length hand-knitted brown wool sleeveless sweater, low scooped neckline. Brown and white striped cotton shirt. Green wool tie. 14 1945. Waist-length hand-knitted green wool sweater, front zip fastening, high collar, long cuffed sleeves, two breast pockets. Cream patterned silk scarf. 15 1944. Black leather shoes with buckle-and-strap fastening. 16 1939. Waist-length hand-knitted brown wool sweater, front zip fastening from under large collar to deep welt, patch-and-flap pockets with button trim, long cuffed sleeves. 17 1940. Dark grey hand-knitted wool shirt, large collar, buttoned strap fastening, short sleeves. Light brown leather belt. 18 1940. Black leather lace-up shoes, pointed toecaps. 19 1946. Light brown leather casual shoes, no toecaps.

1947

1948

1949

1949

1950

1950

1950

Day Wear 1951–1956

1951

1954

1955

1955

1955

1955

1956

1957

1957

1958

1958

1958

1958

Day Wear 1959

1959

1959

1959

1959

1959

1959

1959

1947

1953

1954

1955

1958

1959

Evening Wear 1947–1959

1947

1947

1948

1953

1956

1958

1959

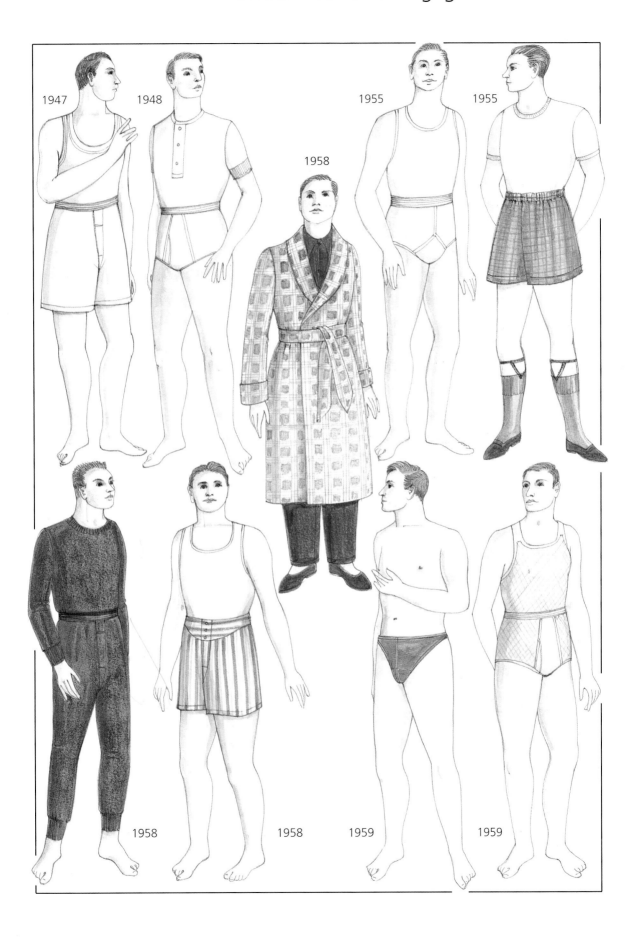

1947

1948

1955

1955

1958

1958

1958

1958

1959

1959

1947

1947

1947

1949

1948

1949

1950

1950

1953

1955

1953

1956

1957

1952

1958

1958

1959

1957

1959

1959

1960

1960

1961

1961

1962

1963

1964

Day Wear 1965–1968

1965

1965

1966

1966

1966

1968

1968

1968

1969

1969

1969

1969

1970

1970

Day Wear 1970–1972

1970

1970

1970

1971

1971

1972

1972

1960

1965

1966

1967

1969

1970

1972

1960

1960

1966

1966

1971

1972

1960

1961

1966

1966

1967

1970

1972

Footwear and Shirts 1960–1972

1961

1960

1960

1960

1961

1961

1961

1961

1962

1963

1965

1965

1968

1969

1972

1969

1972

1972

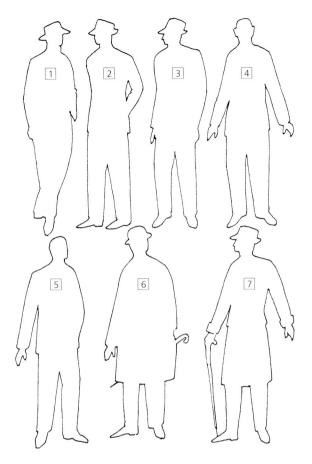

Day Wear 1947–1950

1 1947. British. Single-breasted green wool tweed jacket, three-button fastening, top-stitched collar and lapels, matching edges and flap pockets, ticket pocket on right side only. Cream cloth trousers with turn-ups. Knitted sweater, round neckline infilled with patterned silk scarf. Brown felt trilby hat, shallow crown. Brown suede shoes. 2 1948. British. Double-breasted blue cloth blazer, metal buttons, patch pockets. Grey flannel trousers with turn-ups. Blue and white striped cotton collar-attached shirt. Blue and red striped tie. Black trilby hat, shallow crown. Black shoes. 3 1949. British. Single-breasted tweed jacket, two-button fastening, leather buttons, patch pockets, top-stitched edges, matching collar and lapels. Brown wool trousers with turn-ups. Yellow and green striped scarf. Green felt trilby hat. Brown shoes. 4 1949. British. Cecil Gee. Double-breasted light brown cloth jacket with long roll collar, breast pocket, hip-level piped pockets, inset sleeves with single-button trim. Narrow black cloth trousers with turn-ups. White cotton collar-attached shirt, worn open. Blue and pink spotted silk cravat. Black shoes. 5 1950. British. Collarless wool tweed casual cardigan jacket, high three-button fastening, patch pockets. Narrow trousers with turn-ups. White collar-attached shirt, worn open. Blue and red spotted silk cravat. Brown shoes. 6 1950. British. Knee-length single-breasted wool overcoat, narrow collar, double-breasted lapels, raglan sleeves with single-button trim, diagonal welt pockets. Charcoal grey trousers with turn-ups. Green and white striped cotton collar-attached shirt. Grey and black striped tie. Black bowler hat. Black shoes. Black leather gloves. Rolled umbrella. 7 1950. British. Dark blue wool double-breasted fitted overcoat, large collar, wide lapels, three flap pockets, inset sleeves with deep cuffs. Narrow grey flannel trousers with turn-ups. Grey felt trilby hat, shallow crown. Black shoes. Black leather gloves. Rolled umbrella.

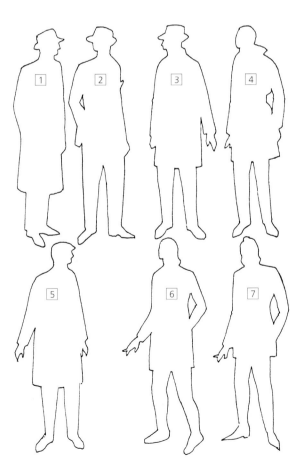

Day Wear 1951–1956

1 1951. British. Knee-length double-breasted grey flannel overcoat, wide lapels, cuffless sleeves with single-button trim, diagonal flap pockets. Straight-cut trousers, wide turn-ups. Collar-attached shirt. Silk tie. Grey felt trilby hat, shallow crown, narrow band, brim turned up at back. Lace-up shoes. Leather gloves. 2 1954. British. Three-piece double-breasted brown wool suit: three-button fastening, wide lapels, breast pocket with pink silk handkerchief; collarless single-breasted waistcoat with welt pockets; straight-cut trousers, no turn-ups. White collar-attached shirt. Green striped silk tie. Brown trilby hat. Lace-up shoes. 3 1955. British. Short single-breasted beige wool overcoat, raglan sleeves, large collar, patch-and-flap pockets, hem decorated with rows of machine stitching, top-stitched edges and detail. Narrow trousers, no turn-ups. Trilby hat. Lace-up suede shoes, no toecaps. 4 1955. British. Short single-breasted blue waterproofed-cotton raincoat, large collar with buttoned flap, vertical welt pockets, hip-level patch-and-flap pockets, inset sleeves with buttoned strap on wrist, buckled belt decorated with rows of machine stitching, matching hem. Narrow trousers. Suede shoes, thick soles, no toecaps. 5 1955. British. Knee-length single-breasted beige wool topcoat with hood, fastening with cord loops and wooden pegs, shoulder yoke, inset sleeves with buttoned strap on wrist, low patch pockets. Brown wool cap. Narrow trousers with turn-ups. Light brown suede lace-up shoes. 6 1955. British. Teddy boy. Long single-breasted pink wool jacket, black velvet collar, matching cuffs and welt pockets. White collar-attached shirt. Narrow black leather tie. Tight ankle-length black trousers. Bright pink socks. Black leather lace-up shoes, thick crepe soles. 7 1956. British. Teddy boy. Two-piece green wool suit: single-button fastening, narrow lapels, black velvet collar, matching piped breast pocket, cuffs and welt pockets; tight ankle-length trousers. Dark blue collar-attached shirt. Black string tie and clip. Yellow socks. Black leather shoes, buckle fastening, long pointed toes.

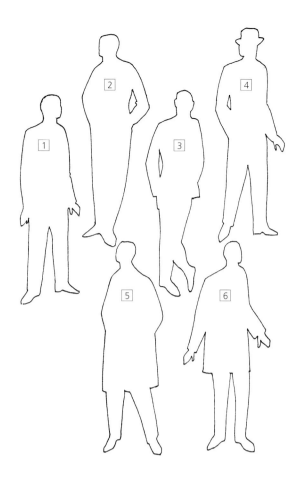

Day Wear 1957–1958

1 1957. British. Cecil Gee. Two-piece grey striped cloth suit: single-breasted jacket with three-button fastening, small collar and narrow lapels, breast pocket, two flap pockets; fitted and tapered trousers, no turn-ups. White cotton shirt with round attached collar. Narrow blue cloth tie. Black shoes. 2 1957. British. Waist-length light brown wool jacket, zip fastening to under small collar, waistband, patch pockets with box pleat decoration and buttoned flap, raglan sleeves with wide buttoned cuffs, top-stitched edges and detail. 3 1958. British. Single-breasted wool jacket, three-button fastening, small collar and narrow lapels, breast pocket, two flap pockets, inset sleeves trimmed with two buttons. Fitted and tapered black cotton trousers, no turn-ups, no creases. Black knitted-cotton crew-neck sweater. Light brown suede ankle-boots. 4 1958. American. Two-piece checked blue cloth suit: single-breasted jacket with three-button fastening, small collar and narrow lapels, breast pocket, handkerchief, two flap pockets, fitted and tapered trousers with turn-ups. Collar-attached shirt. Narrow blue tie and collar pin. Black trilby hat with high crown, wide ribbon band, narrow brim. Black shoes. 5 1958. British. Knee-length single-breasted lightweight wool overcoat, fly fastening, small collar and narrow lapels, raglan sleeves with decorative buttoned straps at wrist-level, diagonal welt pockets. Fitted and tapered light brown wool trousers, no turn-ups. Collar-attached shirt. Striped tie. Brown leather shoes, pointed toes. 6 1958. British. Short single-breasted light brown cotton velvet cord car coat, fastening with three leather buttons to under top-stitched yoke seam; top-stitched large collar, narrow lapels and hems of sleeves and coat, vertical welt pockets. Fitted and tapered charcoal grey cloth trousers, no turn-ups. White cotton collar-attached shirt. Green wool tie. Light brown leather shoes, pointed toes.

Day Wear 1959

1 1959. British. Short single-breasted showerproof beige and black striped jacket, fastening with buttons in sets of two, narrow shoulder yoke, patch pockets, inset sleeves with single-button trim. Fitted and tapered black wool trousers, no turn-ups. Green cotton collar-attached shirt. Plain red wool tie. Light brown leather step-in shoes. 2 1959. British. Single-breasted green cotton cord jacket, two-button fastening, long narrow revers, small collar, patch pockets. Tapered brown cloth trousers, no turn-ups. Dark brown wool collar-attached shirt with top-stitched detail. Narrow yellow wool tie. Brown leather shoes. 3 1959. British. Knee-length showerproof raincoat, double-breasted fastening, raglan sleeves with strap-and-buckle decoration at wrist-level, matching shoulder epaulets, buckled belt, diagonal welt pockets. Narrow trousers, no turn-ups. Collar-attached shirt. Narrow orange wool tie. Brown leather shoes, pointed toes. 4 1959. British. Light grey flannel single-breasted jacket, three-button fastening, long narrow top-stitched lapels, matching small collar, breast flap pockets, two patch pockets with flaps and edges. Tapered trousers, no turn-ups. Grey wool collar-attached shirt. Narrow blue leather tie. Black shoes. 5 1959. British. Short unfitted single-breasted jacket with suede front panel with piped pockets, matching yoke and shirt collar; green knitted-wool sleeves, side and back panels. Fitted charcoal grey trousers, no turn-ups. Black wool polo-neck sweater. Black shoes. 6 1959. British. Short single-breasted blue wool car coat, raglan sleeves with narrow stitched cuffs, matching hem of coat, large collar worn turned up, vertical welt pockets. Fitted and tapered white cotton trousers, top-stitched hems. Yellow cotton sweater. Light brown step-in shoes. Red socks. 7 1959. British. Black and white checked wool jacket, zip fastening from wide waistband to under black knitted wool collar edged in white, inset sleeves with knitted cuffs, matching diagonal pockets. Fitted and tapered white cotton trousers with diagonal hip-level piped pockets, no turn-ups. Black leather step-in shoes.

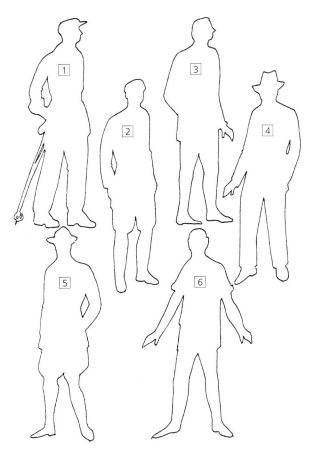

Sports and Leisure Wear 1947–1959

1 1947. American. Ski wear. Cream waterproofed cotton jacket, elasticated waist, zip fastening from hip-level to under large shirt collar, matching fastenings on chest-level pockets, inset sleeves with tight cuffs, jacket lined with thick wool. Dark blue waterproofed cotton gaberdine trousers. Ankle-length black leather ski boots. Red wool cap, large visor. Yellow and red patterned wool scarf. Brown leather mitten gauntlets trimmed in blue. 2 1953. British. Golf. Wool tweed two-piece suit: single-breasted jacket, three-button fastening, narrow lapels and flap pockets; knee-length breeches in matching fabric worn with dark green hand-knitted wool stockings. Collarless hand-knitted brown wool single-breasted waistcoat. White collar-attached shirt. Brown wool tie. Brown wool tweed cap. Brown leather lace-up shoes. 3 1954. British. Tennis. White brushed-cotton collar-attached shirt worn open. White hand-knitted cotton sweater, V-shaped neckline and long cuffed sleeves. Short white cotton shorts, central creases, pockets set into side seams. White socks. White canvas sports shoes, rubber soles. 4 1955. British. Shooting. Single-breasted green wool tweed jacket, fastening with three leather buttons, matching trim on inset sleeves, breast flap pocket, hip-level patch pockets with flaps, leather shoulder yoke on left side only. Trousers straight cut with turn-ups. Yellow wool shirt. Brown wool tie. Hand-knitted brown wool sweater. Trilby hat. Brown leather lace-up shoes, thick soles. 5 1958. American. Riding. Single-breasted fitted brown cloth jacket, three-button fastening, narrow lapels and flap pockets. Collarless single-breasted green cloth waistcoat. Cream cotton jodhpurs. Knee-length leather riding boots. White collar-attached shirt. Pink silk tie. Brown trilby, wide brim. Yellow leather gloves. 6 1959. American. Beachwear. Yellow cotton collar-attached shirt with multi-coloured pattern, collar worn open, single-breasted fastening from neck to straight hip-level hemline, single breast patch pocket with edge piped in white, matching cuffs on short sleeves. Short dark blue shorts, central creases. Brown leather sandals, strap fastening.

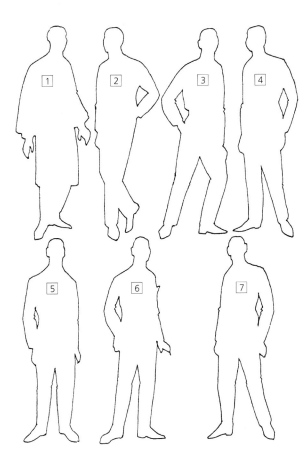

Evening Wear 1947–1959

1 1947. British. Knee-length single-breasted black cloth evening coat, fly front fastening, wide revers, wrist-length shoulder cape in matching fabric lined with red silk, vertical hip-level welt pockets. White shirt, wing collar. Black silk bow-tie. Black suit. Black leather lace-up shoes. White gloves. 2 1947. British. Double-breasted white wool dinner jacket, long shawl collar faced with silk, matching covered buttons, cut-away front, hip-level welt pockets, breast welt pocket, white silk handkerchief. White shirt. Black bow-tie. Black trousers. Black leather lace-up shoes. 3 1948. American. Double-breasted waist-length blue wool battle-dress jacket, blue silk shawl collar, deep waistband, self-fabric buttons, trousers pleated from waist, ribbon band covering outside seam. White shirt, pleated front. Large black silk bow-tie. Black leather lace-up shoes. 4 1953. Italian. Double-breasted waisted pale grey silk dinner jacket, wide revers, self-fabric buttons, breast welt pocket, hip-level piped pockets. White shirt worn with large black velvet bow-tie. Black cloth trousers, braid on outside seam. Black leather lace-up shoes. 5 1956. British. Single-breasted waisted cloth dinner jacket, long collar and wide revers, single self-fabric button fastening, breast welt pocket, hip-level piped pockets. White shirt. Slim red silk bow-tie. Narrow black cloth trousers. Black leather lace-up shoes. 6 1958. French. Single-breasted cream wool dinner jacket, long shawl collar, red silk handkerchief, hip-level flap pockets. White piqué cotton shirt-cum-waistcoat. Black shoestring bow-tie. Narrow black cloth trousers. Black leather lace-up shoes, no toecaps. 7 1959. British. Cecil Gee. Two-piece blue mohair suit: single-breasted waisted dinner jacket, long shawl collar, cuffed sleeves, breast pocket with white silk handkerchief, hip-level piped pockets; narrow trousers. White shirt with frilled strap opening. Black silk under-collar knotted bow-tie. Black suede elastic-sided ankle-boots.

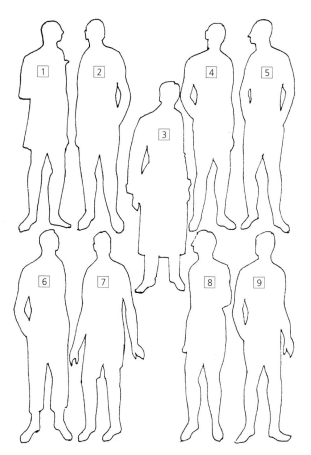

Underwear and Negligee 1947–1959

1 1947. British. Sleeveless white knitted-cotton singlet, low round neckline. Trunks in matching fabric, elasticated waistband, fly-opening.
2 1948. British. Collarless white knitted-cotton vest, short sleeves with ribbed cuffs, high round neckline bound with plain white cotton, matching strap opening and covered buttons. Trunks in matching knitted cotton, elasticated waistband, shaped legs, double front panel with side opening. 3 1958. British. Wrapover black and white checked brushed-cotton dressing gown, long roll collar, deep sleeve cuffs, wide self-fabric tie-belt. Dark blue cotton pyjamas. Red leather slippers. 4 1955. British. Sleeveless white knitted-cotton singlet, low round neckline. Trunks in matching fabric, elasticated waistband, shaped legs, double fabric V-shaped front panel with side opening. 5 1955. American. White knitted-cotton vest, short sleeves, high round neckline. Blue and green cotton boxer shorts, elasticated waistband, wide top-stitched legs. Long knitted socks held in place by elasticated garters and suspenders. Red leather slippers. 6 1958. British. Ski underwear. Collarless double-knitted red cotton vest, long inset sleeves with ribbed cuffs, matching round neckline. Ankle-length drawers in matching double-knit cotton, elasticated waistband, legs with ribbed cuffs. 7 1958. British. Sleeveless white knitted-cotton singlet, low round neckline. Red-green-and-white striped cotton tailored boxer shorts, fitted hip yoke with button fastening, front fly opening, wide top-stitched legs. 8 1959. British. Red nylon briefs, elasticated waistband, high-cut legs, narrow sides, no front opening. 9 1959. British. Sleeveless white knitted-cotton open-mesh singlet; armholes, straps and low round neckline of plain white cotton. Underpants in matching cotton mesh, elasticated waistband, shaped legs, front panel in double thickness of white knitted cotton, side opening.

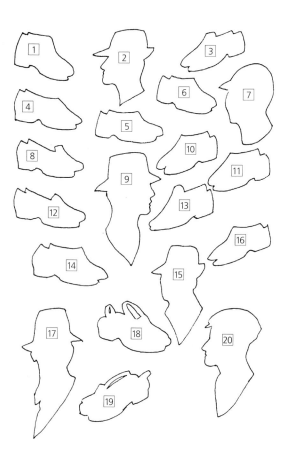

Accessories 1947–1959

1 1947. British. Light brown suede ankle-boots, thick leather soles and heels. 2 1947. American. Natural straw hat, wide brim turned up at back and down at front, high crown swathed with patterned silk scarf. 3 1947. American. Brown leather step-in shoes, brogue decoration. 4 1949. British. Low-cut step-in black leather shoes, thin leather soles, low heels. 5 1949. British. Cream and blue leather lace-up shoes, thin soles, low heels. 6 1948. American. Brown suede shoes, side fastening with leather laces. 7 1950. American. Red cotton sports cap, large visor. 8 1950. British. Black leather step-in shoes, top-stitched detail. 9 1952. British. Grey felt trilby hat, narrow brim trimmed with black petersham, matching wide band on high crown. 10 1953. British. Brown leather lace-up shoes, top-stitched detail. 11 1953. British. Light brown suede lace-up shoes, thick rubber soles and heels. 12 1955. British. Low-cut lightweight cream leather step-in shoes, top-stitched detail. 13 1956. British. Low-cut lightweight grey leather shoes, black leather bow trims, top-stitching. 14 1957. British. Light brown leather step-in shoes, pointed toes, elasticated side vents. 15 1957. British. Light brown brushed-wool trilby hat, plaited band, feather trim. 16 1958. British. Black leather lace-up shoes, pointed toes. 17 1958. British. Green brushed-wool trilby hat, high soft crown, narrow brim. 18 1959. British. Light brown leather sandals, cut-out decoration, strap-and-buckle fastening, thick leather and rubber soles. 19 1959. British. Brown leather sandals, strap-and-buckle fastening, thick leather and rubber soles. 20 1959. British. Checked wool tweed cap, small visor.

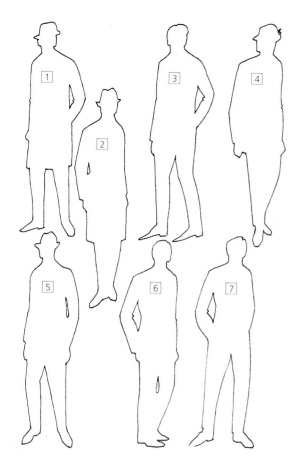

Day Wear 1960–1964

1 1960. French. Knee-length single-breasted wool overcoat, fly fastening to under narrow lapels, small collar, inset sleeves with single-button trim, hip-level diagonal pockets. Tapered grey flannel trousers, no turn-ups. White shirt, small collar. Striped tie. Grey trilby hat, narrow curled brim, tall crown with wide black ribbon band. Black leather ankle-boots, pointed toes. 2 1960. French. Knee-length double-breasted light brown wool coat, large collar and wide lapels, inset sleeves with top-stitched cuffs; matching stitching on flap pockets, edges and seams. Tapered trousers. White shirt. Yellow tie. Light brown felt trilby hat, narrow curled brim, tall crown with wide ribbon band. Brown leather ankle-boots, pointed toes. Brown leather gloves. 3 1961. British. Mod style. Collarless single-breasted jacket, fastening with leather-covered buttons to under high round neckline, matching three-button trim on inset sleeves, four flap pockets. Tight cream cotton trousers, no turn-ups. White shirt. Blue tie. Elastic-sided black leather ankle-boots, pointed toes, high heels. 4 1961. French. Double-breasted wool overcoat, large collar and wide lapels, large patch pockets with shaped buttoned flaps, top-stitched edges and detail. Tapered trousers. Black polo-neck sweater. Felt trilby hat, narrow curled brim, crown with plaited band and feather trim. Black leather ankle-boots, square toes. 5 1962. British. Two-piece cloth suit: single-breasted jacket with three-button fastening to under narrow lapels, flap pockets, no breast pocket, fitted and tapered trousers with no turn-ups. Shirt, small collar. Red leather tie. Trilby hat, narrow curled brim, crown trimmed with wide ribbon band. Two-tone leather step-in shoes. 6 1963. British. Two-piece cloth suit: single-breasted fitted jacket with single-button fastening under long narrow lapels, diagonal flap pockets, breast pocket with silk handkerchief, matching narrow necktie; fitted and tapered trousers. Shirt, small white collar. Black leather elastic-sided ankle-boots. 7 1964. British. Mod style. Single-breasted striped cotton jacket, narrow lapels, flap pockets. Tapered white cotton trousers. Shirt, buttoned collar. Narrow tie. Two-tone leather shoes. White socks.

Day Wear 1965–1968

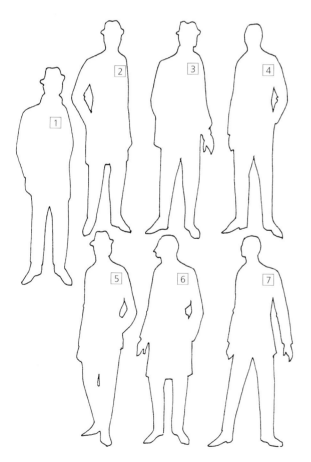

1 1965. American. Short checked wool coat, zip fastening from hem to under fur collar, inset sleeves with buttoned wrist strap, four patch pockets with buttoned flaps. Narrow trousers, no turn-ups. Checked wool scarf. Felt trilby hat, narrow curled brim, high crown with plaited self-fabric band. Suede shoes, thick soles and heels. Leather gloves. 2 1965. German. Knee-length single-breasted camel hair overcoat, narrow lapels and small collar, inset sleeves with button trim, diagonal welt pockets. Narrow tapered trousers. Shirt with buttoned-down collar. Narrow tie. Leather hat, narrow curled brim. Elastic-sided ankle-boots, square toes. 3 1966. German. Short waterproofed blue cotton coat, fly fastening from hem to under knitted polo collar, matching cuffs on inset sleeves, deep yoke with bound pockets, matching vertical hip-level pockets, buttoned strap trim above hem on side seam. Narrow tapered trousers. Brown suede hat, narrow curled brim. Low-cut step-in brown suede shoes. 4 1966. French. Short machine-knitted wool jacket, zip fastening from hip band to under buttoned stand collar, yoke and dolman sleeves cut in one piece, striped machine-knitted front and back panels with large patch pockets in plain fabric with zip openings. Tapered blue cotton trousers. Black leather elastic-sided ankle-boots. 5 1966. British. Two-piece charcoal grey wool and mohair suit: single-breasted fitted jacket with three-button fastening, narrow lapels and small collar, flap pockets, narrow sleeves; narrow tapered trousers. White collar-attached shirt. Red tie. Trilby hat, narrow curled brim, wide ribbon band. Elastic-sided ankle-boots, pointed toes. 6 1968. German. Short double-breasted raincoat, wide lapels and large collar, raglan sleeves with buttoned wrist straps, stitched yoke on right side vertical welt pockets, top-stitched edges and detail. Tapered trousers. Checked cotton collar-attached shirt. Wool tie. Ankle-boots. 7 1968. British. Single-breasted blue cotton denim jacket, four-button fastening to under shirt collar, outsized patch pockets, top-stitched edges and detail. Tapered corded blue velvet trousers. Machine-knitted sweater, high round neckline. Elastic-sided ankle-boots.

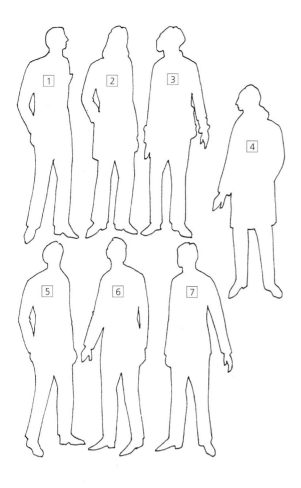

Day Wear 1968–1970

1 1968. French. Pierre Cardin. Two-piece grey cloth suit: double-breasted long fitted jacket with three-button fastening to under narrow lapels, small collar, narrow sleeves, flap pockets; fitted trousers flared from knee-level. White shirt, buttoned collar. Narrow red silk tie. Matching silk handkerchief in breast pocket. Black leather elastic-sided ankle-boots.

2 1969. British. Hippy. Collarless mid-thigh-length jacket, edge-to-edge fastening with two embroidered buttons, matching neck, front and patch pocket edges, inset sleeves with flared hems. Tight blue cotton denim trousers, flared hems. Collarless white cotton T-shirt. Bead and leather thong necklace. Leather boots, pointed toes, high heels.

3 1969. Italian. Single-breasted goatskin coat, strap-and-button fastening, large collar and patch pockets, all seam turnings on outside. Blue cotton denim bib-and-brace overalls, tight legs, flared hems. Yellow sweater. Blue and white striped scarf. Red leather clogs, wooden soles. White socks.

4 1969. German. Hooded pale blue showerproofed cotton coat, loop-and-toggle fastening, deep yoke, large patch pockets, coat lined with brushed cotton and interlined with wadding, top-stitched edges and detail. Straight-cut cream cotton trousers. Brown sweater. Light brown suede lace-up shoes, thick soles and heels.

5 1969. British. Single-breasted fitted brown leather jacket, four-button fastening, large collar and wide lapels, decorative vertical straps between deep yoke and large patch-and-flap pockets, decorative belt around back between vertical straps, hand-stitched edges and detail. Straight-cut blue cotton denim trousers. Black polo-neck sweater. Ankle-boots.

6 1970. British. Two-piece green cotton needlecord suit: single-breasted jacket with three-button fastening, narrow lapels, breast pocket with silk handkerchief, matching necktie, diagonal flap pockets; fitted trousers, flared hems. Brown leather ankle-boots.

7 1970. German. Two-piece white linen suit: single-breasted fitted jacket with high four-button fastening under narrow lapels, large patch-and-flap pockets, no breast pocket; tight trousers, flared hems. Patterned shirt with large collar, worn open. Cream leather ankle-boots.

Day Wear 1970–1972

1 1970. Italian. Cloth jacket, high central zip fastening, large collar and wide revers with rounded edges, matching buttoned yoke, buckled waist-belt, large hip-level flap-and-patch pockets buttoned on each corner of flap, tight sleeves flared at wrists. Brown cloth trousers, slightly flared hems. Yellow knitted-wool polo-neck sweater. Brown suede ankle-boots.

2 1970. German. Single-breasted green wool tweed jacket, high button fastening under small collar and narrow revers, breast flap pocket, matching hip-level pockets, top-stitched detail. Straight green wool trousers. Grey and white striped shirt. Yellow tie. Suede ankle-boots.

3 1970. French. Waist-length leather jacket, asymmetric zip fastening, diagonal pockets with zip fastening, matching opening on hem of sleeve, wide waistband with double-breasted button fastening, detachable lambswool collar. Black cotton denim trousers, slightly flared hems. Black leather shoes, strap-and-button fastening.

4 1971. French. Pierre Cardin. Single-breasted two-tone burgundy suede jacket, stand collar, shaped yoke, large hip-level buttoned flap pockets, some top-stitched detail, self-fabric buttons. Black striped cloth trousers. Black cotton pullover. Black leather step-in shoes.

5 1971. German. Striped wool three-piece suit: single-breasted jacket with high fastening, breast pocket, silk handkerchief, diagonal hip-level flap pockets; collarless waistcoat, high fastening, welt pockets; trousers cut straight from knee. White cotton shirt. Silk tie. Black leather step-in shoes.

6 1972. German. Double-breasted orange and blue striped cloth jacket, wide revers, breast pocket, silk handkerchief, hip-level flap pockets, ticket pocket on right side only. Blue cloth trousers cut straight from knee, deep turn-ups. Dark blue cotton shirt. Yellow and blue patterned silk tie. Black leather shoes, strap-and-buckle fastening.

7 1972. British. Tom Gilbey. Blue cotton jacket, fly front opening, hip-level patch pockets with buttoned flaps, matching breast pocket, split sleeve cuffs with button trim, top-stitched detail. Yellow wool polo-neck sweater. Grey cotton trousers, slightly flared hems. Grey leather step-in shoes.

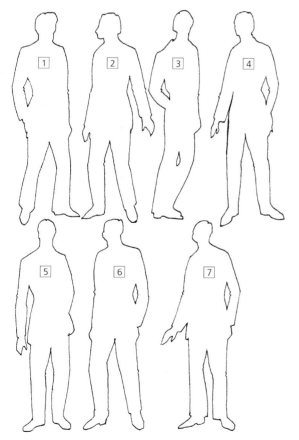

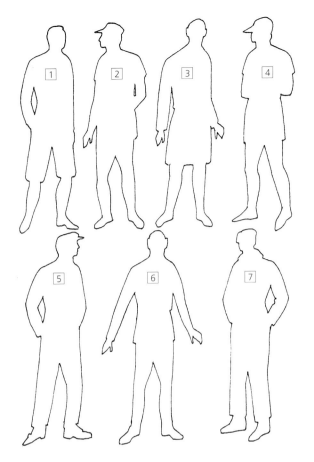

Sports and Leisure Wear 1960–1972

1 1960. French. Golf. Machine-knitted light brown wool V-neck sweater, long cuffed sleeves. Brown velvet knee breeches. Wool shirt, open neck. Patterned silk scarf. Long white knee socks. Brown leather lace-up shoes. 2 1965. German. Beachwear. Hip-length grey cotton shirt, short sleeves, single breast patch pocket, grey and pink checked cotton strap opening and collar; matching shorts. Blue cotton cap. Blue canvas step-in elastic-sided shoes, rope soles. 3 1966. German. Beach wear. Knee-length wrapover white cotton towelling beachrobe, three large patch pockets, self-fabric belt, blue cotton towelling roll collar and sleeve cuffs. 4 1967. American. Tennis. Collarless white knitted-cotton T-shirt, short sleeves. White cotton tailored shorts, matching belt slotted though loops on waistband, fly front, diagonal side pockets, small buttoned flap pocket on right side only. Close-fitting white cotton cap, large visor. White canvas lace-up sports shoes, rubber soles. Short white socks. 5 1969. American. Golf. Collarless single-breasted pink machine-knitted cardigan, long cuffed raglan sleeves, patch pockets. White polo-neck sweater. Pink and brown checked cloth trousers, straight-cut legs. Brown cap. Low-cut dark green leather step-in shoes, fringed turned-down tongues. 6 1970. French. Football. Red knitted-cotton shirt, stand collar piped in white, matching cuffs on long inset sleeves, emblem embroidered in black on left side of chest. Short white cotton shorts. Low-cut black and white leather lace-up boots, pegged soles. Long white socks, cuffs edged with red. 7 1972. French. Ski wear. Three-piece padded and machine quilted green nylon suit: short jacket with zip fastening to under large nylon fur collar, diagonal zipped pockets, matching hems of inset sleeves; collarless waistcoat with zip fastening; ankle-length trousers, zip fly, diagonal pockets, welt pockets on side of hips. Yellow polo-neck sweater. Green ski goggles, chrome frames. Red-brown shiny plastic and leather boots, metal clip fastenings.

Evening Wear 1960–1972

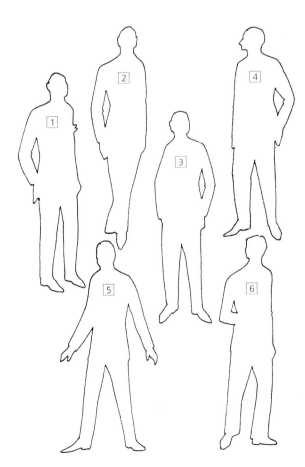

1 1960. British. Single-breasted cream wool dinner jacket, single-button fastening, long roll collar faced with silk. Low-cut collarless single-breasted pink silk waistcoat, matching bow-tie and handkerchief in breast pocket of jacket. Straight-cut black wool trousers, black satin ribbon stripe on outside seam. White collar-attached shirt, buttoned fly fastening. Black shoes. 2 1960. French. Blue mohair two-piece suit: single-breasted jacket with single-button fastening, long roll collar faced with silk, matching covered buttons, hip-level piped pockets; straight-cut trousers. White collar-attached shirt. Black silk bow-tie. Black shoes. 3 1966. Italian. Black silk and mohair two-piece suit: single-breasted jacket with linked-button fastening, narrow lapels edged with black satin, matching satin-covered collar, welt pockets, narrow sleeve cuffs and covered buttons; straight-cut trousers. White collar-attached shirt. Black satin bow-tie. Black satin cummerbund. Black shoes. 4 1966. Italian. Blue silk two-piece suit: single-breasted jacket with single-button fastening, long roll collar edged with black silk braid, matching cuffs and edges of wide front-buttoning cummerbund; straight-cut trousers. White collar-attached shirt. Blue silk bow-tie. Black shoes. 5 1971. Italian. Two-piece silk and mohair evening suit: double-breasted fitted jacket with satin-faced lapels, matching covered buttons, hip-level bound pockets; straight-cut trousers. White shirt, wing collar. Narrow black velvet bow-tie. Black shoes. 6 1972. Italian. Single-breasted patterned-velvet fitted jacket with single-button fastening, wide lapels, narrow sleeves, flap pockets. Fitted black mohair trousers, flared hems. White collar-attached shirt, ruffled front. Black velvet bow-tie tucked under large collar. Black shoes.

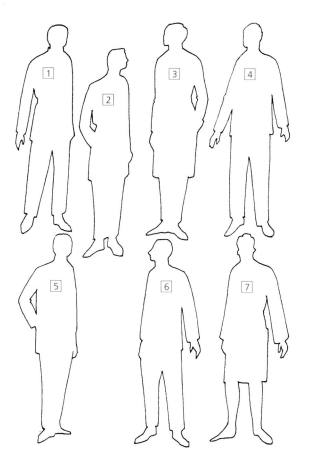

Nightwear 1960–1972

1 1960. French. Two-piece cotton pyjamas: single-breasted jacket with high button fastening to under stand collar, collar piped with light-brown cotton, matching turned back sleeve cuffs and trim on large patch pockets, self-fabric tie-belt; ankle-length straight-cut trousers. Blue leather slippers. 2 1961. British. Short velvet wrapover dressing gown, wide quilted satin roll collar, matching wide stitched sleeve cuffs, trim on large patch pockets and tasseled trim on self-fabric tie-belt. Two-piece blue and white striped cotton pyjamas. Red leather slippers. 3 1966. German. Three-piece green striped silk suit: knee-length wrapover dressing gown, roll collar, wide turned-back sleeve cuffs, self-fabric tie-belt, large patch pockets; pyjamas in matching fabric: single-breasted jacket with button fastening to under shirt collar; ankle-length straight-cut trousers. Black leather slippers. 4 1966. British. Two-piece blue cotton pyjamas: single-breasted jacket fastening to under narrow revers, large shirt collar trimmed with yellow and red cotton inset stripes, matching trim on single breast patch pocket; straight-cut trousers. 5 1967. British. Two-piece patterned-cotton pyjamas, hip-length top, collar cut-in-one with narrow yoke and long sleeves, large hip-level patch pockets; straight-cut ankle-length trousers. 6 1970. French. Two-piece pale green cotton pyjamas: collarless single-breasted jacket with edges bound with black cotton to match hems on inset sleeves and trim on large hip-level patch pockets; straight-cut trousers. Brown leather mules. 7 1972. French. Knee-length collarless wrapover purple cotton dressing gown, self-fabric tie-belt, front edges from neck to hem trimmed with wide gold embroidered braid, matching hems of flared dolman sleeves.

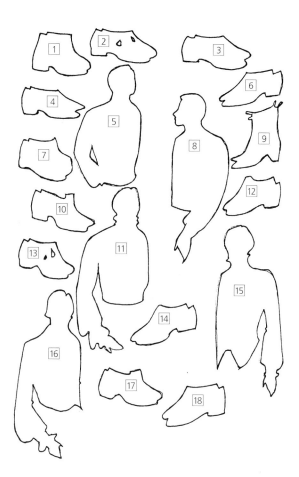

Footwear and Shirts 1960–1972

1 1960. British. Light brown leather lace-up ankle-boots, thick rubber soles. 2 1960. British. Brown leather sandals, open sides, punched hole decoration, strap-and-buckle fastening. 3 1961. Italian. Brown leather lace-up shoes, woven leather decoration, pointed toes. 4 1960. Italian. Winklepickers. Black leather shoes, side-strap-and-buckle fastening, long pointed toes. 5 1961. British. Machine-knitted yellow wool sweater, high round neckline, raglan sleeves. 6 1961. Italian. Green leather shoes, stamped snakeskin pattern, trimmed with black leather tongue, strap-and-buckle fastening, pointed toes, stacked heels. 7 1961. British. Teddy-boy style. Blue suede shoes, wide strap-and-buckle fastening, thick black crepe combined soles and heels. 8 1961. British. Blue leather top, V-shaped neckline, welt pockets, machine-knitted sleeves and back panel. 9 1962. Italian. Black leather elastic-sided boots, long pointed toes, high stacked heels. 10 1963. Italian. Black leather step-in shoes, strap-and-buckle trim, square toes. 11 1968. British. Mr Fish. Blue silk shirt, ruffled collar and matching sleeve cuffs, wide yoke, front fastening with self-fabric rouleau-bow fastening. 12 1965. British. Light brown suede lace-up shoes, rubber soles and heels. 13 1965. Italian. Brown leather sandals, open sides, strap-and-buckle fastenings. 14 1972. British. Black leather shoes, wide strap-and-buckle fastening, brogue decoration. 15 1969. British. Mr Fish. Collarless patterned-silk brocade waistcoat worn open, plain silk back. Striped shirt, stand collar with pleated edge, matching strap opening and cuffs of full sleeves. 16 1969. British. Mr Fish. Pale green crepe shirt, ruffled front strap opening to under long collar, full sleeves with ruffled cuffs. 17 1972. British. Brown suede elastic-sided shoes, thick soles. 18 1972. British. Brown leather step-in shoes, concealed elastic gusset under high tongues.

1973

1974

1974

1974

1975

1975

1975

Day Wear 1975–1978

1975

1976

1976

1976

1977

1977

1978

1978

1978

1979

1979

1980

1980

1980

1981

Day Wear 1982–1984

1982

1983

1983

1983

1984

1984

1984

Sports and Leisure Wear 1973–1984

1973

1976

1978

1979

1980

1982

1984

Footwear 1973–1984

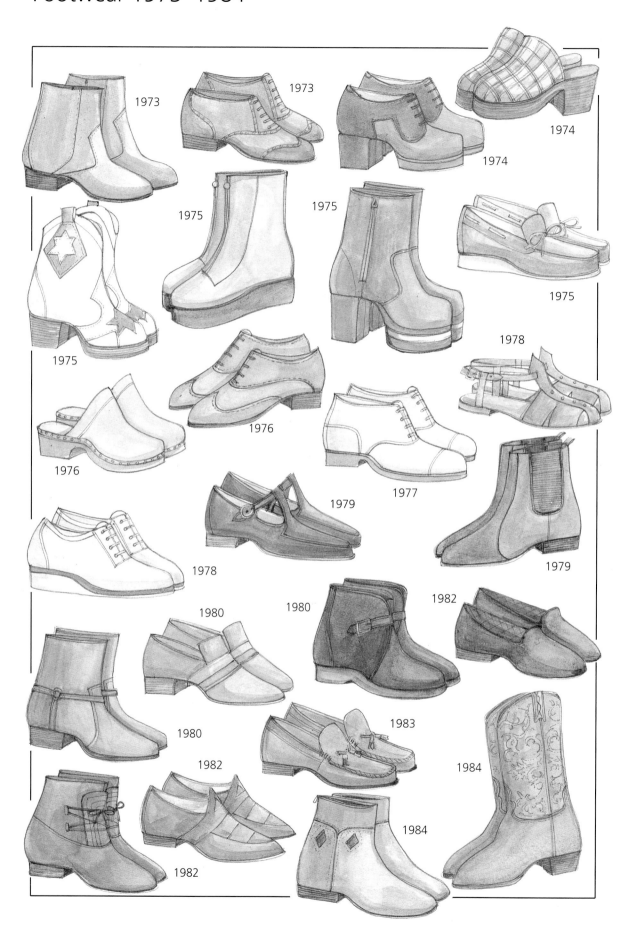

1973

1973

1973

1974

1974

1975

1975

1975

1975

1976

1976

1976

1977

1978

1978

1979

1979

1980

1980

1980

1980

1982

1982

1982

1982

1983

1984

1984

1973

1974

1974

1975

1979

1980

1984

1982

1984

Evening Wear 1973–1984

1973

1974

1976

1978

1981

1984

1985

1985

1985

1985

1986

1986

1986

1987

1988

1988

1988

1989

1989

1989

1989

1989

1990

1990

1991

1991

1991

Day Wear 1992–1995

1992

1992

1993

1992

1993

1994

1994

1995

1985

1986

1986

1987

1993

1994

1995

Evening Wear 1985–1995

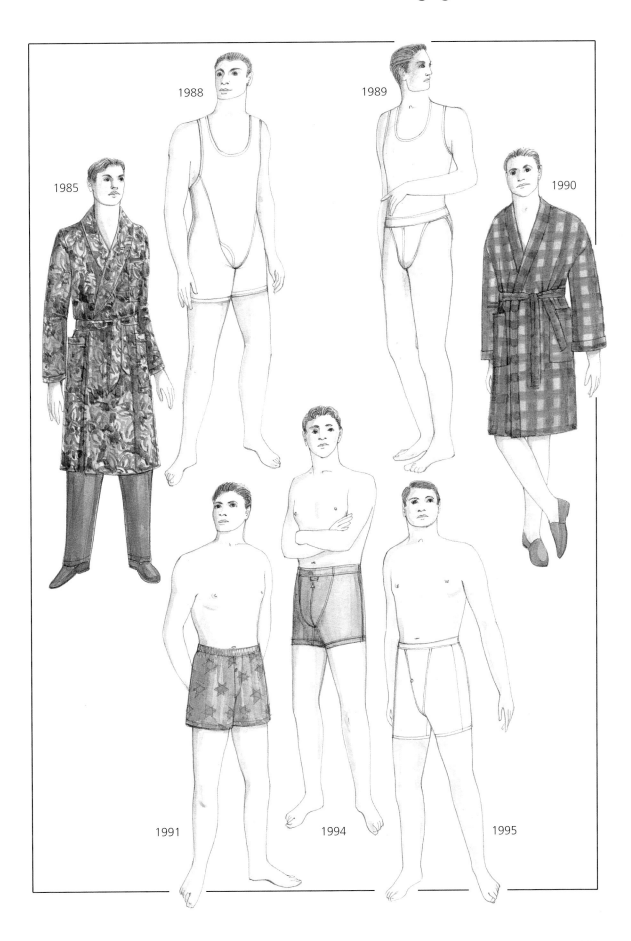

1988

1989

1985

1990

1991

1994

1995

1985

1985

1985

1986

1986

1986

1986

1987

1987

1988

1987

1988

1988

1989

1988

1989

1990

1990

1989

1990

1991

1990

1991

1991

1993

1993

1994

1993

1995

1995

1995

1995

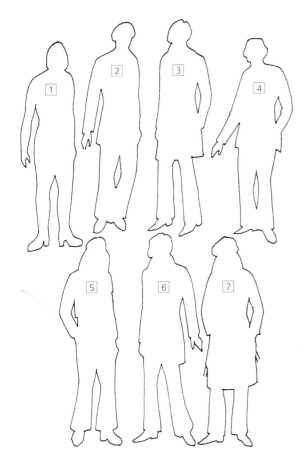

Day Wear 1973–1975

1 1973. British. Pop star. Sleeveless black leather top, zip fastening to under high round neckline, shaped yoke with top-stitched decoration, tight trousers in matching black leather. Long black leather boots, high heels, thick platform soles, decorative inset red stripe. Wide leather belt, decorated silver buckle. 2 1974. Italian. Three-piece checked cloth suit: single-breasted jacket with three-button fastening to under wide lapels, large patch pockets; collarless single-breasted waistcoat; tight flared trousers, wide turn-ups. Dark blue shirt, wide collar. Red patterned silk tie. Black leather moccasin shoes. 3 1974. Italian. Short cream wool coat, double-breasted fastening to under wide lapels, large collar, tight sleeves, welt pockets. Flared trousers with turn-ups. Red shirt. Light-blue tie. Brown leather boots, platform soles, stacked heels. 4 1974. Italian. Two-piece tweed suit: single-breasted jacket, wide lapels, patch pockets, tight sleeves; flared trousers with wide waistband belt in matching fabric. Coloured collar-attached shirt. Striped tie. Cream and brown uneven striped sweater, V-shaped neckline. Brown leather boots, platform soles. 5 1975. British. Waist-length light brown leather jacket, zip fastening to under large sheepskin collar, inset sleeves with knitted cuffs, flap pockets with stud fastenings, matching patch-and-flap pockets. Orange cotton shirt, long pointed collar, worn open. Multi-coloured waist-length sweater, V-shaped neckline. Tight denim trousers, large patch pockets, flared hems. Multi-coloured patchwork leather clogs, high heels, platform soles. 6 1975. British. Short double-breasted sheepskin-lined coat, strap-and-button fastening, matching decoration on tight sleeves, large sheepskin collar, patch pockets. Brown polo-neck sweater. Patchwork blue denim flared trousers. Leather boots, stacked heels, platform soles. 7 1975. Italian. Double-breasted green checked knee-length coat, wide lapels and large collar, raglan sleeves with buttoned-strap decoration, tied buckled belt, diagonal welt pockets. Long knitted scarf, fringed hem. Flared trousers. Boots with platform soles.

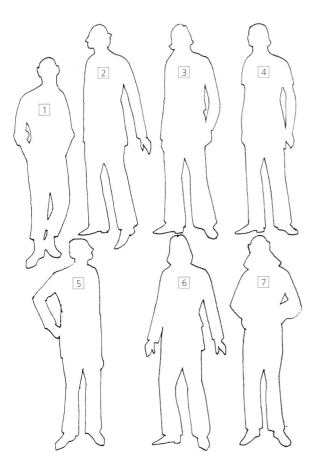

Day Wear 1975–1978

1 1975. British. Skinhead. Checked cotton shirt worn with sleeves rolled up and collar open. Button-through white knitted-cotton vest, long sleeves. Tight mid-calf-length cream cotton trousers. Elasticated braces. Buckled leather belt. Long black leather lace-up boots. 2 1976. Italian. Fitted two-piece single-breasted cream linen suit: two-button fastening, wide lapels, welt pockets, narrow shoulders, fitted sleeves; tight trousers flared from knee. Blue cotton shirt. Wide striped silk tie. Elastic-sided ankle-boots. 3 1976. American. Waist-length blue denim jacket, narrow shoulders, tight sleeves, chest-level patch pockets with buttoned flaps, top-stitched edges and detail. Fitted blue denim shirt fastening with metal studs. Tight denim jeans, flared from knee. Black leather belt. Black leather elastic-sided boots. 4 1976. Italian. Lightweight natural lined two-piece safari suit: three-button fastening, short sleeves, epaulets, chest-level patch pockets with buttoned flaps, large hip-level patch pockets, top-stitched edges and detail; tight trousers flared from knee. Collarless short-sleeved green silk shirt. Ankle-boots. 5 1977. Italian. Fitted two-piece single-breasted lined tweed suit: wide lapels, narrow shoulders, fitted sleeves, patch pockets; tight trousers flared from knee. Pink cotton shirt, large collar. Wide striped silk tie. Elastic-sided ankle-boots. 6 1977. British. Fitted two-piece single-breasted blue denim suit: narrow shoulders, wide lapels, fitted sleeves, single-button fastening, side panel seams, flap pockets; tight trousers flared from knee. Collar-attached shirt. Silk scarf. Black leather ankle-boots. 7 1978. Italian. Waist-length wool tweed jacket, zip fastening, large collar, raglan sleeves gathered into cuffs, vertical welt pockets, elasticated hem. Tight cotton-cord trousers flared from knee. Brown wool tweed shirt, buttoned-down collar. Checked wool tweed tie. V-neck hand-knitted sleeveless sweater. Hand-knitted brimless cap. Two-tone lace-up leather shoes.

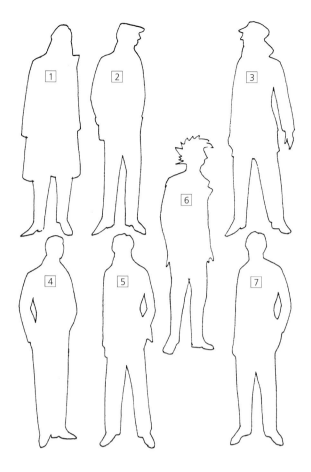

Day Wear 1978–1981

1 1978. Italian. Three-piece brown cloth suit: single-breasted jacket with two-button fastening and flap pockets; collarless single-breasted waistcoat; narrow trousers, no turn-ups. White cotton collar-attached shirt, patterned silk tie. Light brown wool and cashmere double-breasted overcoat, wide lapels, large collar, flap pockets. 2 1978. Italian. Long single-breasted wool jacket, knitted shawl collar, matching cuffs of raglan sleeves and trim on patch pockets. Hand-knitted wool sweater, V-shaped neckline. Checked wool shirt. Narrow cotton-cord trousers. Leather step-in shoes, contrast trim. 3 1979. German. Short double-breasted blue fitted overcoat, wide lapels, large collar, flap pockets. White polo-neck sweater. White cotton trousers. Blue cotton denim cap. Black elastic-sided boots. 4 1979. Italian. Short leather jacket, off-centre zip fastening to under long roll collar, two-piece sleeve with top-stitched seams; matching yoke seam, waist seam and patch pockets; strap decoration on side hips and sleeve cuffs. Brown polo-neck sweater. Green wool scarf. Narrow wool tweed trousers. Brown boots. 5 1980. British. Single-breasted jacket with two-button fastening, narrow lapels, collar turned up. Light green silk scarf. Pink cotton sweater, high round neckline, worn with silk scarf. Narrow cream linen trousers. Brown shoes. 6 1980. British. Punk. Sleeveless black leather jacket, off-centre zip fastening, decorated with various studs, pins, clips and badges. Short brightly coloured ripped cotton T-shirt. Black cotton vest. Tight cotton trousers. Two black leather studded belts. Black leather dog collar. Long black leather lace-up Dr Marten boots. Head shaved with central strip left long and dyed bright orange, spiked and kept in place with glue and strong hairspray. Large earring. Arms heavily tattooed. 7 1981. British. Single-breasted cream linen jacket, single-button fastening under long shawl collar, flap pockets. Dark blue cotton collar-attached shirt. Narrow green striped silk tie. Narrow black linen trousers, no turn-ups. Black leather step-in shoes.

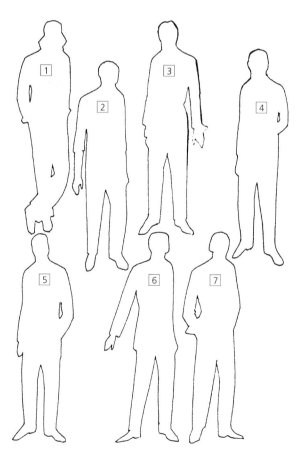

Day Wear 1982–1984

1 1982. American. One-piece green heavy-duty cotton jumpsuit, zip fastening from crotch to under shirt collar, diagonal chest-level zipped pockets, high waist-level flap pockets, patch-and-flap pockets with side zip detail above knee-level, inset shirt sleeves; straight-cut trousers, decorative zip fastening on inside seam from hem to below knee-level. White moulded plastic sandals. 2 1983. American. Hip-length red leather jacket, zip fastening from hipband to under stand collar, various decorative zipped pockets, white leather inset yoke, cuffed sleeves zipped into armholes and worn pushed up arms. White collar-attached shirt, collar worn open. Tight blue leather trousers, knee-level seams. Black leather boots. 3 1983. German. Two-piece pale blue cotton suit: double-breasted jacket fastening from waistband to under stand collar with press studs, chest-level flap pockets, large patch pockets, cuffed inset sleeves, padded shoulders; straight-cut trousers pleated from waist, no central creases. White T-shirt. White training shoes (trainers). 4 1983. American. Short single-breasted grey and black tweed jacket, knitted waistband and matching sleeve cuffs, vertical welt pockets, narrow lapels. Grey brushed-cotton collar-attached shirt. Narrow grey wool tie. Straight-cut black cloth trousers pleated from waist. Low-cut black leather step-in shoes. 5 1984. British. Blue and yellow striped cloth jacket, single-breasted two-button fastening, flap pockets. Lilac knitted-cotton shirt. Straight-cut plain blue cloth trousers. White leather belt. Low-cut black leather step-in shoes, fringed tongues. Purple socks. 6 1984. British. Single-breasted brushed-wool jacket, large patch pockets. Collarless single-breasted knitted wool waistcoat. Brushed-cotton collar-attached shirt. Striped wool tie. Straight-cut trousers. Lace-up leather shoes. 7 1984. Italian. Single-breasted checked cotton jacket, single-button fastening, flap pockets, padded shoulders. White cotton shirt, collar worn open. Straight-cut white cotton trousers, pleated from waist; buckled belt in matching fabric. White leather sandals, strap-and-buckle fastening.

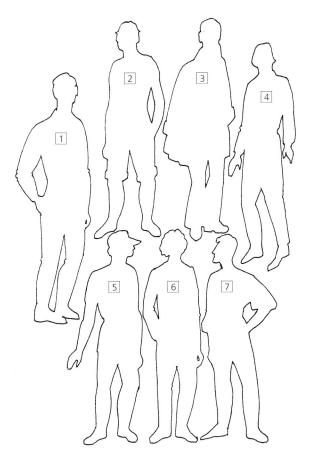

Sports and Leisure Wear 1973–1984

1 1973. Italian. Ski wear. Hip-length multi-coloured elasticated and waterproof top, polo-neck, long sleeves with padded elbow patches and inset stripes; tight pants with stripe on outside seams, slightly flared hemline. Knitted cap. Dark goggles. Padded multi-coloured leather gloves. Long ski boots, metal strap-and-clip fastenings. 2 1976. Italian. Beachwear. Multi-coloured striped cotton bib-and-brace, bib with adjustable straps, large divided patch pocket with small flap on one side, wide waistband; short trousers with turn-ups, hip-level pockets, top-stitched decoration. 3 1978. Italian. Casual travel. Thigh-length loosely woven brown cotton T-shaped edge-to-edge coat, wide flared wrist-length white cotton sleeves with wide cuffs, matching collar and front facings. Red-white-and-blue knitted-cotton collarless T-shirt. Tight blue denim jeans, flared from knee to hem. Wooden clogs with leather uppers. Large leather shoulder bag. 4 1979. American. All-in-one heavy-duty cotton jumpsuit, front zip fastening to under shirt collar, matching vertical zip pockets and hems of trousers, inset sleeves with buttoned cuffs, top-stitched edges and detail. Collarless T-shirt. Trainers. 5 1980. Italian. Tennis. Short-sleeved knitted white cotton mixture shirt, decorated with horizontal stripes of black; shorts with elasticated waistband, high-cut sides. White canvas shoes. White cotton ankle-socks. Dark plastic visor on white stretch-cotton band. 6 1982. Italian. Jogging suit. Red jersey two-piece: top with low scooped neckline bound with yellow padded jersey, matching hem and sleeve head, sleeves gathered into narrow cuffs; narrow pants. Black and yellow trainers. 7 1984. Italian. Holiday wear. Collarless plain and striped cotton shirt, dolman sleeves gathered into cuffs. Cotton canvas trousers, wide waistband decorated with buckled straps, hip-level pockets, patch-and-flap pockets above knee-level seams, top-stitched decoration. Multi-coloured trainers.

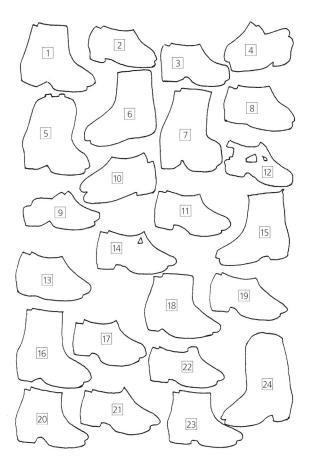

Footwear 1973–1984

1 1973. Grey leather ankle-boots, top-stitched detail, low stacked heels. 2 1973. Brown suede brogues. 3 1974. Red leather lace-up shoes, thick platform soles, high square heels. 4 1974. Patchwork leather clogs, wooden platform soles, high heels. 5 1975. White leather cowboy boots, silver and brown leather star trim, platform soles, high stacked heels. 6 1975. Light brown suede boots, front zip fastening, thick rubber platform soles and wedge heels. 7 1975. Green leather boots, zip fastening on outside seam, high leather-covered square heels, thick platform soles with inset stripe of silver leather. 8 1975. Low-cut blue leather casual shoes, white leather bow-trim, white rubber soles and wedge heels. 9 1976. Light brown leather clogs, wooden soles and heels, metal stud trim. 10 1976. Green leather and light brown canvas lace-up shoes, low stacked heels. 11 1977. White leather lace-up shoes, black soles and heels. 12 1978. Brown leather sandals, strap-and-buckle fastening, low heels. 13 1978. White canvas lace-up shoes, wedge heels with decorative inset red stripe. 14 1979. Blue leather sandals, buckle-and-strap fastening. 15 1979. Black leather elastic-sided boots, thin soles, low stacked heels. 16 1980. Brown leather boots, self-leather strap-and-buckle trim, stacked heels. 17 1980. Light green leather step-in shoes; three colour inset stripes. 18 1980. Brown suede fur-lined ankle-boots, strap-and-buckle fastening, crepe soles. 19 1982. Black velvet house slippers lined with quilted red silk. 20 1982. Blue leather ankle-boots, decorative self-leather outside tongues and laces. 21 1982. Green leather step-in shoes, tan suede trim, low stacked heels, pointed toes. 22 1983. Brown leather moccasins, decorative leather stitching and trim. 23 1984. Grey leather ankle-boots, dark grey leather cuffs and trim, back zip opening. 24 1984. Light brown leather cowboy boots, decorative top-stitched uppers, stacked heels, pointed toes.

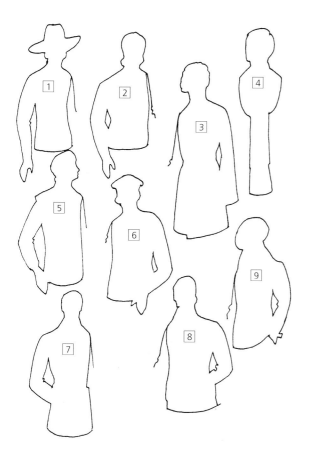

Knitwear 1973–1984

1 1973. American. Machine-knitted fitted sweater, V-shaped neckline, main body green, long tight inset sleeves, ribs of neckline and hem pale cream, pattern at waist-level. Dark blue cotton shirt, long pointed collar. Green felt hat, tall crown, wide brim. Sunglasses. 2 1974. British. Machine-knitted fitted cotton sweater with horizontal bands of pattern on white background, wide V-shaped neckline, cuffs of long inset sleeves and ribbed hem in plain white. Dark pink cotton shirt, long pointed collar. 3 1974. Italian. Long machine-knitted collarless wrapover wool coat, banded in grey, orange, brown and white, long inset sleeves with wide flared hems, tie-belt, large patch pockets. Machine-knitted orange cotton polo-neck sweater. 4 1975. Italian. Long pale blue wool scarf, fringed hems. Black polo-neck sweater. Blue cotton shirt, pointed collar. 5 1979. British. Grey machine-knitted wool sweater, wrapover collar, long inset sleeves with narrow ribbed cuffs, matching hem. Collarless and sleeveless brown machine-knitted wool waistcoat, shaped hem, welt pockets. Brimless hand-knitted grey wool pull-on hat. 6 1980. British. Hand-knitted beige wool sweater, allover raised pattern, wide V-shaped neckline, long inset sleeves. Beige wool shirt. Striped wool tie. Checked wool cap. 7 1982. French. Machine-knitted wool single-breasted jacket, fastening to under shirt collar with leather buttons, matching yoke, long inset sleeves with turned-back ribbed cuffs, matching edges of patch pockets, collar and tie-belt. Green cotton shirt. 8 1984. British. Machine-knitted grey cotton sweater, long raglan sleeves with narrow turned-back ribbed cuffs, matching hem, low wrapover collar and insert. 9 1984. Rastafarian. Red-yellow-and-green banded hand-knitted sweater, high round neckline, long inset sleeves. Outsized hand-knitted white wool hat banded with red, yellow and green. Dreadlocks.

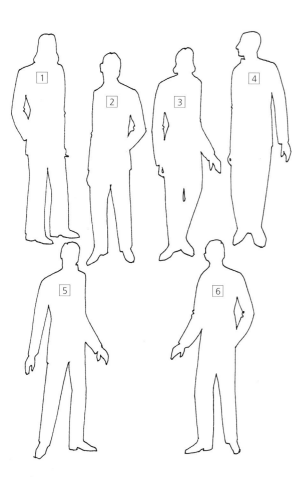

Evening Wear 1973–1984

1 1973. British. Two-piece black silk and mohair evening suit: double-breasted fitted jacket, wide silk lapels, matching covered buttons, hip-level flap pockets, side-back vents; flared trousers, satin ribbon on outside seam. White cotton shirt, deep collar. Large black silk bow-tie. Black shoes. 2 1974. American. Single-breasted red velvet fitted jacket, two-button fastening under wide lapels and large collar, flap pockets, narrow sleeves. Collarless single-breasted black velvet waistcoat. White shirt, long pointed collar. Large black velvet bow-tie. Straight-cut black cloth trousers. Black step-in shoes. 3 1976. Italian. Two-piece black striped cloth suit: double-breasted jacket, low fastening under long silk lapels, matching covered buttons, four patch pockets; straight-cut trousers. White shirt with small collar. Narrow black silk bow-tie. Black shoes. 4 1978. British. Three-piece blue cloth suit: single-breasted jacket, single-button fastening under wide lapels, single breast pocket, hip-level piped pockets; collarless single-breasted waistcoat; straight-cut trousers. White collar-attached shirt, pleated front. Black velvet bow-tie. Black shoes. 5 1981. Italian. Double-breasted cream silk jacket, satin lapels, matching covered buttons, piped pockets. White silk shirt, attached wing collar. Large black silk bow-tie. Black silk straight-cut trousers. Black shoes. 6 1984. American. Two-piece black cloth evening suit: short double-breasted waistcoat jacket with long silk lapels, matching covered buttons, single breast pocket with red silk handkerchief; matching narrow red silk bow-tie; straight-cut trousers with pleats from waist. White shirt with attached wing collar. Black shoes.

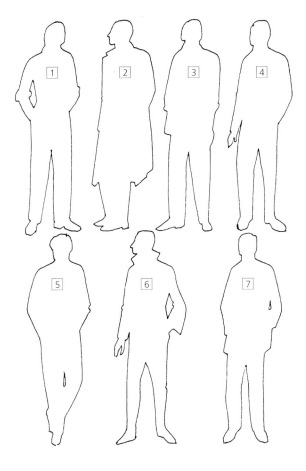

Day Wear 1985–1986

1 1985. British. Double-breasted hip-length dark blue wool jacket fastening with two buttons on hip band, long narrow lapels, inset sleeves rolled up to elbows, diagonal piped pockets, epaulets. Blue cotton shirt, collar worn open. Striped tie. Green and blue checked cloth straight-cut trousers with turn-ups. Leather step-in shoes. 2 1985. British. Single-breasted checked cotton jacket with patch pockets. White collar-attached shirt worn open. Straight-cut plain blue cotton trousers with turn-ups. Single-breasted light brown cotton raincoat, two-piece inset sleeves with buttoned strap matching epaulets, top-stitched edges and detail. Low-cut brown leather step-in shoes. White socks. 3 1985. British. Two-piece white cotton suit: single-breasted unstructured jacket with button fastening to under shirt collar, patch pockets with buttoned flaps, inset sleeves rolled up to below elbow, top-stitched edges and detail; straight-cut trousers pleated from waist, no creases or turn-ups. Blue and white striped cotton shirt, buttoned collar points. White leather lace-up shoes. 4 1985. British. Waist-length blue wool jacket with double-breasted fastening under wide lapels and large collar, breast flap pockets, padded shoulders, wide sleeves with stitched hems, button trim. Collarless blue and white striped knitted-cotton T-shirt. Straight-cut cotton trousers, stitched hems, no creases or turn-ups. Lace-up shoes. 5 1986. Italian. Two-piece brown cloth suit: double-breasted jacket; long narrow lapels, breast and flap pockets, wide padded shoulders; straight-cut trousers, no turn-ups. White cotton collar-attached shirt. Red silk tie. Brown suede lace-up shoes. 6 1986. American. Blue cotton denim shirt, stud fastening, matching sleeve cuffs and patch-and-flap pockets, collar worn turned up, epaulets, top-stitched edges and detail. White knitted-cotton singlet. Tight blue cotton-denim trousers worn at knees. Brown leather belt with large silver buckle. White trainers. White socks. 7 1986. British. Single-breasted brown cotton jacket, patch pockets, narrow lapels, stitched cuffs. Knitted red cotton shirt. Straight-cut beige cotton trousers, pleats from waist, deep turn-ups. Brown suede lace-up shoes.

Day Wear 1987–1989

1 1987. British. Single-breasted red wool jacket, single-button fastening under narrow lapels, patch pockets, breast pocket with patterned silk handkerchief. Brown machine-knitted sweater, low V-neck, fine cable-stitch design. White cotton shirt, small collar. Linen trousers, pleats from waist, narrow hems with no turn-ups. Black lace-up shoes. 2 1988. British. Knee-length grey cotton raincoat, knitted collar, raglan sleeves; front fastening with self-fabric straps, loops and buttons; belt with leather buckle, hip-level welt pockets, top-stitched edges and detail. Yellow polo-neck sweater. Narrow trousers. Lace-up shoes. 3 1988. British. Two-piece black cotton suit: double-breasted jacket, breast patch pocket and hip-level piped pockets; straight-cut trousers pleated from waist, no turn-ups. White shirt, narrow stand collar. Black knitted-cotton shirt, collar with red stripe, worn open. Lace-up shoes. 4 1988. British. Knee-length coat, zip fastening from strap and button above hem to under knitted stand collar, matching knitted cuffs of inset sleeves, dropped shoulderline, diagonal welt pockets. Striped cotton polo-neck sweater. Narrow trousers. Hat with flat-topped crown and straight brim. Leather boots. 5 1989. Italian. Giorgio Armani. Single-breasted linen jacket with two-button fastening, narrow lapels and small collar bound with contrasting leather, matching pockets and edges. Collarless grey silk T-shirt. Light brown linen trousers, pleats from waistband, narrow hems, no turn-ups. Brown leather step-in shoes. No socks. Sunglasses. 6 1989. American. Short blue denim jacket, button fastening from waistband to under upturned shirt collar, deep yoke, patch pockets with shaped buttoned flaps, inset sleeves with shirt cuffs. Pink cotton shirt. Tight denim trousers. Buckled leather belt. White trainers. 7 1989. American. Short grey leather jacket lined with sheepskin, matching collar, zip fastening, padded shoulders, inset sleeves with shirt cuffs, vertical and diagonal welt pockets. Black knitted-cotton shirt. Blue denim straight-cut trousers. Brown suede lace-up boots.

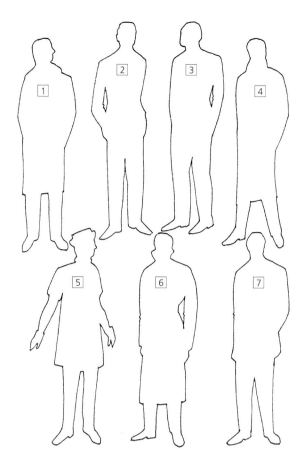

Day Wear 1989–1991

1 1989. British. Knee-length blue wool hooded overcoat, fastening with two self-fabric straps and wooden pegs and two wooden buttons at neckline, stitched yoke, large patch pockets, top-stitched edges and detail. Red wool scarf. Narrow trousers. Lace-up leather shoes. 2 1989. Italian. Single-breasted green wool jacket, three-button fastening, wide padded shoulders, flap pockets. White wrapover shirt secured with small pin. Multi-coloured patterned silk waistcoat. Trousers with pleats from waist, narrow hems with turn-ups. Lace-up leather shoes. 3 1990. French. Pierre Cardin. Single-breasted wool jacket, single-button fastening under narrow lapels, wide padded shoulders, side vents, flap pockets, breast pocket with yellow silk handkerchief; matching yellow shirt with small round collar. Silk tie. Narrow trousers. Step-in leather shoes, thick soles and heels. 4 1990. Italian. Giorgio Armani. Long double-breasted grey wool overcoat, wide padded shoulders, inset two-piece sleeves, large patch pockets. Yellow wool scarf. Narrow cloth trousers. Lace-up leather shoes. 5 1991. British. Raver. Outsized white knitted-cotton T-shirt printed with large multi-coloured letters, short baggy sleeves, round neckline. Blue scarf. Ankle-length white cotton trousers. Cotton gloves patterned with luminous paint. Straw hat, shallow crown, upturned brim. Black leather ankle-boots, thick soles and heels. 6 1991. Italian. Verri. Long brown double-breasted padded cotton overcoat, raglan sleeves decorated with straps at wrist-level, wide padded shoulders, large collar worn turned up, patch pockets with flap, top-stitched edges and detail. Narrow trousers. Leather shoes. 7 1991. British. Single-breasted yellow wool jacket, two-button fastening, narrow lapels, patch pockets, padded shoulders; collarless waistcoat in matching fabric with welt pockets. Light brown linen shirt. Yellow silk tie. Trousers pleated from waist, narrow hems with turn-ups. Step-in leather shoes.

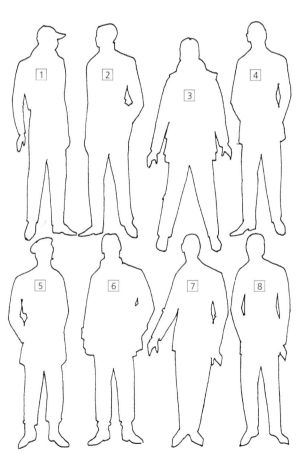

Day Wear 1992–1995

1 1992. American. Waist-length brown leather jacket, zip fastening from knitted waistband to fur collar, matching fastening on hem of tight sleeves, various zipped pockets. Collarless T-shirt. Blue denim jeans. Red suede baseball cap. Leather lace-up ankle-boots. 2 1992. Italian. Dolce & Gabbana. Two-piece single-breasted pale grey linen suit: jacket with three-button fastening, four patch pockets; trousers with pleated waist, cut straight from knee, turn-ups. Knitted cream cotton polo-neck sweater. Leather shoes. 3 1993. German. Techno. Sleeveless combat jacket, zip fastening, four patch pockets with flaps, four zipped pockets. Black cotton collarless T-shirt, long sleeves. Heavy cotton camouflage trousers, knee-level patch-and-flap pockets. Black leather belt. Ankle-boots. 4 1992. Italian. Gianni Versace. Single-breasted blue wool jacket, three-button fastening, wide padded shoulders, breast pocket, flap pockets. Collarless single-breasted multi-colour patterned waistcoat. Straight-cut trousers, turn-ups. Black leather step-in shoes. 5 1993. Japanese. Yohji Yamamoto. Two-piece double-breasted blue cloth suit: high fastening to under narrow lapels, four patch pockets with buttoned flaps, waist-level vertical bound pockets, inset sleeves with decorative wrist-level buttoned strap; ankle-length trousers with turn-ups. White silk shirt. Blue cloth beret. Black socks. Black lace-up shoes. 6 1994. French/Japanese. Kenzo Homme. Hip-length unfitted striped wool tweed jacket, dropped shoulderline, wide cuffs, large collar, outsized patch pockets. Collarless T-shirt. Striped cotton shirt. Long plain blue cotton shirt. Unfitted striped cotton trousers tucked into thick socks. Wide black leather belt. Brimless knitted cap. Leather ankle-boots. 7 1994. British. Hardy Amies. Three-piece single-breasted tweed suit: high fastening to under narrow lapels, breast pocket with silk handkerchief, flap pockets; collarless single-breasted waistcoat; straight-cut trousers with turn-ups. Silk shirt. Striped wool tie. Leather brogues. 8 1995. French. Joseph Homme. Two-piece striped wool suit: two-button fastening, narrow lapels, small collar, sleeves with two-button trim; narrow ankle-length trousers. Black cotton polo-neck sweater. White silk shirt. Black leather brogues.

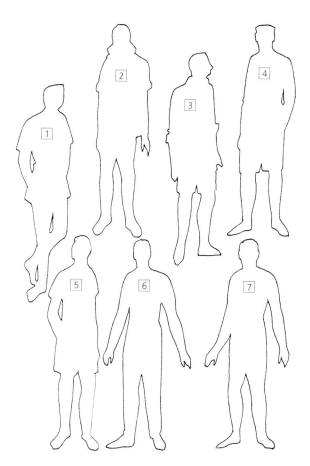

Leisure Wear 1985–1995

1 1985. Italian. Beachwear. Collarless blue knitted-cotton T-shirt, short baggy sleeves, round neckline bound with red knitted cotton, matching inset shoulder stripes and appliqué outsized number nineteen on chest. Short white cotton shorts, elasticated waistband, pockets in side seams, cuffed hems. 2 1986. American. Beachwear. Dark blue cotton shirt patterned with outsize lemons and lemon leaves, single breast patch pocket and short cuffed sleeves; short shorts with elasticated waistband in matching fabric. 3 1986. Italian. Beachwear. Two-piece beige striped cotton suit: single-breasted jacket, patch pockets, narrow lapels, sleeves rolled to elbow; knee-length tailored shorts in matching fabric. Green and yellow patterned cotton shirt. Beige canvas step-in shoes, wedge heels. 4 1987. British. Sailing. Wide blue and white striped cotton sweater, plain white polo-neck collar and cuffs. Knee-length blue striped cotton tailored shorts, pleats from waistband, turn-ups. Dark blue cap. Blue canvas shoes, rubber soles. 5 1993. Italian. Beachwear. Collarless blue cotton baggy T-shirt, wide short sleeves banded with white stripes, matching hems of main body and long baggy shorts. 6 1994. British. Exercise wear. Sleeveless black stretch-cotton vest, low scooped neckline. Cream cotton pants, pleats from elasticated waistband, legs narrow to hem, pockets in side seams. White canvas trainers, rubber soles. 7 1995. British. Surfing. All-in-one red and black stretch nylon bodysuit, low-cut armholes, scooped neckline, front zip fastening from waist to neckline.

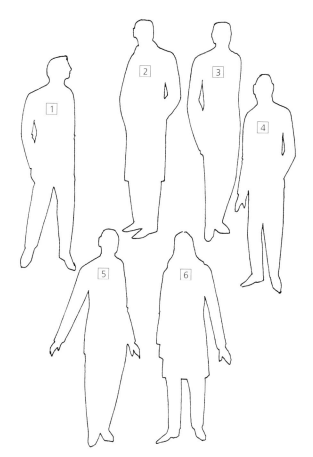

Evening Wear 1985–1995

1 1985. British. Two-piece black wool suit: single-breasted waisted jacket with single-button fastening, narrow lapels faced with black silk-satin, matching buttons, piped pockets; narrow trousers, no turn-ups. White cotton shirt, attached wing collar. Black silk-satin bow-tie. Black shoes. 2 1988. British. Knee-length black wool overcoat, large Persian lamb collar, fly fastening, raglan sleeves with deep turned-back cuffs, single-button trim, diagonal welt pockets. Narrow trousers, silk stripe on outer seam, no turn-ups. White collar-attached shirt. Large black silk bow-tie. Low-cut step-in black patent-leather pumps, petersham ribbon bow trim. 3 1989. British. Three-piece suit: single-breasted waisted jacket, single-button fastening, lapels faced with black silk, piped pockets; single-breasted waistcoat with welt pockets, long collar, no lapels; straight-cut trousers, no turn-ups. White shirt with attached wing collar. Large black silk bow-tie. Black shoes. 4 1990. French. Lanvin. Three-piece suit: single-breasted patterned red silk brocade jacket, single-button fastening, piped pockets; red velvet roll collar, matching buttons, turned-back sleeve cuffs, collarless waistcoat and straight-cut trousers. White silk shirt, attached wing collar. Red silk bow-tie. Black shoes. 5 1991. French. Yves Saint Laurent. Two-piece black silk suit: long single-breasted waisted jacket, button fastening to under high stand collar, narrow sleeves, diagonal welt pockets; straight-cut trousers with narrow hems. Black silk polo-neck sweater. Black shoes. 6 1995. Belgian. Dries van Noten. Two-piece washed black velvet suit, long single-breasted coat with three-button fastening under narrow lapels and small collar, hip-level flap pockets; narrow trousers, no turn-ups. White silk collar-attached shirt worn outside trousers, wide cuffs show under hem of sleeves. Black shoes.

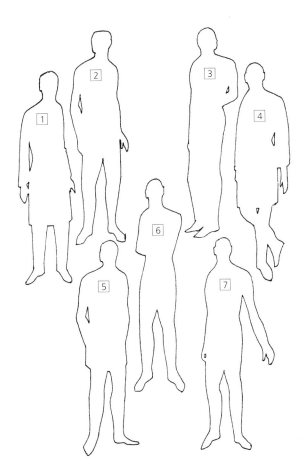

Underwear and Negligee 1985–1995

1 1985. Brown-yellow-and-orange patterned silk dressing gown with wrapover front, self-fabric belt, long roll collar, inset sleeves and three large patch pockets. Blue silk pyjama trousers. Red leather slippers.
2 1988. White knitted-cotton-and-nylon all-in-one bodysuit, low scooped neckline, deep armholes, front side opening set into shaped panel seam, short legs with stitched hems. 3 1989. White knitted-cotton singlet, scooped neckline, deep armholes. White knitted-cotton-and-nylon briefs, double-fabric pouch, cut-away sides, elastic waistband.
4 1990. Wrapover blue and green checked towelling bathrobe, neck and front edges widely bound with self-fabric, matching tie-belt and cuffs of wide sleeves, large hip-level patch pockets. Red leather slippers.
5 1991. Yellow star-patterned green cotton boxer shorts, single-button fastening on fly front, elasticated waistband. 6 1994. Knitted dark grey cotton and nylon shorts, front zip fastening, wide elastic waistband, top-stitched detail. 7 1995. White knitted-cotton-and-nylon shorts, elastic waistband, side-front opening in panel seam, single-button fastening.

Footwear 1985–1995

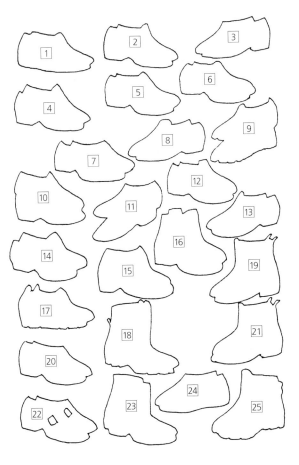

1 1985. White leather lace-up shoes, padded upper edges, man-made soles and heels. 2 1985. Cream leather step-in low-cut casual shoes, low stacked heels. 3 1985. Snakeskin-effect red leather low-cut step-in shoes, low heels. 4 1986. Light brown leather low-cut step-in shoes, brogue decoration. 5 1986. Green leather step-in casual shoes, fringed tongues. 6 1986. Blue leather lace-up shoes, white trim, white man-made soles and heels. 7 1987. Brown leather step-in shoes, shaped strap over instep with cut detail, low heels. 8 1987. Red leather step-in shoes, shaped strap over instep, top-stitched detail, low heels, thin soles. 9 1987. White canvas lace-up trainers, red stripe decoration, man-made textured soles and heels. 10 1988. Low-cut black leather step-in shoes, fringed tongues with strap-and-buckle trim. 11 1988. Light brown suede lace-up shoes, man-made soles and heels. 12 1988. Tan leather step-in shoes, fringed tongues with strap decoration, low stacked heels.
13 1989. Brown leather step-in shoes, brogue decoration, low heels. 14 1989. Black leather step-in shoes, cross-over strap-and-buckle decoration, low heels. 15 1990. Beige suede lace-up ankle-boots, man-made soles and heels. 16 1990. Brown leather boots, strap-and-buckle fastening. 17 1990. Lace-up white canvas trainers, red trim, black man-made textured soles and heels. 18 1993. Long brown leather lace-up boots, padded upper edges, thick man-made soles and heels 19 1991. Black leather lace-up boots, thick soles and heels. 20 1991. Brown leather shoes, strap-and-buckle fastening. 21 1993. Brown leather ankle-boots, strap-and-buckle back fastening, heavy soles and heels.
22 1994. Brown leather sandals, cut-out sides, strap-and-buckle fastening. 23 1995. Beige suede lace-up ankle-boots, man-made soles and heels. 24 1995. Trainers, man-made soles and heels. 25 1995. Brown leather lace-up boots, heavy soles and heels.

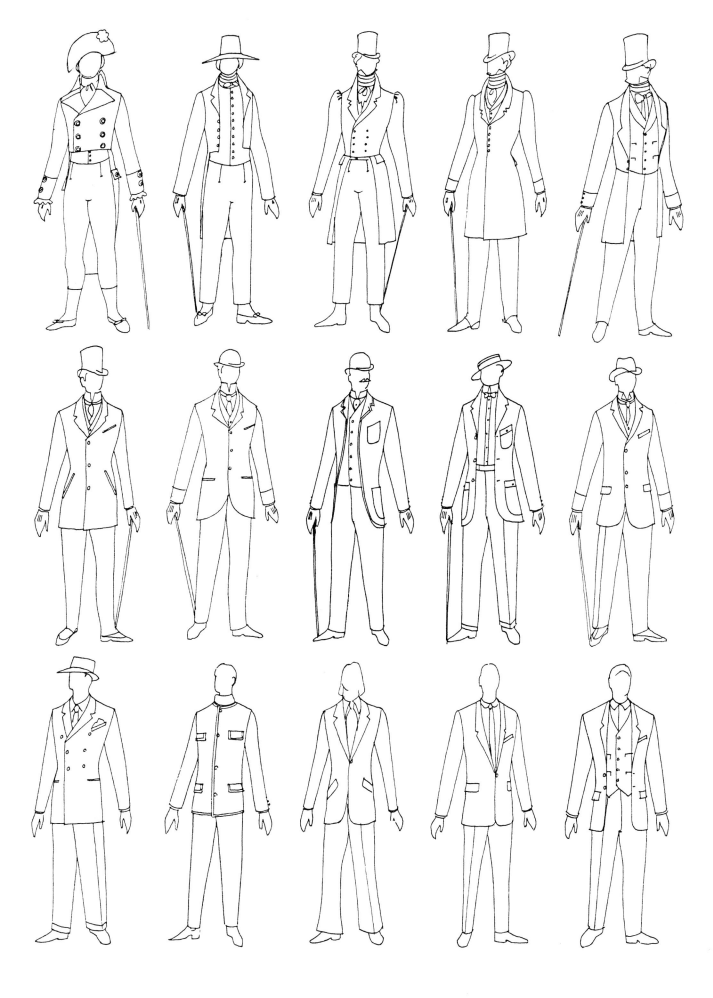

Chart of the Development of Men's Fashion

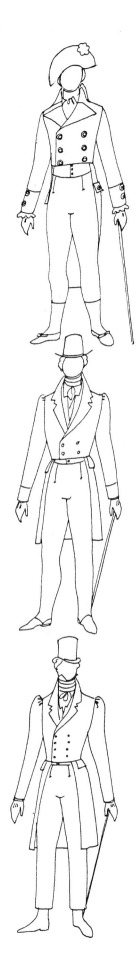

1789   1799

Coat	Fitted, single- or double-breasted, worn open or closed, high stand collars, wide revers, tight sleeves with cuffs, silk, later wool cloths.
Waistcoat	Fitted, single- or double-breasted, high stand collars, embroidered and striped silk fabrics fashionable.
Breeches	Fitted, fall fronts, buckled at knee, silk.
Pantaloons	Fitted, fall fronts, mid-calf or ankle-length, cotton.
Shirt	Stand collars, frilled fronts and cuffs, fine linen.
Colour	Red, blue, green, grey, black; white, cream and pale colours for breeches, pantaloons and waistcoats.
Accessories	Tricorn and bicorn hats, fine linen stocks, leather gloves, embroidered or striped stockings, shoes with large bows, flat pumps, walking canes.

1800   1809

Coat	Fitted, knee-length, single- or double-breasted, worn open or closed, high stand collars, wide revers, tight sleeves with or without cuffs, wool cloths.
Waistcoat	Fitted, single-breasted, high fastenings, stand collars, embroidered or striped silks.
Pantaloons	Fitted, ankle-length or long with stirrups, cotton.
Shirt	Stand collars, full sleeves, not visible.
Colour	Dark colours, black, blue, green, grey, brown; pale colours for waistcoats and pantaloons.
Accessories	Hats with tall crowns and narrow or wide brims, linen stocks, leather gloves, flat pumps, short boots, walking canes.

1810   1819

Coat	Fitted, single- or double-breasted, cut-away fronts, M-notch collars, fitted sleeves with or without cuffs, gathered sleeve head, wool cloths.
Waistcoat	Fitted, single-breasted, high fastenings, stand collars, embroidered silk.
Pantaloons	Fitted, ankle-length, cotton.
Trousers	Fitted, tight to ankle, stirrups under instep, cotton.
Shirt	High collar points, frilled fronts and cuffs, fine linen.
Colour	Dark colours, black, blue, brown, grey, combination of black and bright colours, light-coloured trousers.
Accessories	Top hats, leather gloves, stocks, short boots worn with spats, flat pumps, walking canes.

1820

1829

Coat	Fitted into waist, single-breasted, worn open or closed, large M-notch collar, wide revers, sleeves gathered into armhole, with or without cuffs, flap pockets in waist seam, full skirts, wool cloths.
Waistcoat	Fitted, single-breasted, collar and revers, shawl collars, plain or embroidered silk or matching coat.
Trousers	Fitted, narrow at ankles, straps under instep, cotton.
Shirt	High collar points, pleated fronts, fine linen.
Colour	Dark colours, black, blue, grey, brown, green, bright coloured waistcoats, pale trousers, black trousers.
Accessories	Top hats with tall crowns and curled brims, stocks, gloves, ankle-boots, walking canes.

1830

1839

Coat	Fitted into waist, double-breasted, large collars, wide revers, fitted sleeves with gathered head, full skirts, flap pockets, wool cloths.
Waistcoat	Fitted, single- or double-breasted, with or without collars, pointed and shaped fronts, silk or matching coat.
Trousers	Fitted, narrow at ankles, straps under instep, later gathers from waist, cotton or fine wool.
Shirt	High collar points, pleated fronts, fine linen.
Colour	Dark colours, black, blue, grey, brown; pale grey, cream or white for trousers, later black; contrasting colours for waistcoats, or matching coat.
Accessories	Top hats with tall crowns and curled brims, stocks, bow-ties, gloves, short boots, walking canes.

1840

1849

Coat	Fitted into waist, full knee-length skirts, single-breasted, large collars, wide revers, wool cloths, velvet collars.
Waistcoat	Fitted, single-breasted, collar and revers, shawl collars, welt pockets, silk or matching coat.
Trousers	Gathered from waist, narrow legs, strapped under instep, plain wool cloths, later checked cloths.
Shirt	High collar points, pleated fronts, linen.
Colour	Dark colours, black, blue, brown, grey; pale colours for trousers, or black or coloured checks.
Accessories	Top hats with tall crowns, stocks, cravats and bow-ties, gloves, pocket handkerchiefs, ankle-boots, walking canes.

1850   1859

Coat	Fitted, above knee-length, single-breasted, fly fastenings, fitted sleeves with or without cuffs, narrow collar and revers, piped pockets, breast pockets, wool cloths.
Waistcoat	Fitted, single-breasted, collarless, welt pockets, silk or matching coat.
Trousers	Straight-cut, narrow at ankles, wool cloths, checked cloth popular.
Shirt	High stiff collar points and sleeve cuffs, pleated fronts, linen.
Colour	Dark colours, black, blue, grey, brown, green; coats and trousers in matching colour; waistcoats in bright colours.
Accessories	Top hats, stocks, cravats and bow-ties, pocket handkerchiefs, leather gloves, spats worn with ankle-boots and shoes, walking canes.

1860   1869

Coat/jacket	Semi-fitted, thigh-length, single-breasted, three-button fastening, narrow sleeves with stitched cuffs, small collars, narrow lapels, braided edges, piped pockets, wool cloths.
Waistcoat	Fitted, single-breasted, collarless, cloth matching jacket.
Trousers	Narrow; checked cloths popular.
Shirt	High stiff stand collars and cuffs, later turned-down collars, linen and fine cotton.
Colour	Dark and muted, blue, grey, brown, black popular; trousers and waistcoats matching jackets.
Accessories	Top hats, bowler hats, cravats, bow-ties and neckties, leather gloves, ankle-boots and lace-up shoes.

1870   1879

Coat/jacket	Semi-fitted, thigh-length, single- or double-breasted, high fastenings, narrow lapels, sleeves cuffed or cuffless, flap and welt pockets, breast pockets, wool cloths.
Waistcoat	Fitted, single-breasted, collarless, high fastenings, welt pockets, silk, velvet, matching jacket.
Trousers	Narrow; wool cloths.
Shirt	High stiff collars and cuffs, wing collars, plain fronts, linen and fine cotton.
Colour	Dark and subdued, blue, brown, grey, green, black popular; trousers, jackets and waistcoats often matching.
Accessories	Top hats, bowlers, homburgs, cravats, bow-ties and neckties, gloves, short boots, lace-up shoes, some spats, walking canes.

1880   1889

Jacket	Fitted, narrow shoulders, single-breasted, high fastening, small collar, narrow lapels, fitted sleeves with or without cuffs, braided edges, piped pockets, patch pockets, wool cloths.
Waistcoat	Fitted, single-breasted, collarless, high fastenings, silk, plain wool cloths.
Trousers	Narrow to hems; plain wool cloths.
Shirt	Stiff stand collars and cuffs, later turned-down collars, plain fronts, fine linen and cottons.
Colour	Black, subdued blue, grey, brown, green; waistcoat, jacket and trousers matching.
Accessories	Top hats, bowler hats, caps, cravats, bow-ties and neckties, gloves, ankle-boots, lace-up shoes, spats, walking canes.

1890   1899

Jacket	Semi-fitted, narrow shoulders, single-breasted, high fastening, small collar, narrow lapels, patch pockets, flap pockets, braided edges, wool cloths, tweeds.
Waistcoat	Fitted, single-breasted, collarless, high fastenings, plain wool cloths, patterned velvets.
Trousers	Narrow to hems; wool cloths.
Shirt	Stiff stand collars and cuffs, turned-down collars, plain fronts, linen, cotton.
Colour	Dark, subdued, blue, grey, brown, green, black popular, later lighter and clearer colours.
Accessories	Top hats, bowler hats, homburgs, cravats, bow-ties and neckties, gloves, elastic-sided boots, lace-up shoes, walking canes.

1900   1909

Jacket	Fitted, narrow shoulders, single-breasted, three-button fastenings, narrow cuffless sleeves, patch and flap pockets, small collars, narrow lapels, wool cloths, linen and cotton.
Waistcoat	Fitted, single-breasted, collarless, high fastenings, wool cloths to match jacket, sometimes not worn.
Trousers	Straight, narrow hems, turn-ups, centre creases, wool cloths.
Shirt	Stiff stand collars and cuffs, plain fronts, plain linen, later striped cotton with attached collars.
Colour	Dark colours as before, some lighter: cream, brown, grey.
Accessories	Bowler hats, boaters, homburgs, caps, bow-ties and neckties, leather and cotton gloves, elastic-sided boots, lace-up shoes, walking sticks.

1910

Jacket	Semi-fitted, single-breasted, three-button fastenings, narrow lapels, flap pockets, breast pockets, wool cloths.
Waistcoat	Fitted, single-breasted, collarless, high fastenings, welt pockets, cloth matching jacket, sometimes not worn.
Trousers	Straight, narrow hems with turn-ups, centre creases, cloth often matching waistcoat and jacket.
Shirt	Stiff stand collars, wing collars, later collar-attached, plain white cotton, later striped cotton.
Colour	Subdued, striped and plain cloths, blue, brown, grey, some lighter colours, cream, beige, light brown, grey.
Accessories	Bowler hats, homburgs, boaters, trilbies, neckties, bow-ties with matching pocket handkerchiefs, leather and cotton gloves, elastic-sided boots, lace-up shoes.

1919

1920

Jacket	Fitted into waist, narrow shoulders, single- or double-breasted, high fastenings, narrow lapels, patch pockets, flap pockets, breast pockets, wool cloths, tweeds, linens.
Waistcoat	Fitted, single-breasted, collarless, high fastenings, often matching jacket, sometimes not worn or replaced with knitted waistcoat or sweater.
Trousers	Straight, narrow hems with turn-ups, centre creases, become wide to end of period, cloth matching jackets.
Shirt	Collar-attached, some buttoned collars, plain or striped cottons.
Colour	Subtle, blue, brown, green; light colours, cream, light brown, beige; brighter colours for knitwear.
Accessories	Trilbies, caps, boaters, ties and bow-ties, gloves, knitted sweaters and scarves, pocket handkerchiefs, lace-up boots and shoes.

1929

1930

Jacket	Fitted, single- or double-breasted, three-button fastenings, wide shoulders, diagonal pockets, breast pockets, wool cloths, tweeds, linens.
Waistcoat	Fitted, single-breasted, collarless, matching jacket cloth, sometimes not worn, knitted waistcoats popular.
Trousers	Straight, wide hems with turn-ups, centre creases, cloth matching jacket and waistcoat, grey flannel popular.
Shirt	Collar-attached, plain coloured or striped cotton.
Colour	Subtle, beige, grey, brown, light blue, some light colours; bright colours used for accessories.
Accessories	Bowler hats, trilbies, homburgs, boaters, narrow ties, bow-ties, pocket handkerchiefs, silk scarves, leather gloves, lace-up boots and shoes, rolled umbrellas.

1939

1940   1949

Jacket	Fitted into waist, single- or double-breasted, wide padded shoulders, wide lapels, piped, patch and flap pockets, breast pockets, wool cloths.
Waistcoat	Collarless, single-breasted, cloth matching jacket, often not worn.
Trousers	Wide, pleated from waist, wide hems with turn-ups, centre creases, cloth matching jacket, grey flannel trousers popular.
Shirt	Long pointed collars, plain or striped cotton.
Colour	Subdued, blue, brown, grey; grey flannel with white chalk stripe popular.
Accessories	Trilbies, homburgs, wide ties, pocket handkerchiefs, lace-up shoes, brogues.

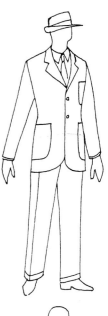

1950   1959

Jacket	Semi-fitted, single-breasted, three-button fastenings, narrow lapels, flap pockets, breast pockets, late period waist-length jackets with zip fastenings, wool and wool mixture cloths, later some suedes and leathers.
Waistcoat	Collarless, single-breasted, worn only as part of three-piece suit to match jacket cloth.
Trousers	Straight-cut with turn-ups, later narrow, tight at ankle, no turn-ups, wool cloths, man-made, denim popular.
Shirt	Collar-attached, plain colours, small collars, cotton, man-made fabrics.
Colour	Subtle, blue, green, brown, grey, mixed colour tweed jackets, light coloured trousers.
Accessories	Narrow ties, matching silk pocket handkerchiefs, knitted sweaters, scarves, elastic-sided boots, lace-up shoes with pointed toes.

1960   1969

Jacket	Unfitted, narrow shoulders, single- or double-breasted, small collars, narrow lapels, some collarless, flap pockets, wool cloths, man-made cloths, leather popular.
Waistcoat	Fitted, single-breasted, collarless, cloth matching jacket, leather popular, often not worn.
Trousers	Fitted, narrow at hem, no turn-ups, later fitted, flared from knee to hem, no turn-ups, wool cloths, man-made cloths, denim popular.
Shirt	Small collars, plain coloured cottons.
Colour	Subtle, blue, green, brown, black popular; light grey and beige fashionable for trousers.
Accessories	Narrow ties, polo-neck sweaters, elastic-sided boots with stacked heels and pointed toes.

1970 — 1979

Jacket	Fitted, narrow shoulders, one-, two- or three-button fastenings, deep collars, wide lapels, narrow sleeves, flap pockets, top-stitching, wool cloths, man-made cloths, denim, leather and suede popular.
Waistcoat	Only worn as part of three-piece suit, fitted, single-breasted, collarless.
Trousers	Fitted, flared from knee to hem, with or without turn-ups, wool cloths, man-made cloths, denim.
Shirt	Fitted, tight sleeves, large cuffs, large collars with long points, cotton, lawn, denim, silk, bright colours, patterned and striped.
Colour	Subtle colours for suits; jackets, trousers and shirts in bright, clear, contrasting and discordant colours.
Accessories	Wide ties, silk scarves, knitted scarves, large trilby hats, shoes with high heels and platform soles.

1980 — 1989

Jacket	Semi-fitted, cut large, wide padded shoulders, narrow collars and lapels, single-breasted, single-button fastenings, patch or flap pockets, plain wool cloths, leather and suede, denim.
Waistcoat	As part of three-piece suit, single-breasted, collarless, later fashion statement, single-breasted, cut large, bright colours, big patterns, silk, satin, lurex, embroidered denim.
Trousers	Cut straight, narrow hems, no turn-ups, later pleated from waist, wide legs, with or without turn-ups, wool cloths, cotton, linen, denim, suede, leather.
Shirt	Body cut large, full sleeves, small cuffs, small collars, often without tie, cotton, linen, silk, silk tweed, denim, leather.
Colour	Subtle colours for three-piece suits, bright colours for jackets and waistcoats, light colours or black for trousers.
Accessories	Narrow silk ties, silk pocket handkerchiefs, waistcoats, step-in shoes, cowboy boots, training shoes.

1990 — 1995

Jacket	Semi-fitted, wide shoulders, single- or double-breasted, small collars, narrow lapels, flap or patch pockets, wool cloths, leather, suede, denim.
Waistcoat	Cut large, collarless, single-breasted, welt pockets, silk, brocade, denim.
Trousers	Pleated from waist, straight legs, narrow hems with or without turn-ups, wool cloths, cotton, linen, denim.
Shirt	Semi-fitted, small collars, fly fastenings, often worn without a tie, cotton, silk, denim.
Colour	Subtle colours for suits, some bright colours for jackets, waistcoats multi-coloured, trousers in lighter colours.
Accessories	Narrow silk or leather ties, polo-neck sweaters, step-in casual shoes, ankle-boots, training shoes.

Concise Biographies of Designers, Tailors and Outfitters

Amies, (Sir) Hardy (Edwin) 1909–.

Born London, England. Joined the fashion house of Lachasse, London, in 1934 as managing designer. Opened his own house in 1946. Amies was the first woman's couturier to design for men. During the 1960s his menswear collection was created in conjunction with the tailoring firm of Hepworth's. He is best known for fine fabrics and excellent tailoring.

Armani, Giorgio 1935–.

Born Piacenza, Italy. Joined Nino Cerruti in 1961 as a menswear designer. Worked as a freelance fashion consultant during the early 1970s. Established his own company in 1975 and presented his first ready-to-wear men's line in the same year. He is best known for his unpadded, unstructured garments.

Beene, Geoffrey 1927–.

Born Haynesville, Louisiana, USA. Studied at the Traphagen School of Fashion in New York, as well as at the Ecole de la Chambre Syndicale de la Haute Couture and the Académie Julian in Paris. While a student, he also attended the tailoring studio of the House of Molyneux. From 1951 to 1963 he worked in New York for several major ready-to-wear companies before setting up his own business in 1963 designing for both men and women. He is best known for his craftsmanship and attention to detail.

Brooks Brothers

Clothing company, established in 1818 in New York, USA. Pioneers of ready-to-wear clothes for men from the late 19th century on. Best known for their button-down shirt, introduced in 1900.

Burberry, Thomas 1835–1926.

Store owner. Born Dorking, Surrey, England. Trained as a draper and opened his own business in 1856. He specialized in producing waterproof coats made from gaberdine. The 'Burberry' has become the classic British raincoat, the most popular style being the trenchcoat, first produced for military use during World War I.

Cardin, Pierre 1922–.

Born Venice, Italy. Apprenticed to a tailor at the age of 14. Moved to Paris in 1944 and worked for Paquin and Schiaparelli before joining Dior where he remained for 3 years. He started his own firm in 1950 and showed his first haute couture collection in 1953, opening his first shop one year later. He launched his menswear collections in 1960, using students as models. Among his earliest outfits were the collarless jacket that would soon be made internationally famous by the Beatles.

Caumont, Jean-Baptiste 1932–.

Born Béarn, France. Studied in Paris. Worked for Balmain during the 1960s and illustrated for *Vogue* and *Marie Claire*. Established his own ready-to-wear line in Milan in 1965. 'Caumont Monsieur', his ready-to-wear men's range, started in 1970.

Cerruti, Nino (Antonio) 1930–.

Born Biella, Italy. Took over his family's textile business in 1950. During the 1960s he launched a collection of knitwear for both men and women and in 1967 showed his first ready-to-wear collection of menswear. Best known for his subtle colours, fine fabrics and excellent tailoring.

Dolce & Gabbana (Domenico Dolce and Stefano Gabbana)

Dolce born 1958 in Palerma, Sicily. Gabbana born 1962 in Milan, Italy. Dolce and Gabbana met in 1980, when they were both working with a Milanese designer. They started their own company in 1982 and launched the Dolce & Gabbana label in 1985. Their first menswear collection was shown in 1990.

Fish, Michael

Fish served as an apprentice to a tailor in London's Jermyn Street and Savile Row. In the early 1960s he introduced the wide 'kipper' tie, in colourful, bold designs. In 1966 he opened his own shop, 'Mr Fish', which catered to a clientele including pop stars and aristocrats.

Gaultier, Jean Paul 1952–.

Born Paris, France. Worked for Pierre Cardin, Jacques Esterel and Jean Patou. Started his own label in 1979. Gaultier launched his first ready-to-wear menswear collection in 1984. He takes his inspiration from streetstyle and his collections are controversial and avant-garde. In 1984 he showed a man's suit with a 'skirt' composed of wide-legged pants which folded over each other to give the effect of a sarong.

Gee, Cecil

Store owner. Born London, England. Gee trained as a jeweler in Hatton Garden in London before becoming at the age of 18 a window-dresser for a leading menswear shop. He started his own menswear business, 'G-Man', in London in the 1930s and during this period introduced the collar-attached coat shirt, which opened from under the collar to the hem. In the 1940s he imported the colourful 'American Look'. The 1950s saw the opening of the first of the Cecil Gee shops. These were instrumental in popularizing the elegant 'Italian' style prevalent in the late 1950s and early 1960s.

Gigli, Romeo 1949–.

Born Castelbolognese, Faenza, Italy. Worked briefly in a men's tailoring company in New York before returning to Italy and setting up his own label in 1982. Showed his first collection in 1983. Gigli designs for both men and women. He is known for his imaginative cutting and original feeling for fabric.

Gilbey, Tom 1938–.

Born London, England. Gilbey started his fashion house and showed his first collection in 1968. The following year he was awarded a Fashion Oscar. Since 1969 he has worked as a consultant and designer for a wide range of manufacturers. In 1982 he launched his line of waistcoats, for which he is now best known.

Joseph (Joseph Ettedgui) 1936–.

Born Casablanca, Morocco. Ettedgui started as a hairdresser in London in the late 1950s and began showing Kenzo sweaters in his salon in 1964. Soon after, he opened the first Joseph boutiques, as a showcase for British and international designers. He also produces his own labels, including a menswear collection, Joseph Homme, which he established in 1988.

Kawakubo, Rei 1942–.

Born Tokyo, Japan. Studied at Keio University in Tokyo. Joined the Tokyo textile company Asahi Kasei in 1964. Kawakubo became a freelance fashion designer in 1966 and formed Comme des Garçons in Paris in the 1970s. She is best known for her non-traditional, draped clothing, in sombre colours.

Kenzo (Kenzo Takada) 1939–.

Born Hyogo, Japan. Studied at the Bunka Fukuso Gakuin school of fashion in Tokyo before moving to Paris in 1965 where he became a freelance designer. He opened his own shop, Jungle Jap, in Paris in 1970. His first collection of menswear was launched in 1983 under the name Kenzo Homme.

Lanvin, Jeanne 1867–1946.

Born in Brittany, France. The Lanvin Monsieur collection was launched by Jeanne Lanvin in 1926. In 1972, the men's ready-to-wear collection was created. This was designed by Patrick Lavoix from 1976 to 1991. In 1992, Dominique Morlotti took over. He continues the Lanvin tradition of classic clothing – maintaining a balance between comfort and refinement.

Lapidus, Ted (Edmond) 1929–.

Born Paris, France. Son of a tailor. Studied in Paris and Tokyo before opening a boutique in Paris in the 1950s. In the 1960s his designs followed the prevailing unisex style. He is best known for his well cut, classic designs for both men and women.

Lauren, Ralph (Ralph Lipschitz) 1939–.

Born New York, USA. Studied at the City College in New York. After working for a firm producing neckties, he launched his own first collection of menswear, 'Polo', in 1968 and in 1971 produced a collection for women. From 1972, under the label 'Ralph Lauren', he produced sophisticated and well-tailored Ivy-league-style collections for both men and women.

Miyake, Issey 1935–.

Born Hiroshima, Japan. While studying fashion in Paris in the early 1960s, Miyake worked for Guy Laroche and Hubert Givenchy. In 1969 he moved to New York and joined Geoffrey Beene. His first collection of womenswear was shown in New York in 1971 and two years later he produced his first collection in Paris. His ready-to-wear menswear was launched in the 1980s. Miyake is best known for his wrapped and layered look and for his innovative use of fabrics.

Montana, Claude 1949–.

Born Paris, France. Studied in Paris. Worked for a brief period in London as a costume jewelry designer. In 1977 Montana launched his first womenswear collection in Paris. His menswear collections were developed during the 1980s. He is best known for his use of leather.

Mugler, Thierry 1948–.

Born Strasbourg, France. During the 1960s Mugler worked for a ballet company and as a window-dresser in Paris. In 1971 he produced a collection of womenswear under the name Café de Paris. Two years later he showed his first collection under his own name. Mugler produces clothes for both men and women. He is best known for the theatricality and sexiness of his designs.

Nutter, Tommy 1943–1992.

Born London, England. Started his tailoring career at the age of 17 working for G. Ward & Company. He opened his own establishment, 'Nutters', in 1969 and made his name in 'Swinging London' as a maverick Savile Row tailor. He created suits for movie stars and members of the popular music world (The Beatles' 'Abbey Road' album cover contains three Nutter suits). He introduced extra-wide lapels and padded shoulders, and often used several contrasting suitings in one jacket. He left 'Nutters' in the 1970s but later opened another shop, 'Tommy Nutter', at 19 Savile Row.

Saint Laurent, Yves (Henri Donat Mathieu) 1936–.

Born Oran, Algeria. Saint Laurent studied in Paris. In 1953 he won a competition sponsored by the International Wool Secretariat and was subsequently hired by Christian Dior. Saint Laurent took over as director in 1957, after Dior's death. In 1962 he opened a house under his own name. His first collection of menswear was shown in the 1980s.

Savile Row

Street in London's Mayfair district, the name of which has become synonymous with craft tailoring. The first generation of Savile Row tailors occupied the area in the late 18th century, the first tailoring firm in Savile Row itself being established in 1806.

The term 'Savile Row' covers an area roughly between New Bond Street and Regent Street to the east and west, and Oxford Street and Piccadilly to the north and south. It includes more than 50 tailoring firms. Some of the oldest and best known are Adeney & Boutroy (tailors to many movie stars, including Tony Curtis, Rod Taylor and Trevor Howard); Anderson & Sheppard (a highly successful firm, patronized by the present Prince of Wales); Tom Brown (specializing in serving old Etonians); Davies & Son; Gieves & Hawkes (originally tailors to the British Navy and probably the most successful of all London tailors); Johns & Pegg; Kilgour, French & Stanbury (makers of Fred Astaire's tailcoat in *Top Hat*); Henry Poole (one of Savile Row's most famous tailors, known for its tradition of understated elegance; patronized by Edward, Prince of Wales); and Rose & Kent (tailors to the Duke of Edinburgh).

In the 1960s these older establishments were joined by such firms as Nutters of Savile Row (run by Tommy Nutter and Edward Sexton) and Rupert Lycett-Green's Blades.

Smith, Paul 1946–.

Born Nottingham, England. Started his career in fashion at a Nottingham clothing warehouse. He opened his own shop, in Nottingham, in 1970, selling clothing by such designers as Kenzo and Margaret Howell. After taking evening classes in design, he created his own label and showed his first collection in Paris in 1976. He is an immensely successful designer with shops all over the world, including 147 shops in Japan. He is known for his simplicity of style, and for practical clothes enlivened by offbeat fabrics and colours.

Valentino (Valentino Garavini) 1933–.

Born Voghera, Italy. Studied in Milan and at the Chambre Syndicale de la Haute Couture in Paris. Worked for Jean Dessès and Guy Laroche before opening a couture house in Rome in 1959. His first ready-to-wear collection for men was shown in the early 1980s. Best known for his superb cutting and for the elegance of his designs.

Van Noten, Dries 1960–.

Born Antwerp, Belgium. While studying fashion at the Royal Academy of Fine Arts, Antwerp, Van Noten designed several freelance childrenswear collections. In 1986 he was backed by the Belgian government to present a collection of mainly menswear at the London Fashion Designers' Show. He opened a shop in Antwerp in 1989 serving both men and women. He is known for his well-cut clothes and for his use of unusual fabrics, such as washed velvet.

Versace, Gianni 1946–.

Born Reggio, Calabria, Italy. Trained for five years in his mother's dressmaking atelier. Moved to Milan, where he worked for Genny and Callaghan. Showed a highly successful leather collection for Complice in 1975. Opened his own business in 1978, producing his first menswear collection that same year. He is best known for leather garments and for leather-trimmed knitwear.

Yamamoto, Yohji 1943–.

Born Tokyo, Japan. After studying law, Yamamoto took a course in fashion design at the Bunka Fukuso Gakuin school of fashion in Tokyo. Between 1968 and 1972 he worked as a freelance fashion designer. In 1972 he formed his own company, and in 1976 showed his first collection in Japan. His first menswear collection was presented in 1984. Yamamoto is best known for his unconventional approach to clothes, involving an unstructured, loose wrapping of the body.

Sources for Men's Fashion

Baynes, Ken, and Kate Baynes, *The Shoe Show: British Shoes since 1790*, 1979.

Bentley, Nicolas, *Edwardian Album: Photographic Excursion into a Lost Age of Innocence*, 1974.

Black, J. Anderson, and Madge Garland, *A History of Fashion*, 1975.

Blum, Stella, *Everyday Fashions of the Twenties*, 1981.

Boucher, François, *A History of Costume in the West*, 1965.

Bradfield, Nancy, *Historical Costumes of England*, 1958.

Broby-Johansen, R., *Body and Clothes: An Illustrated History of Costume*, 1966.

Brooke, Iris, *A History of English Costume*, 1937.

Buckley, V. C., *Good Times*, 1979.

Byrde, Penelope, *The Male Image: Men's Fashion in Britain 1300–1970*, 1979.

Cardin, Pierre, *Pierre Cardin: Past, Present and Future*, 1990.

Chenoune, Farid, *A History of Men's Fashion*, 1993.

Contini, Mila, *Fashion*, 1965.

Creed, Charles, *Made to Measure*, 1961.

Cunnington, C. W., and P. E. Cunnington, *The History of Underclothes*, 1951.

——, *Handbook of English Costume in the Nineteenth Century*, 1959.

——, and Charles Beard, *A Dictionary of English Costume*, 1960.

Dorner, Jane, *Fashion in the Twenties and Thirties*, 1973.

——, *Fashion in the Forties and Fifties*, 1975.

Drake, Nicholas, *The Fifties in Vogue*, 1987.

Evelyn, Hugh, *History of Costume: 1600–1800*, 1967.

Ewing, Elizabeth, *Fur in Dress*, 1981.

Ginsburg, Madeleine, *Victorian Dress in Photographs*, 1988.

Gordon, Colin, *A Richer Dust: Echoes from an Edwardian Album*, 1978.

Hamilton-Hill, Margot, and Peter Bucknell, *The Evolution of Fashion 1066 to 1930*, 1967.

Hansen, Henny Harald, *Costume Cavalcade*, 1956.

Harrison, Michael, *The History of the Hat*, 1960.

Howell, Georgina, *In Vogue: Six Decades of Fashion*, 1975.

Kelsall, Freda, *How We Used to Live: 1936–1953*, 1981.

Kennett, Frances, *The Collector's Book of Twentieth-Century Fashion*, 1983.

Laver, James, *Costume*, 1963.

——, *Costumes through the Ages*, 1961.

——, *How and Why Fashions in Men's and Women's Clothes Have Changed over the Past 200 Years*, 1950.

——, and Amy de la Haye, *Costume and Fashion: A Concise History*, 1995.

Langner, Lawrence, *The Importance of Wearing Clothes*, 1959.

La Vine, W. Robert, *In a Glamorous Fashion*, 1981.

Martin, Richard, and Harold Koda, *Jocks and Nerds: Men's Style in the Twentieth Century*, 1989.

Moke, Johnny, and Jan McVeigh, *Mods!*, 1979.

Mulvagh, Jane, *Vogue: History of 20th Century Fashion*, 1988.

O'Hara, Georgina, *The Encyclopaedia of Fashion*, 1986.

Polhemus, Ted, *Streetstyle*, 1994.

——, and Lynn Proctor, *Fashion and Anti-Fashion: An Anthology of Clothing and Adornment*, 1978.

Robinson, Julian, *The Fine Art of Fashion: An Illustrated History*, 1989.

——, *Fashion in the Thirties*, 1978.

Sansom, William, *Victorian Life in Photographs*, 1974.

Speller, Reggie, *'Scoop', What a Picture!: Photographs of the Thirties and Forties*, 1981.

Stevenson, Pauline, *Edwardian Fashion*, 1980.

Sykes, Christopher Simon, *The Golden Age of the Country House*, 1980.

Viera, Mark A., *Hollywood Portraits: Classic Scene Stills 1929–1941*, 1988.

Waugh, Norah, *The Cut of Men's Clothes, 1600–1900*, 1964.

Wheatcroft, Andrew, *The Tennyson Album: A Biography of Original Photographs*, 1980.

Wilcox, R., Turner, *The Mode in Costume*, 1942.

——, *Five Centuries of American Costume*, 1963.

——, *Dictionary of Costume*, 1969.

Winter, Gordon, *A Country Camera, 1844–1914*, 1966.

——, *A Cockney Camera*, 1971.

——, *The Golden Years: 1903–1913*, 1975.

Worswick, Clark, *An Edwardian Observer*, 1978.

Yarwood, Doreen, *English Costume: From the Second Century to 1967*, 1975.